Ashraf Ragab

Navigation in Suez Canal

Ashraf Ragab

Navigation in Suez Canal

Rules of Navigation and Passage Procedures
in Suez Canal

VDM Verlag Dr. Müller

Impressum/Imprint (nur für Deutschland/ only for Germany)

Bibliografische Information der Deutschen Nationalbibliothek: Die Deutsche Nationalbibliothek verzeichnet diese Publikation in der Deutschen Nationalbibliografie; detaillierte bibliografische Daten sind im Internet über http://dnb.d-nb.de abrufbar.

Alle in diesem Buch genannten Marken und Produktnamen unterliegen warenzeichen-, marken- oder patentrechtlichem Schutz bzw. sind Warenzeichen oder eingetragene Warenzeichen der jeweiligen Inhaber. Die Wiedergabe von Marken, Produktnamen, Gebrauchsnamen, Handelsnamen, Warenbezeichnungen u.s.w. in diesem Werk berechtigt auch ohne besondere Kennzeichnung nicht zu der Annahme, dass solche Namen im Sinne der Warenzeichen- und Markenschutzgesetzgebung als frei zu betrachten wären und daher von jedermann benutzt werden dürften.

Coverbild: www.ingimage.com

Verlag: VDM Verlag Dr. Müller Aktiengesellschaft & Co. KG
Dudweiler Landstr. 99, 66123 Saarbrücken, Deutschland
Telefon +49 681 9100-698, Telefax +49 681 9100-988
Email: info@vdm-verlag.de

Herstellung in Deutschland:
Schaltungsdienst Lange o.H.G., Berlin
Books on Demand GmbH, Norderstedt
Reha GmbH, Saarbrücken
Amazon Distribution GmbH, Leipzig
ISBN: 978-3-639-28516-1

Imprint (only for USA, GB)

Bibliographic information published by the Deutsche Nationalbibliothek: The Deutsche Nationalbibliothek lists this publication in the Deutsche Nationalbibliografie; detailed bibliographic data are available in the Internet at http://dnb.d-nb.de.

Any brand names and product names mentioned in this book are subject to trademark, brand or patent protection and are trademarks or registered trademarks of their respective holders. The use of brand names, product names, common names, trade names, product descriptions etc. even without a particular marking in this works is in no way to be construed to mean that such names may be regarded as unrestricted in respect of trademark and brand protection legislation and could thus be used by anyone.

Cover image: www.ingimage.com

Publisher: VDM Verlag Dr. Müller Aktiengesellschaft & Co. KG
Dudweiler Landstr. 99, 66123 Saarbrücken, Germany
Phone +49 681 9100-698, Fax +49 681 9100-988
Email: info@vdm-publishing.com

Printed in the U.S.A.
Printed in the U.K. by (see last page)
ISBN: 978-3-639-28516-1

Tables of Contents

Preface:

- The **Suez Canal** is a canal in Egypt. Opened in 1869, it allows water transportation between Europe and Asia without circumnavigation of Africa or carrying goods overland between the Mediterranean and the Red Sea.

- The opening of the Suez Canal in 1869 created the first salt-water passage between the Mediterranean and Red seas. The Red Sea is about 1.2 m higher than the eastern Mediterranean, so the canal serves as a tidal strait that pours Red Sea water into the Mediterranean.

- The canal is 192 km long. It is single lane with 4 passing places north and south of the Great Bitter Lake, and links the Mediterranean Sea to the Gulf of Suez on the Red Sea.

- The canal is owned and maintained by the Suez Canal Authority (SCA) of the state of Egypt.

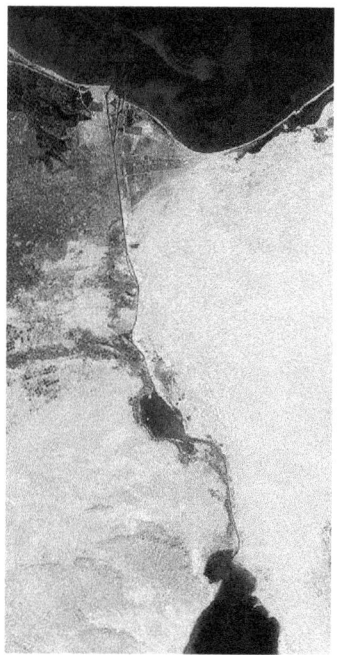

- The canal allows passage of ships up to 150,000 tons displacement. It permits ships up to 16 m (53 ft) draft to pass, and improvements are planned to increase this to 22 m (72 ft) by 2010, allowing passage of fully-laden supertankers.

- Some supertankers are too large. Others can offload part of their cargo onto a canal-owned boat and reload at the other end of the canal.

- The main alternative is travelling around Cape Agulhas. This is the route for ships which are too large, and was the route in the past before the canal was constructed, and when the canal was closed.

- Also, before the canal's opening in 1869, goods were sometimes offloaded from ships and carried overland between the Mediterranean and the Red Sea.

- The canal has no locks due to the flat terrain, and the sea level difference between each end is inconsequential.

- There is one shipping lane with several passing areas. On a typical day, three convoys transit the canal, two southbound and one northbound. The first southbound convoy enters the canal in the early morning hours and proceeds to the Great Bitter

Lake, where the ships anchor out of the fairway, awaiting passage of the northbound convoy. The northbound convoy passes the second southbound convoy, which moors in a bypass near El Qantara. The passage takes between 11 and 16 hours at a speed of around 8 knots (15 km/h). The low speed helps prevent erosion of the canal banks by ships' wakes.

Timeline of Suez Canal development:

- ➤ Circa 1799 — Napoleon I of France conquered Egypt and ordered a feasibility analysis. This reported a supposed 10 meter difference in sea levels and a high cost, so the project was set on standby.
- ➤ Circa 1840 — a second survey found the first one incorrect. A direct link between the Mediterranean Sea and the Red Sea would be possible and not be as expensive as expected.
- ➤ Circa 1854 — The French consul in Cairo, Ferdinand Marie de Lesseps, created the "Companies Universally du Canal Maritime de Suez".
- ➤ 25 Apr 1859 — The French were allowed to begin canal construction (Said Pasha acquired 22% of the Suez Canal Company, the remainder controlled by French private holders).
- ➤ 16 Nov 1869 — The Suez Canal opened; operated and owned by Suez Canal Company.
- ➤ 25 Nov 1875 — Britain became a minority share holder in the Suez Company, acquiring 44% of the Suez Canal Company. The remainder was controlled by French syndicates.
- ➤ 25 Aug 1882 — Britain took control of the canal.
- ➤ Mar 1888 — The Convention of Constantinople guaranteed rite of passage of all ships through the Suez Canal during war and peace.
- ➤ Nov 1936 — Suez Canal Zone established, under British control.
- ➤ Jun 1956 — Suez Canal Zone restored to Egypt.
- ➤ 26 Jul 1956 — Egypt nationalized the Suez Canal.
- ➤ Nov 1956 to 22 Dec 1956 — French, British, and Israeli forces occupied the Suez Canal Zone.
- ➤ 22 Dec 1956 — Restored to Egypt.
- ➤ June 1967 to 10 June 1967 — Canal closed and blockaded by Egypt, against Israel, sparking the Six-Day War.
- ➤ June 1975 — Suez Canal reopened.

Suez Canal advantages considering in being:[1]

- ➤ Longest canal in the world with no locks
- ➤ Compared with other waterways, the percentage of accidents is almost none.
- ➤ Passage proceed day and night
- ➤ Liable to be widened and deepened when required coping with the expansion in ship sizes.

---

[1] http://www.suezcanal.gov.eg/sc.aspx?show=10

Chapter 1: General

1.   Suez Canal Technical Future:

"The Suez Canal is the water channel to the west of the Sinai Peninsula, a route length of 163 km in Egypt between Port Said on the Mediterranean and Suez on the Red Sea. The channel is divided into two parts, north and south of Lakes Time. It allows ships to cross the canal from the Mediterranean countries of Europe and Asia without access to the long road - via the Cape of Good Hope on Africa. Additionally, during digging of the canal some movement was discharged through the tonnage of ships and transfer of land to the Red Sea."

1.1. Development of Suez Canal:

After the construction of the Suez Canal, which took 10 years, it opened in the year 1989. The canal was anything other than what we know today.

During years, the development of the canal alters due to the demands of the shipping market.

The table below shows the development of Canal until today.[2]

ITEM	UNIT	1869	1956	1962	1980	1994	1996	2001	2008	Percentage increase (1869-2001)
WIDTH AT 11M DEPTH	M	44	60	90	160	210	210	210	210	477%
MAX DRAFT OF SHIPS	FEET	22	35	38	53	56	58	62	68	282%
OVERALL LENGTH	KM	164	175	175	190.25	190.25	190.25	190.25	190.25	116%
DOUBLED PARTS	KM	-	29	29	78	78	78	78	78	269%
WATER DEPTH	M	10	14	15.5	19.5	20.5	21	22.5	23.5	225%
CROSS SECTIONAL AREA	M2	304	1100	1800	3600	4300	4500	4800	4800	1579%
MAX. TONNAGE (DWT)	TON	5000	30,000	80,000	150,000	180,000	185,000	210,000	210.000	4200%

---

[2] http://www.rafimar.com/homepage/suez_canal.html#transit

1.2. Characteristics of the current canal:

The Canal properties serve today nearly the needs of all types of vessels. However, this does not mean that the development of the Canal has stopped. Every day the authorities are working together with many investors on the improvement of the Canals properties to facilitate the use of the Canal.

In the table below, the current characteristics of the Canal are described:[3]

Overall length	193 km
From the fairway buoy to Port Said lighthouse	22.5 km
From the waiting area to the southern entrance	15 km
From Port Said to Ismailia	78.5 km
From Ismailia to Port Tewfik	83.65 km
The length of doubled parts	68 km
Width at water level	300/365 m
Width between buoys	180/205 m
Maximum permissible draught for ships	68 ft./20.73 m
The canal depth	21m
Maximum permissible air draft	68 m
Cross sectional area	4500/4800 m2

1.3. Environmental statistics of the Canal:[4]

"Since the very first opening of the Suez Canal at 1869, it has played a big role in maritime transport. During the course of the years, the Suez Canal is always improving its properties to meet the demand of the ships."

For the current status of the ship traffic on the Suez Canal is as follows: [5]

Total number of vessels calling at Suez Canal	20384 ship
Net Tonnage	844.4 million Ton
Container Vessels	7718 ship
Net Tonnage of Container Vessels	437806 Thousand tons
Cargo volume from North to South	286028 Thousand ton
Cargo volume from South to North	424047 Thousand ton
Total cargo volume	700.027 Thousand Ton
Containerized cargo from North to South	141381 Thousand Ton
Containerized cargo from South to North	177107 Thousand Ton
Total of Containerized cargo	318488 Thousand Ton

---

[2] http://www.rafimar.com/homepage/suez_canal.html#transit

[4] For further information about recent Statics please check http://www.suezcanal.gov.eg/TRstat.aspx?reportId=1

[5] http://www.emdb.gov.eg/english/inside_e.aspx?main=suezcanal&level1=statistics

Over the last 8 years the number of vessels passing the Suez Canal has been increased to more than 5000 Vessels than in the year 2000. This just proves the increasing importance of the Suez Canal throughout the years.

Statistics from the Egyptian Maritime ministry show the increase in the total number of vessels passing the Suez Canal:[6]

1.3.1. Traffic of Vessels Crossing Suez Canal:

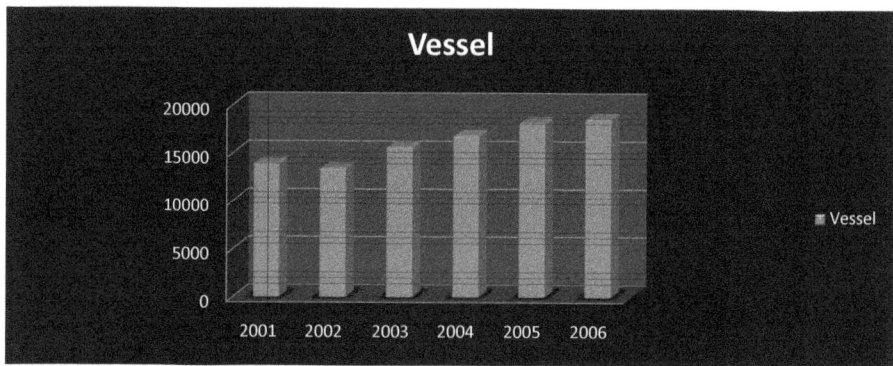

1.3.2. Net Tonnage of Vessels Crossing Suez Canal:

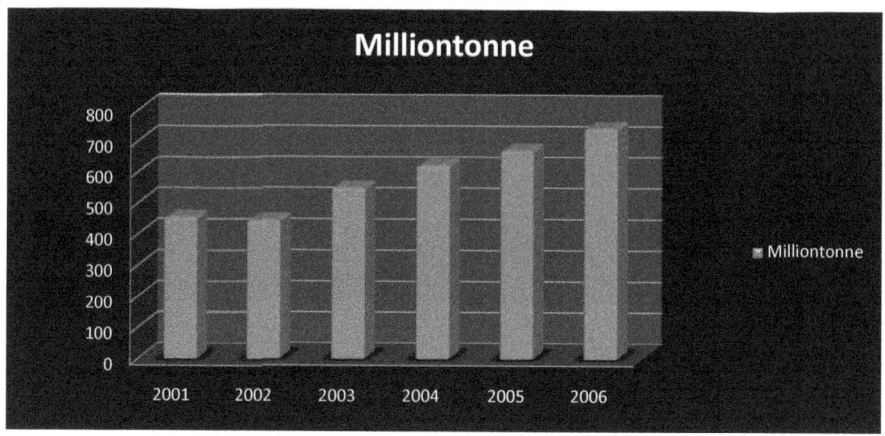

---

[6] http://www.emdb.gov.eg/english/inside_e.aspx?main=suezcanal&level1=totals

1.3.3. Number of Containers Crossing Suez Canal

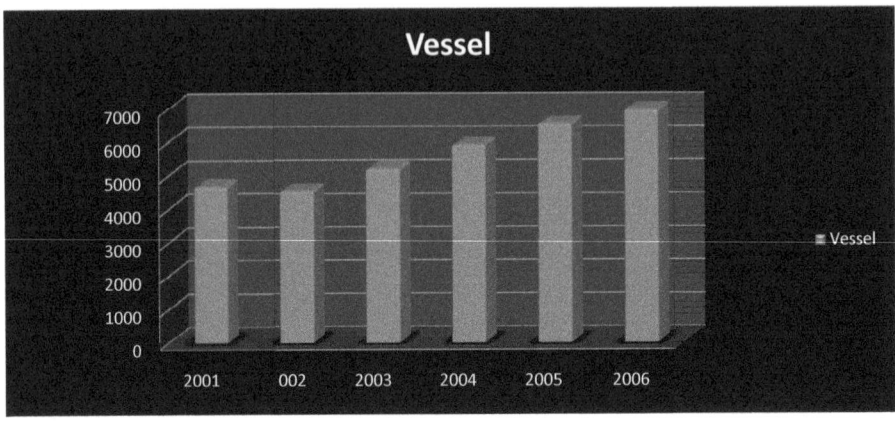

1.3.4. Total Cargo Crossing Suez Canal

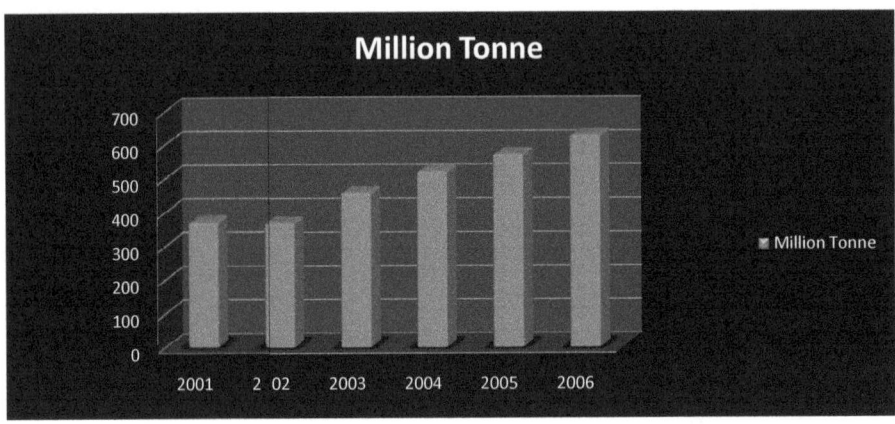

2. Authorities Structure:

"The Suez Canal Authority (SCA) is a state owned authority, which owns and maintains the Suez Canal. It was set up by Egypt to replace the then privately nationalized company in the 1950s, which resulted in the Suez Crisis. After the UN intervened, Egypt agreed to pay millions of dollars to shareholders of the nationalized Suez Canal Company."

The Suez Canal is controlled and organized in many small agencies under the Ministerial service for transportation. The tasks of Maritime transport are carried out and organized again under the Department of the Maritime Transport Sector. This sector operates under the instruction and organization of the Minister of Transport.

The structure adopted by the Central Body of Organization and Administration, which is currently being elaborated, includes a number of counseling, assisting and executive activities. The main Authorities that control movements on the Suez Canal are the Port Said Authority and the Red Sea Port Authority.

2.1. Goals of the Authorities instruction:

1. Setting goals and policies of bodies, organizations and entities, as well as the Follow-up implementation and coordination between them
2. The development of Egyptian ports to keep pace with progress in the shipping industry and add competitiveness and modernization of infrastructure facilities and the transition from performing the role of the crossing to be a link in a multimodal transport and distribution center.
3. Coordination with everyone to unite and to review and audit decisions, laws and legislation (government bodies - ministries - bodies' ports - Rooms navigation - users of the port).
4. Raise the efficiency of workers in maritime transport in accordance with international standards to improve the efficiency of maritime transport and provide the possibility of export of labor freely.
5. To enter an era of information technology in the maritime transport sector.
6. Achieve safe navigation in the territorial waters in accordance with international standards and the reduction of accidents and pollution confrontation.
7. Encourage private sector participation in all activities of maritime transport vessels and his Aims.
8. Marketing and shipping activities to attract investments in all shipping activities.
9. Follow up the developments of shipping and the predictability to keep pace and increase the volume of transit trade in Egypt.

2.2. Reference of the Ministry of Transport:

- Planning to ensure the upgrading of facilities and the development of maritime transport in line with global developments in the context of the economic and social Development plan of the State.
- Policy-making for the establishment of the Ports and Lighthouses and development to ensure sufficient upgrading to cope with the volume of world trade and coordination between the bodies of ports.
- To provide a means to aid navigation in territorial waters to ensure the safety of navigation.
- Supervision and control over the implementation plans to ensure the safety of maritime transport units and movement of all fixed and mobile installations as well as equipment and machinery that are actively shipped in coordination with the Competent organizations of the State

2.3. Structure of Egyptian Maritime Authorities:[7]

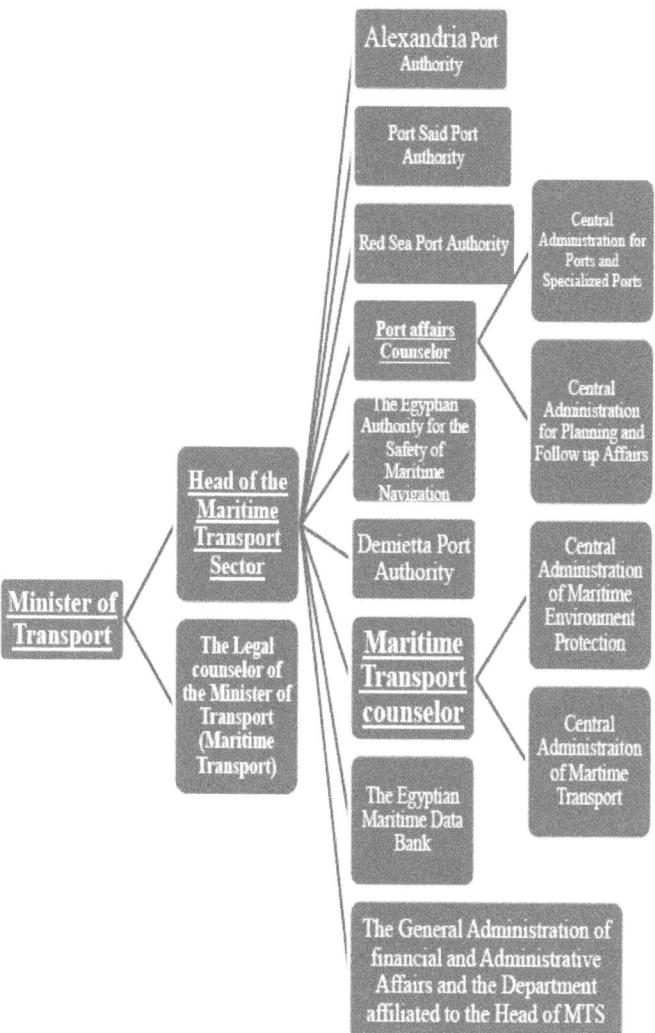

3. Tariffs for Suez Canal transit:

"The Suez Canal Authority announces that the transit dues for the year 2008/2009 will be as shown in the table below, as per <u>circular no. 1/2007</u>. This circular takes effect as of April 1st 2008". See table of transit charges below.[8]

Tariff	Vessel type	Condition	First 5000	Next 5000	Next 10000	Next 20000	Next 30000	Next 50000	Rest
08-01	Tankers of Crude Oil	Laden	7,65	4,80	3,90	1,70	1,50	1,40	1,30
		Ballast	6,50	4,08	3,32	1,45	1,28	1,19	1,11
08-02	Tankers of Petroleum Products	Laden	7,65	4,80	3,90	2,35	2,30	2,20	2,10
		Ballast	6,50	4,08	3,32	1,45	1,28	1,19	1,11
08-03	Dry Bulk Carriers	Laden	7,65	5,20	4,40	1,40	1,30	1,25	1,20
		Ballast	6,50	4,42	3,74	1,19	1,11	1,06	1,02
08-04	LPG Carriers	Laden	7,65	4,90	3,90	2,80	2,60	2,50	2,50
		Ballast	6,50	4,17	3,32	2,38	2,21	2,13	2,13
08-05	LNG Carriers	Laden	7,65	5,30	4,90	3,40	3,30	3,20	3,10
		Ballast	6,50	4,51	4,17	2,89	2,81	2,72	2,64
08-06	Chemical and Other Liquid Bulk	Laden	8,00	5,50	4,70	3,00	2,90	2,80	2,80
		Ballast	6,80	4,68	4,00	2,55	2,47	2,38	2,38
08-07	Container Ships	Laden	7,65	5,00	4,00	2,80	2,60	2,05	1,95
		Ballast	6,50	4,25	3,40	2,38	2,21	1,74	1,66
08-08	General Cargo Ships	Laden	7,65	5,50	4,00	3,00	2,90	2,85	2,80
		Ballast	6,50	4,68	3,40	2,55	2,47	2,42	2,38
08-09	RO - RO Ships	Laden	7,65	5,30	4,30	3,10	2,90	2,80	2,70
		Ballast	6,50	4,51	3,66	2,64	2,47	2,38	2,30
08-10	Vehicle Carriers	Laden	7,65	5,00	3,85	2,75	2,60	2,05	1,95
		Ballast	6,50	4,25	3,27	2,34	2,21	1,74	1,66
08-11	Passenger Ships	Laden	7,65	5,00	4,30	3,05	3,00	2,90	2,80
		Ballast	6,50	4,25	3,66	2,59	2,55	2,47	2,38
08-12	Special Floating Units	Laden	8,30	5,10	4,80	3,40	3,20	2,90	2,80
		Ballast	0,00	0,00	0,00	0,00	0,00	0,00	0,00
08-13	Other Vessels	Laden	8,00	5,00	4,40	3,20	3,10	2,90	2,80
		Ballast	6,80	4,25	3,74	2,72	2,64	2,47	2,38

---

[8] http://www.lethsuez.com/tariff_08.aspx

The special drawing right SDR is an international reserve asset created by the International Monetary Fund to supplement existing reserves. It is valued on the basis of a basket of five currencies and can be used in a wide variety of transactions and operations among official holders.

Remarks :

1. If in ballast, Chemical / Oil Tankers are to be charged at the same rate as Oil tankers.

2. Combined Carriers (OBO) when transiting in Ballast, combined Carriers are to be charged at the same rate applied to Ballast Bulk Carriers.

3. Combined Ballast Gas Carriers LNG/LPG Transit Dues for combined Ballast Gas Carriers are to be calculated according to the last shipment transported through the Suez Canal, in case the last cargo was LNG.

4. Container vessels or Lash vessels carrying containers or lashes over the weather deck will be subject to the following surcharges on the Suez Canal Dues:-

2%	For vessels carrying one tier of containers or lashes.
4%	For vessels carrying two tiers of containers or lashes.
6%	For vessels carrying three tiers of containers or lashes.
8%	For vessels carrying four tiers of containers or lashes.
10%	For vessels carrying Five tiers of containers or lashes.
14%	For vessels carrying Six or more of containers tiers.

    this, however, shall be increased of the rate of 1% for each extra tier exceeding 6 tiers :

15%	For Vessels carrying seven tiers of containers.
16%	For Vessels carrying eight tiers of containers.

5. Containerships are to be exempted from extra dues on the top tier in the following two cases:
    If the top tier contains no more than ten containers (TEU).
    If the top tier has a protrusion of not more than 4 feet.

6. Any vessel carrying only containers to be treated as FCC (fully cellular container vessel)

7. The acceptable currencies for payment of transit dues.

- U.S. Dollar	- Sterling pound	- Euro
- Japanese yen	- Canadian dollar	- Swedish kroner
- Danish kroner	- Norwegian kroner	- Swiss franc

8. Transit Dues Rates are determined on the basis of SDR (Special Drawing Rights) SDR unit consists of :

U.S Dollar	45 %
Euro	29 %
Yen	15 %
Pound sterling	11%

13

4. Representation of differences between Suez Canal passage and travelling around Cape Agulhas.

4.1. Economic Differences:

"The geographical position of the Suez Canal makes it the shortest route between East and West as compared with the Cape of Good Hope. The Canal route achieves a saving in distance between the ports north and south the Canal, which can be translated into other savings in time, fuel consumption and ship operating costs."

In this part, we show an example for the difference between crossing the Suez Canal and taking the route around Africa. This Example is just to show how effective passing through the Suez Canal can be.

First: Ship Detail example:
MV "Y"
LOA= 188.10 m
BOA= 32.00 m
Speed= 20 Kn.
HF consumption per day: 65t/day by 20 Kn.
International Tonnage: GRT= 23652/NRT= 10596
Suez Tonnage: GRT= 24728/NRT=20232[9]

Route A: Transit in Suez Canal
Departure: Hamburg (Germany)
Destination: Singapore (Singapore)
Distance: 8513 NM
Time to proceed: 17 Days /18 Hours by constant speed of 20 Kn.
HF Consumption: Time of Trip x HF Consumption per day = 17, 75 days x 65 t/day = **1170t**

Route B: Round Cape Agulhas
Departure: Hamburg (Germany)
Destination: Singapore (Singapore)
Distance: 12006 NM
Time to Proceed: 25 days by constant speed of 20 Kn.
HF Consumption: Time of Trip x HF Consumption per day = 25 days x 65 t/day = **1626t.**

---

[9] The Suez Canal NRT or/and GRT are calculated by the Dockyard. There is no official formula to calculate this value. It is dependent on the specified volume of each vessel, which would be calculated separately by the shipyard and classification company.

As shown in the example before, the difference between the two routes is large. There is a difference between consumption and travel time, which is important in the efficiency interests of the passage of shipping through the Suez Canal. This example serves only to represent the effectiveness of Suez Canal passage for companies.

Here are some other routes saving facts, which show by how much you can save for each route example:[10]

From	To	Distance (N. Miles)		Saving
		S. C.	CAPE	%
Ras Tanura	Constantza	4,144	12,094	66
	Lavera	4,684	10,783	57
	Rotterdam	6,436	11,169	42
	New York	8,281	11,794	30
Jeddah	Piraeus	1,320	11,207	88
Jeddah	Liverpool	3,902	10,702	63.5
Bombay	Rotterdam	6,337	10,743	41
Bombay	Marseille	4,558	10,362	56
Shanghahai	Genoa	8,670	13,619	36.3

The distance between Jeddah (Saudi Arabia) and the Port of Costanzia (Black Sea) is 11771 miles via the Cape of Good Hope, whilst it is only 1698 miles via the Suez Canal (SC), thus a saving of 86% in distance is achieved.

A saving of 23% in distance is also achieved by using the SC for the trip from Rotterdam in Holland to Tokyo in Japan, if compared with the route round the African coast.

As illustrated by the aforementioned factors, transit through the Suez Canal is always getting more attractive for the economy and the Shipping lines.

---

[10] http://www.rafimar.com/homepage/suez_canal.html#transit

4.2. Approximate calculation for Suez Canal Passage fees:

In this section, I describe the calculation of a ships cost, assuming it runs through Suez Canal. This serves merely as an approximation of how the costs for Suez Canal passage are calculated.

First: Ship Detail example:
MV "Y"
LOA= 188.10 m
BOA= 32.00 m
International Tonnage: GRT= 23652/NRT= 10596
Suez Tonnage: GRT= 24728/NRT=20232

Canal Tolls breakdown :	
First 5000 : 5000 * 7,65	38 250,00
Next 5000 : 5000 * 5	25 000,00
Next 10000 : 10000 * 4	40 000,00
Next 20000 : 232 * 2,8	649,60
Next 30000 : 0 * 2,6	0,00
Next 50000 : 0 * 2,05	0,00
Rest: 0 * 1,95	0,00
Total SDR :	103 899,60
USD/SDR Exchange rate :	1,5382
Canal tolls	159.818,36 USD

Calculation Process:
Vessel Particulars Tariff: 08-07
SCNT: 20232
GRT: 23652
SDR: Varies with the dollar exchange rate (in this Example 1, 5382)
Draft: 11.50 m
Beam: 30.00 m
Laden or Ballasted: Laden
North- or Southbound: Northbound
Calculation result
Canal Tolls:	159.818, 36 USD
Tugs (0 tug(s)):	000.000, 00 USD
Mooring / Projector:	002.352, 50 USD
Pilot age:	000.262, 75 USD
Disbursements:	005.479, 71 USD

TOTAL: 167.913, 32 USD[11]

---

[11] Total transit cost does not include Agencies Transit fees or various kinds of deck cargo. This is only estimation.

Chapter 2: Passage Procedures:

1. Allowances for Entrance:

1.1. General allowances:

- Transit through the Suez Canal is open to vessels of all nations subject to them complying with the conditions stated in the present Rules of Navigation.
- All references and circulars are organized and regulate by the SCA (Suez Canal Authorities) Vessels also have to comply with the provisions of the International Regulations for SOLAS and its amendments, MARPOL 73/78, as well as the provisions of the International Regulations for Preventing Collisions at Sea and all laws, orders, and regulations issued by the Egyptian Government.
- As long as the vessel size matches the Suez Canal properties and may pass through the passage, however, the SCA have some rules for some vessels, which are not allowed to transit through the Suez Canal.
- If the vessel has no means for lifting mooring boats and the ship's boats are not suitable for mooring in the Canal, the vessel shall not be allowed to transit the Canal.
- The SCA reserves the right to refuse access to Canal Waters for any vessel in case of carrying prohibited cargoes, and in case of none or erroneous declaration on the presence of dangerous cargo on board, such as ammunition, explosives, radioactive substances, etc.

1.2. General Prohibition:[12]

According to the rules of navigation from the SCA a vessel will not be allowed to transit the Canal in any of the following cases:[13]

- Any vessel whose Tropical Load Line is submerged, or Plimsoll Marks not plainly visible (Overloaded).
- Vessels considered by the Suez Canal Authorities as dangerous for navigation.
- If carrying dangerous cargo and not conforming to (Chapters 12, 13 and 14) of the Rules of Navigation or carrying prohibited cargoes.
- If having a list of more than 3 degrees.
- If trimmed in a way causing poor maneuverability.
- If having deck loads protruding from vessel's sides in a manner endangering the safety of transit.
- If the vessel is fragile or loaded in a manner that dangerously affects her stability.
- If her draught is in excess of the maximum permitted, according to rules of Navigation.
- For VLCC's and ULCC's if there is bad weather.

---

[12] These regulations are for all kind of ships and both the south-and north convoy Passage.

[13] (Art. 47) of the SCA Navigation Rules

- The SCA may consider delaying the vessel's entry to the Canal in the event of bad weather.
- Any vessel without anchors.

1.3. Special Prohibitions for South Convoy:

There are some special prohibitions for the second southbound Convoy Passage, which have been specified by the SCA.

The following vessels are not allowed to join the second southbound convoy:
- Vessels with an arrival draught of more than 42 feet (12.80 m).
- Vessels with a beam over 148 feet (45.11 m).
- Vessels over 90000 Suez Canal Gross Tonnages.
- Container vessels over 90000 Suez Canal Gross Tonnage need pre- approval from the SCA.
- Liquefied inflammable gas vessels (LPG, LNG, or similar Loaded or Ballast N.G.F. vessels).
- Tankers carrying chemicals with a flashpoint below 23 degree centigrade.
- Vessels carrying uncontainerized radioactive materials Group 1.
- Vessels not fitted with double bottom carrying chemicals in bulk.
- Vessels carrying dangerous wastes.
- Heavy lifters (semi – submersible) carrying heavy lift units with tonnage exceeding the lifting capacity of their individual cranes.
- Vessels carrying deck cargo protruding more than half the vessel's breadth on any side, with a maximum of 15 meters on each side if breadth exceeds 30 meters.
- Navy ships

2. Canal traffic system[14]

The Canal is uses a convoy system allowing ships to transit at a fixed speed with a fixed distance between every two passing ships.

Three convoys pass through the Canal every day, two southbound against one northbound. Each of the three convoys follows a certain system from the moment it enters the Canal, respecting the speed limits and the emergency stopping distance between every two ships within the one convoy.

2.1. North Passage Process:[15]

There is only one northbound convoy daily, starting at around 0600 hours and clearing the Canal Port Said end the same day at around 1600 hours.

2.1.1. General:

- Two hours before arrival at the Suez pilot station, vessels should contact the harbor office by VHF channel 14-16 in order to provide details of transit.
- A pilot boat can be contacted via VHF channel 14
- Vessels have to advise the Agent Office 48 hours before the ETA.
- Time limit to join the North Passage 0100 LT= GMT+3 Hours.
- Time limit regarding Cargo Vessels & Chemicals Tanker or Palm oil is 0300 LT.
- Time limit regarding Bulk Vessel, Container, RORO Vessel more than (GRT 44000 t.) or Draft more than (38 f./11.58m), Tankers and Gas Carriers is 0100 LT.
- Vessels arriving after 0500 LT may join the Group, if the traffic condition permits. In this case, an extra charge will be added.
- The SCA considers the arrival time at the Port Said pilot station by passing South of Latitude 31° 28.7` N regardless of anchorage time.

2.1.2. North Passage Process:

- The North bound convoy has a free run from Port of Suez until Port Said.
- It passes through the East Kabrit channel, the Eastern dredged channel in the Bitter Lakes, the East channel of the Diversion, the East channel of Lake Temsah, the East channel of Ballah loop and the East channel from KM. 17 Northward.
- In the event that the northbound convoy has to stop in the Bitter Lakes due to the traffic situation of the southbound convoy or an emergency, **the following must be considered:**
  - ○ Container vessels heading the convoy will drop anchor in the suitable East Anchorage Areas of the Bitter Lakes.

---

[14] These Information are based on the actual Information from the SCA, See
http://www.suezcanal.gov.eg

[15] http://www.suezcanal.gov.eg/NR.aspx?node=81

- o VLCC's will anchor in the suitable East Anchorage according to their draught.
- o All other vessels will anchor in the East Area corresponding to their draught.
- o Three berths are available in Kabrit East Branch in case of emergency.

- LPG, LNG in ballast or loaded, and chemicals loaded in bulk for safety measures are included in the Tankers Group.
- Vessels complete transit of the Canal in approximately 10 hours in the northbound convoy.
- Northbound convoy commences at 0600 hours LT at KM 160 and consists of two groups of vessels

2.1.2.1. Group A:
- Arrival Limit 0100 LT on passing north of Latitude 29° 42, 8 N. extendable to 0300 LT.
- Vessels classified as First Group:
  - o 3rd & 4th generation containerships over 40,000 SGRT & similar
  - o Lash Carriers over 35,000 SCGRT
  - o LPG-LNG (Loaded or NGF)
  - o Loaded VLCC'S, Conventional or Chemical Tankers
  - o Heavy Bulk carriers and other vessels with a draft over 38 FT or a length over 950 FT)
  - o Navy ships

2.1.2.2. Group B:
- Start after the entrance of the First North Group.
- Arrival Limit 0300 LT on passing north of Latitude 29°48, 33´ N. extendable to 0400 LT.
- Vessels classified as Second Group:
  - o Cargo and other vessels anchored in Suez Anchorage's.
  - o All other Vessels.

2.2. South Passage:[16]

There are 2 southbound Convoys daily passing the Suez Canal. The first southbound group starts at 0100 LT and proceeds directly to the Great Bitter Lakes. The second southbound Convoy starts at 0700 LT and proceeds directly to Ballah Loop.

2.2.1. General:

- Two hours before arrival at the Suez pilot station, vessels should contact the harbor office by VHF channel 14-16 in order to provide details of transit.
- A pilot boat can be contacted via VHF channel 14.
- Fifteen miles before arrival at the fairway buoy, vessels should contact the harbor office via VHF channel 12 or 16 in order to provide full details of transit.
- Vessels have to advise the Agent Office 48 hours before the ETA.
- Time limit to join the first South Passage is 1900 LT=GMT+3 Hours
- Time limit to join the Second South Passage is 0300 LT=GMT+3 Hours.
- Vessels arriving after 1900 LT may join the Convoy, if Traffic conditions permit. In this case, an extra charge will be added.

2.2.2. First South Passage Process:

- All vessels, which are entitled to transit the Suez Canal, can join the first southbound convoy.
- Vessels complete the transit of the Canal in approximately 12 to 14 hours in the southbound convoy.
- This convoy has a free run to the Bitter Lakes, passes through the East branch of the Ballah by-pass, the East channel of Lake Temsah, the Diversion West channel and anchors in the Western Anchorage's in the Bitter Lakes.
- The route sequence continuing from the Bitter Lakes will be Warships, LPG, LNG vessels, the 4th Generation Containerships, 3rd Generation Containerships over 40.000 SCG and LASH over 35.000 SCGT, followed by VLCC's in ballast and then other vessels.
- The first ship of the southbound convoy will regulate the speed to cross the last northbound vessel abeam of Kabrit station and consists of 3 groups of vessels.
- This Convoy is separated into 3 Groups:
  - **Group A:** Vessels in Port Said Harbor.
  - **Group B:** Vessels anchored in the Northern Anchorage Area consisting of 4th Generation Containerships, 3rd Generation Containerships, VLCC's in ballast over 42 feet draught, LPG, LNG, N.G.F *(LPG, LNG, N.G.F. vessels may join group A.)*. Vessels in ballast or loaded and LASH over 35.000 SC. G.T. This group will be headed by the Containerships and the first vessel will enter through Port Said East Approach channel in due time to join Group A at Km. 17.
  - **Group C:** Vessels anchored in Southern Anchorage Area will enter through Port Said West channel in due time to join Group B at Km. 17.

---

[16] http://www.suezcanal.gov.eg/NR.aspx?node=81

21

2.2.3. Second South Passage Process:

- Starts from 0630 hours to 0900 hours. The forming and depth of this convoy is subject to situation of traffic and the time limit.
- 3rd & 4th Generation Container ships with more than one propeller astern shall be ahead of this convoy to anchor at Temsah Lake (maximum two vessels).
- Vessels will make fast (anchor) in Ballah West Branch *(Maximum capacity 15 vessels according to the NR. of berths at Ballah Loop.)*, and continue route after the last Northbound vessel clears KM 61.
- Dimensions of vessels that can make fast (anchor) at Ballah West Branch should not exceed those indicated in the following table, excluding Tankers over 90000 Tons SC.G.T.
- Vessels not allowed to join this convoy are the following:
    - o Loaded Tankers (or Bulk carriers) carrying Petroleum Grade A or similar substances (Flash point below 23°C or 73°F)
    - o Liquefied inflammable gas vessels (LPG, LNG, or similar Loaded or Ballast N.G.F. vessels).
    - o Vessels not fitted with double bottom carrying chemicals in bulk.
    - o Vessels carrying radioactive substance Group 1.
    - o Vessels carrying dangerous wastes.
    - o Heavy lifters (semi-submersible) carrying heavy lift units with tonnage exceeding the lifting capacity of their individual cranes.
    - o Vessels carrying deck cargo protruding more than what is stated in Art. 26 of the Rules of Navigation.

Chapter 3: Passage preparation and responsibility[17]

Like any port and canal in the world, there are certain documents and preparation, which are needed to be done, before proceeding to the canal. In this Chapter are lists with all cases, documents and preparations needed to have a clear passage through the Suez Canal.

1. Arrival Notice:[18]

Due to the increase in Canal traffic, priority will be given to vessels notifying the S.C.A (Suez Canal Authority) 5 days in advance of the intended transit, provided the vessel arrives within the time limits stipulated.

A fine is imposed by the S.C.A. if the vessel does not transit on the notified date, therefore it is imperative to alter or cancel any such notification at least 24 hours in advance Vessel should advise following details (through its Canal Transit Agent) to Suez Canal Authority:

- The name and type of vessel.
- Year built - flag - call sign - MMSI no.
- Ex-name/s (if any).
- Classification society- P&I club rep. office in Egypt.
- Vessels Suez Canal I.D (SCID) number.
- Suez Canal GRT/NRT tonnage.
- International DWT/GRT/NRT tonnage
- LOA/Beam
- Arrival draft FW/AFT (trim not to exceed 4 ft by stern).
- ETA
- Last port and port bound to.
- Date of last transit (if any)
- Whether ballast or loaded stating nature of cargo on board and total quantity.
- For liquid Cargo: Flashpoint of cargo and whether vessel fitted with double bottom tanks.
- For bulk Cargo: If vessel also carrying empty/full bags and/or general cargo - quantity of same.
- If carrying any dangerous cargo stating quantity and class according to IMCO's regulations.
- If carrying any military cargo or vessel under time charter to military forces.
- Whether vessel carries floating units on deck or heavy pieces over 250 MT on/under deck.

---

[17] In compliance with Rules of Navigation Chapter 2

[18] In compliance with art 13 of Rules of Navigation

- Number and size of any containers onboard - if stowed on or under deck - number of tiers of containers on deck - if top tier contains more than 10 containers - if top tier has a protrusion of more than 4 ft.
- Number of crew and their nationalities.
- Whether ship requires hiring projector for transit.
- Whether vessel is in compliance with Suez Canal regulation regarding mooring boats and which of the provided alternatives will be followed.[19]
- If ship's machinery/equipment is in good working condition or not.
- If garbage removal service will be required or not.
- Vessels INMARSAT TLX/TEL/FAX numbers – email.
- Name of master.
- Any requirements (provisions, bunkers, fresh water, cash, bunker sample delivery, etc.)

In case of (garbage removal) is not required; please ensure that you do not sign any invoice/voucher for same because they will not be able to be rejected afterwards and vessel will be liable for Payment of same.

This information is just a notice for the SCA to inform about the situation of current Vessel transiting the Canal. This also allows an overview for the Authorities, which leads to comfortable passage process.[20]

1.1.Arrival Registration:

To avoid missing convoys and/or delays, Fifteen miles before arrival to fairway buoy, vessel should contact the harbor office by VHF channel 12 or 16 for answering questions related with vessels particulars and arrival details such as draft, nature/quantity of cargo, cranes capacity, etc.

The Master of a vessel destined to transit the Suez Canal Could use the following methods:

1.1.1. At Port Said :

- Port management (Listening) :
  Call sign: (Port Said 16) 156.800 MHz
- Pilot vessel and Radar guidance :
- Outside the Harbor :
  Call sign : (Port Said 12) 156.600 MHz
- Inside the Harbor :
  Call sign : (Port Said 13) 156.650 MHz
- Admeasurements Office :
  Call sign: (Port Said 73) 156.675 MHz

---

[19] (see Rules of Navigation Annex 2)

[20] If any change of information above, before arrival the Suez Canal, Master should inform the Agent immediately about it, so that the SCA make the right preparation, and for avoiding any misunderstanding.
In due time before arrival a copy of the International Tonnage Certificate 1969 (ITC-69) must be sent per email or fax to the Agent.

1.1.2. At Suez Port :
- Port management (Listening) :
  Call sign: (Suez 16) 156.800 MHz
- Pilot vessel and Radar guidance :
- Outside the Harbor :
  Call sign : (Suez 11) 156.550 MHz
- Inside the Harbor :
  Call sign : (Suez 14) 156.700 MHz
- Admeasurements Office :
  Call sign : (Suez 74) 156.675 MHz

2. Vessel Dimensions and Drafts:
There is some regulation and restrictions about Drafts and Dimensions of vessels, which allowed entering the canal. These are as follow:

Height: Max Air draft = 68 meters
Length: No restrictions
Beam: max. 245 ft.
Draft: maximum draft for loaded vessels is authorized in relation to beam. (See BEAM/Draft Table in Annex No.2)

3. Documents needed for Transit:
3.1.General Documents:
Documents required by the Suez Canal authorities:[21]
One copy of each of the following documents must normally be presented not later than 90 minutes after the registered arrival time and in any event the documents should not be presented later than one hour after the arrival time limits.
- Suez Canal Special Tonnage Certificate issued by recognized classification society.
- Certificate of registry.
- GA/engine room/capacity plan
- Statistical declaration
- Copies of cargo manifest for cargo onboard.
- Declaration concerning any dangerous cargo.
- Declaration concerning double bottom tanks and the lower parts of the high tanks.
- Declaration concerning vessels in ballast.
- Declaration concerning state of navigability
- Classification certificate
- Piping plan and general arrangement plan for LPG/LNG vessels
- All other known documents and valid certificates which every sailing and seaworthy vessel must have, should be onboard.[22]

---

[21] These Documents are required for all kind of vessels (see Annex No.2).

[22] Normal Documents must be also ready as such Crew List, Radio Certificates, and Cargo Manifest etc.

3.2.For First Time Transit:

When a ship is to sail through the Suez Canal for the first time, all the above documents must be accompanied by the following:

- 3 Copies of Ship's registry certificate.
- 3 Copies of Suez Canal special tonnage certificate.
- 3 Copies of Ship's general arrangement plan
- 3 Copies of Ship's engine room plan.
- 3 Copies of Ship's capacity plan.

3.3.Vessel Arriving in Ballast:

When a ship is to sail through the Suez Canal in ballast, all the above documents must be accompanied by the following:

- Suez Canal Special Tonnage Certificate
- Crew List
- Certificate of registry.
- General Arrangement Plan
- Engine Room Plan
- Capacity Plan
- In-Ballast Declaration
- Classification Certificate[23]

3.4.Tanker Vessels:

For Tanker Vessels transiting through Suez Canal, all the above documents must be accompanied by the following:

- Copy of Capacity Plan
- Declaration concerning double bottom tanks and the lower parts of the high tanks.
- Piping plan and general arrangement plan for LPG/LNG vessels
- In addition Master will fill other Formal Documents to be presented by Agents and Authorities.

---

[23] Important: Even though copies of the documents are presented to the SCA, this does not preclude that the original certificates may be requested from the master during transit for checking.

4. Authorities' Personnel:

For every Passage, Authorities Personal will have to come on Board, to check the required Equipments and Documents needed for safe Transit.

For own safety and smooth Passage, please prepare for all documents needed for Passage before boarding the SCA Authorities Personal.

4.1. Quarantine officials (1 doctor and his assistant)

Please note that the quarantine officials may board vessel and the quarantine doctor will collect the following:

- One copy of the crew list.
- One copy of the last port calls list
- One copy of vaccination list.
- Maritime declaration of health (if not available, the form will be provided by the quarantine doctor).

4.2. Harbor master

Please note that the harbormaster may board vessel in order to:

- Check vessels draft/trim and general condition.
- Check whether both anchors are in good working order.
- Check whether cranes are in good working order.
- Record vessels maximum maneuvering speed.
- Record dead slow ahead speed.

4.3. Suez Canal inspector

- Please note that the following blank documents will be presented by the Suez Canal inspector for completion and will be collected by him [24]
- Please also note that the Suez Canal inspector will collect the following:
  - o One copy of the crew list.
  - o One copy of the last port calls list.
  - o One copy of cargo manifest.
  - o One copy of certificate of registry signed and stamped by master.
- The Suez Canal inspector will also require seeing vessels original Suez tonnage certificate.
- Please also note that in special cases the Suez Canal inspector is at liberty to collect original plans to be returned at a later date when SCA have completed their measurement formalities.

---

[24] See point 3.1. General Documents

4.4. Suez Canal engineer[25]
- Please note that the Suez Canal engineer will board vessel in order to check Suez Canal projector (searchlight) and its electrical connections
- In case vessel does not have a projector or the existing one is not approved by the Suez Canal engineer a shore portable projector will be provided.

4.5. Suez Canal mooring men[26]
- In case vessels Suez GRT is less than 5,000 MT three mooring men will board vessel (one mooring boat will be used for transit).
- In case vessels Suez GRT is more than 5,000 MT six mooring men will board vessel (two mooring boats will be used for transit).
- Mooring men will remain on board during transit.

4.6. Suez Canal electricians
- In case vessel has her own projector one electrician for its operation will remain on board during transit.
- In case vessel is provided with shore projector two electricians for its operation will remain on board during transit.

4.7. Suez Canal pilots[27]
- Please note that at least 5 pilots will board vessel during Suez Canal transit.
- Each pilot will be relieving the previous pilot and there will be max two pilots on board at the same time.
- A suitable (officer class) accommodation is to be put at each pilot's disposal.
- In case of no suitable accommodation vessel may be delayed and will pay extra dues (USD 300 for each pilot).

---

[25] In compliance with art 28 of Suez Canal Rules of Navigation

[26] In compliance with art 20 of Suez Canal Rules of Navigation

[27] In compliance with art 6 of Suez Canal Rules of Navigation

5. Communications due transit:[28]

UHF Radiotelephonic in the Canal:

- UHF voice communication system was built to cover the entire Canal and its approaches to facilitate communication between pilots and the main movement office at Ismailia and the port management offices.

  The Canal pilot uses a special portable UHF personal transceiver which has the following frequencies.

Ch. No.	Reception Frequency MHz	Transmission Frequency MHz	Function
1	415.35	412.85	Vessels from North (SB)
2	415.60	413.10	Vessels from South (NB)
3	415.85	413.35	Emergency (EM)
4	416.60	141.10	In Port of Suez Harbor HP(T)
5	416.35	413.85	In Port Said Harbor HP (S)
6	416.13	413.60	Emergency Critical Vessels (out of convoy) (EMC)

- Escort tugs-towing tugs will use special portable UHF transceiver set which has the following frequencies :

  Ch.1:414.750MHz
  Ch.2:414.775MHz
  Ch.3:414.800MHz

- Sending SUQ to Suez Canal Authority Head Office Ismailia is per following Numbers:

TELEX	:	581 1622570
FAX	:	+20 64 392518

---

[28] In compliance with Chapter 9 of Rules of Navigation

5.1. Special Communication due the ISPS:

Quick connections for Suez Canal Authority according to (ISPS) as follows:-

Inmarsat - A	tel.	871-1622570	
	fax	871-1622574	
	telex	581-1522570	
Inmarsat - B	tel.	71-362213310	
	fax	871-362213312	
	data	871-362213313	
	telex	581-362213314	
Inmarsat - C	telex	581-462299911	
International	telex	0091-63528	
	fax	0020643393517 0020643393230	or
Chief marine office	tell	0020643393116 0020643393128	or
Chief team movement office	tell	0020643393205	
Chief movement office	tell	0020643392005	
Movement office	fax	0020643392518 0020643392514	or
Radio telex		Sel. call (4820)	
		Freq. Tax / Rx	
		1612 / 2142	
		4250 / 4205	
		4250 / 6310	
MMSI. no.		0062211 20	
VHF	CH	68 (24hrs/7days)	
E-mail		ismradio@hotmail.com	

6. Crew change in Suez Canal:[29]

Arriving and departing crewmembers are looked after through Agent offices, which the company is working with.

- **Joiners**
  - Information required prior arrival;
    - Personal Details "Name, Rank, Nationality, Date of Birth, Passport number and Seaman's book number".
    - Full flight details including any connecting flight(s).
    - Copy of passport prior to arrival should be faxed to your Agency in Egypt.

  - Documents required upon arrival:
    - Valid seaman's book.
    - An introductory letter from the owners stating ship's name, the port ship arrives and the Canal agent's name.
    - Contract of employment.
    - Officers should also carry their license of competency.
    - Visas

Visas can be granted on arrival at Cairo airport. For certain countries, however, an entry visa is required prior to arriving in Cairo.

As per Egyptian authorities, crewmembers from following countries:
- India
- Pakistan
- Bangladesh
- Somalia
- Sri Lanka
- Turkey,

, are expected to send data and information, including a copy of their passport and visa, to the agent 72 hours prior to arrival at Cairo Airport.

- **Off Signers**
  - Documents required for off signers
    - Personal Details "Name, Rank, Nationality, Date of Birth, Passport number and Seaman's book number".
    - Full flight details including any connecting flight(s).
    - PTA reference NOS.
    - Ticket collection place.

---

[29] The information here are based on various requirements of various agents, please respect any other needs of information of your Agency.

31

7. Special instructions for Master:

Master should provide following in first ETA telex:

- Full particulars of ship (SCGRT, SCNRT, DWT, DRAFT, BEAM, LOA, NATIONALITY, CALL SIGN, EX NAMES. Date of last transit, Type of cargo and quantity, or if in ballast, gas free or not and IMO class of any dangerous cargo), if no changes since last transit, please state ''particulars no change''.

Master should include following in his last ETA telex to the agent:

- ''No bam boats or others are allowed to board my vessel except the officials, please advise port police accordingly "

Please note:

- Information / instructions concerning all other matters should be directed to the Agent, who will coordinate and authorize additional requirements.

Special information for master to avoid unexpected expenses:

- Master should know that only authorized personnel are allowed to board his ship and he can always ask for their official license and/or identification card.

Important:

- Do not sign any vouchers/invoices for services not rendered.
- All vouchers/invoices should state amount and type of service requested.
- Before signing any presented document, master should clarify necessity of particular service offered.
- Service requested should be rendered and in a satisfactory manner before signing.
- Do not sign/stamp any blank paper. No blank space below signature. ¨
- Always keep a photocopy of signed papers onboard.
- All spirits (incl. wines) and excess cigarettes must be properly manifested and together with any "x" rated materials to be placed in bonded store room prior to arrival and request / insist sealing by customs officer.
- Officers/crew to be warned to comply, or otherwise ship may be detained and may be charged for "smuggling".

Chapter 4: Navigation Rules

In this Chapter I just handle about most important Navigation Rules of the Suez Canal transit, which may be a kind of help progress for safe transit. All the information here included, are based on the Main Navigation Rules of the SCA for transiting in Suez Canal.

1. Responsibilities:[30]

- *When on Canal waters or at its ports or roads, any vessel or floating structure of any description are responsible for any damage and consequential loss she may cause either directly or indirectly to herself or to CA properties or personnel or to third party.*
- *The vessels' or floating structures' owners and/or operators are responsible without option to release them from responsibility by limited liability.*
- *The words (owners and /or operators) for the purpose of the present article shall be considered to mean person/persons or corporate body responsible for the vessel at the time of navigational accident or incident.*
- *Moreover, the vessel guarantees to indemnify the CA in respect of any claim against the latter by reason of any damage, whatsoever she may cause either directly or indirectly to third party.*
- *The vessel waives the right to claim the SCA for any damages caused by third party that she may sustain while on Canal Waters.*

2. Pilot age[31]

- *Pilot age is compulsory for all vessels, whatever is their tonnage when entering, leaving, moving, changing berth or shifting on Canal Waters or Port Said and Suez harbors.*
- *Any exemption must be explicitly authorized by the Suez Canal Authority.[32]*

3. Anchorage

- *Masters must avoid anchoring or using the thrusters in the Canal, except in case of absolute necessity.[33]*
- *The sounding of a whistle or siren is prohibited except for giving any authorized or required signal, as mentioned in Part III, Art 92.*
- *Anchor station is to be established during bad weather or poor visibility and when advised by the pilot.[34]*

---

[30] in compliance with art 4 of Navigation Rules

[31] in compliance with art 6 of Navigation Rules

[32] For extra information about detailed info please look up to art11 of Navigation Rules

[33] in compliance with art 65 of Navigation Rules

4. Mooring boats[35]

- *Vessels transiting the Canal must have mooring boats as mentioned hereafter hired from the Suez Canal Mooring Company approved by SCA*
- *In case no mooring boats from the said company are available, ship's boats if suitable for mooring in the Canal can be used and must be manned by shore crew , hired from the SC mooring company, each boat is to be manned by three men.*
- *One mooring boat or one motor boat for vessels under 2500 tons gross, SC.G.T.*
- *One motor boat for vessels from 2500 to 5000 tons gross, SC.G.T.*
- *Two motor boats or one motor boat and one mooring boat for vessels from 5000 SC.G.T. To 30000 SC.G.T.*
- *Two motor boats for vessels over 30000 tons gross, SC.G.T.*
- *Ships may ask for additional motor boats or mooring boats according to Master's request.*
- *These mooring boats must be in constant readiness for lowering to run the ropes to the mooring posts without any delay during the transit of the vessel*
- *Ships must be fitted with well maintained lifting appliances capable of lifting mooring boats of 4 tons weight (Including crew members).*
- *Ships may carry extra mooring boats as passengers for the interest of navigation. However, L.P.G, L.N.G, and Loaded Tankers are not allowed any extra boats.*
- *The handling of mooring boats must be carried out well clear from the ship's propellers.*
- *Masters are requested to reduce speed during lifting or lowering operations of mooring boats, an officer must be in charge, to avoid accidents that may endanger the life of mooring men.*
- *If the vessel has no means for lifting mooring boats and ship's boats are not suitable for mooring in the Canal, the vessel shall not be allowed to transit the Canal.*

5. Suez searchlights[36]

- *Before transiting the Canal, the vessel should be provided with a searchlight (projector) complying with the following conditions and specifications:*
- *It should be placed on the bow in the axis of the vessel and show the Canal clearly.*
- *Specifications are as follows :*
  - *Minimum range of radiation of single beam 1800 m. ahead (Brightness of 1 LUX approx, at the atmospheric transmission factor T = 0.85).*
  - *The power of the lamp must give a luminous intensity of single light beam not less than 3 x 106 (3 million) candles, which is equivalent to a high efficiency incandescent lamp of :*
    - i. *2000 watts for vessels up to 30000 SC.G.T.*
    - ii. *3000 watts for vessels over 30000 SC.G.T.*

---

[34] in compliance with art 45 of Navigation Rules

[35] in compliance with art 20 of Navigation Rules

[36] in compliance with art 28 of Navigation Rules

iii. Or any kind of lamps which fulfill the specifications, under item (2) above and to be of the non-explosive type.

- The drum and stand should be of high corrosion resisting material and can be operated both horizontally and vertically.
- The front glass must be of hardened type and can stand rapid cooling.
- The reflector must be in two halves of precise ground glass mirror of highest quality or of polished aluminum having at least 95% the reflective capacity of the glass mirror.
- The two halves of the reflector can be brought together (zero position) to make a single reflector light beam and can be parted to give two separate light beams each of 5 degrees at least on the horizontal level with adjustable dark sector from 0 to 10 degrees.
- The searchlight drum must be watertight (pressure test 0.25 kg/cm2) and gastight (according to the classification rules for the vessel's electric appliances within the dangerous area) and provided with a vent - out of which a flexible hose can be fitted on the drum to dissipate the heated air out of the searchlight in addition to a safety vent. On vessels carrying Petroleum products, L.N.G. or inflammable substances or vessels Not Gas Free, exit of hot air must be effectuated in a place devoid of inflammable gas.
- The searchlight must be equipped with 2 lamps carrier that can be turned into position to let the lamp exactly in the focus of the reflector, and the current must be switched on automatically.
- The electric system (switches, plug, socket and cables) must be of 1st class marine type.
- The degree of protection IP 55 or similar standards.
- The searchlight must have a certificate for the „Type Test „. This type test must include illuminate test to fulfill the above specifications, issued by one of the Classification Societies (Lloyd's Register, etc.) .The original to be submitted to Suez Canal Officials and thereby, after test by SCA Inspector, the searchlight can be accepted.

- On all vessels of whatever type, electric cables installations for searchlight and all electric connections leading to it must be permanently fixed, insulated and gastight.
  - At the end of the cables, a fixed and gastight socket should be installed close to the searchlight.
- On board vessels, electrically propelled or having electrically driven gear (steering, winches, etc.) the number of generators and their individual power output must be sufficient to ensure uninterrupted functioning of the searchlight in the event of stoppage of one of the generators, No exception to this rule will be allowed except when there is an independent generator and circuit on board specifically set apart for the searchlight.
- A portable projector can be hired locally from the Canal Mooring and light Company (weight of projector about 22 KGs).
- For vessels fitted with their own projector, two shore electricians should operate it during the transit.

- *Vessels with special cases :*
  - *L.P.G. and L.N.G. vessels, without any exceptions, must be provided with their own searchlight.*
  - *Vessels entering the Canal, direct from sea, must be provided also with their own searchlight.*
  - *New built tugs and yachts up to 1500 tons SCGT can transmit the Canal with their own Projectors, on condition that the unit is equipped with at least 2 projectors, each with a capacity of not less than 1000 watts for each.*
- *If electrical connections and/or searchlight are not in conformity, the vessel is liable to transit only in day-time and therefore, subject to delay. An additional due of (4 300 U.S. Dollars) will be imposed when the searchlight and/or electrical connections are not conform for the 3rd transit and each following.*

6. Signals and lights

All signals used in Canal Waters are mentioned in Chapter 11 of Navigation Rules.

Art 91 handles all generalities of Signals

Art 92 handles all Sound Signals

Art 93 handles all Visual Signals

Please be aware that all signals mentioned in Navigation Rules are obligations to enter the Suez Canal

7. Tugs

All information about tugs and requirements are listed in Chapter 3, Section 3 of Navigation Rules.

8. Overtaking[37]

- *Vessels proceeding in the same direction are not allowed to overtake one another while underway in the Canal Waters and ports unless authorized by the Suez Canal Control Office.*
- *An additional due of (750 U.S. Dollars) will be imposed for violation of this rule.*

9. Buoy age[38]

- *The navigable channel is marked by pairs of light buoys.*
- *On the east side: **Green** buoys showing **Green light**.*
- *On the west side: **Red** buoys showing **Red light**.*

---

[37] in compliance with art 73 of Navigation Rules

[38] in compliance with art82 of Navigation Rules

- *In the straight parts, the distance between each pair is 1.5 kilometers.*
- *In the north section and 1.0 kilometer in the south section.*
- *In the curves, the distance will be less than 1.0 kilometer.*
- *All buoys in the Canal and its approaches are fitted with radar reflectors.*

For further information about Buoy age please look up in Art 83 of Navigation Rules.

10. Accidents[39]

- *Whenever a vessel is underway and accidentally going to stop, she must if other vessels are following, attract their attention by giving five or six short blasts on the whistle or siren also contact movement control office by all means of connections (SUQ. VHF, Fax... etc.). The master must immediately contact stating:*
  "I am reducing speed and may have to stop and make fast"
  Vessels stopping accidentally at night, must in addition, immediately replace their White light astern by a Red light.
- *In case of grounding, the Master must immediately hoist the signal shown in Part III, Art. 92 of these Rules, and send a radio message whether a tug is required or not, whether or not passage is clear for the tug and whether lightening is necessary, sounding, statement of fact ... etc.*
- *When a vessel runs aground, Suez Canal Officials are alone empowered to order and direct all operations required to get the vessel afloat and if needed get the vessel unloaded and towed. Nevertheless, Masters remain responsible for all damages or accidents of any kind which may be the direct or indirect consequence of the grounding.*
- *All attempts on the part of other vessels to get off a vessel aground are strictly prohibited.*
- *Once afloat, and the Canal Officials find it necessary to tow or escort the vessels by one tug or more tugs, the vessel must from that moment, pay towage charges as mentioned in Part IV. p. 190. Moreover, it is understood that the vessel bears all expenses necessary for repairs of any damage or breakdown which might interfere with her getting underway, regardless of the time when such damage or breakdown takes place.*
- *When a vessel grounds or stops outside the Canal itself or if the grounding or stoppage is due to a collision, all charges for getting the vessel afloat, towing, unloading, etc..., are paid by the vessel and must be settled as per statement drawn up by CA before the vessel leaves Port Said or Port of Suez.*
- *Whenever a collision appears probable, vessels must not hesitate to run aground should this be necessary to avoid the collision.*
- *When a vessel or any floating units of any description runs aground or strands or sinks or is left abandoned, either in the Canal itself or in one of its port, Waiting and anchorage Areas and CA deems it as an obstruction or a menace to navigation in Canal, the Authority has the right to take of its own accord such action as may be*

---

[39] in compliance with art 59 of Navigation Rules

necessary for the purpose of removing or destroying the vessel or floating structure by whatever means CA may select and at the risk and expense of the owner, or the person responsible for the vessel or the floating structure. In this case the SCA has the right to sell the vessel or the floating structure of the wreck salvaged or all of them together in public auctions with a view to covering all kinds of expenses.

11.Leak[40]

- *In Case a leak occurs or is discovered, when the ship in approaching channel, sea waiting areas and Harbor the Master must inform the Suez Canal Port Office at once.*
- *When in Canal or anchored in lakes, the Master must inform immediately the Movement Control Office. At the same time he must make the appropriate International Signal and Call attention by sounding a prolonged blast on the whistle or siren; and take all necessary measures to stop the leakage and ensure the safety of the vessel and environmental protection.*
- *The CA officials, whose decision shall be final, may order any action deemed necessary in the best interest of all concerned; change of berth or mooring, beaching or taking the vessel out to sea.*
- *The Master, the Owner and/or Operator of the vessel are nevertheless responsible for all damages or accidents arising directly or indirectly from the salvage operations.*
- *The Master, the Owner and/or Operators of vessel shall be liable to indemnify for any damage that may occur from pollution directly or indirectly to the environment and shall pay all expenses incurred for its removal, cleaning costs and all costs and compensation for any damage to the environment. (E.E.P.A No. 4, 1994 shall be applied)*

12.Pollution[41]

1. Discharge of substances polluting water :
Vessels must not discharge or throw into the Canal water any objects or any polluted ballast water, heavy slops, engine or fire room polluted bilge water, oil, wastes (2) or any other substances that will cause pollution.
The Egyptian Environmental Protection, Art. No. 4, 1994 prohibits the discharge of any polluting substances into water. The Provisions of this action. will apply for any discharge of polluting substances. -If for any reason a leakage of any polluting material from a vessel, the Master, the Owners and/or Operators of the vessel shall be liable to indemnify any damage that may occur from the pollution directly or indirectly to the environment and shall pay all expenses incurred for its removal and compensations. Moreover, she shall pay for all claims regarding cleaning costs and all environmental economic losses caused from the pollution.

---

[40] in compliance with art 60 of Navigation Rules

[41] in compliance with art 64 of Navigation Rules

Oil pollution notification :

Whenever a vessel observes an oil slick or an oil mixture discharge in the sea waiting areas, Approach Channels, Port Said harbor, Canal and anchorage areas in lakes, she must inform SCA with the following information at once:

1. *The time of observation.*
2. *The location and place and area covered by the slick.*
3. *The directions of movement of the slick.*
4. *The approximate oil thickness if possible.*
5. *If known; the name of vessel causing the slick.*
6. *The meteorological and oceanographic conditions, if possible.*
7. *Any other in formations.*

Annexes

1. Shortcuts

- ❖ A.
  - ➢ AB: alongside berth
  - ➢ Abm: abeam
  - ➢ AC: Admiralty Chart
  - ➢ AFT: Aft wards
  - ➢ ALL: Admiralty List of Lights
  - ➢ ALRS: Admiralty List of Radio Signals
  - ➢ Alt: Altitude
  - ➢ ALL: Alternating Light
  - ➢ Anch: Anchorage
  - ➢ App: apparent
  - ➢ Appr.: approaches
  - ➢ Art.: Article
- ❖ B.
  - ➢ BOA: Breadth over All
  - ➢ Bkwtr: Breakwater
  - ➢ Bn: Beacon
  - ➢ Bol: Bollard
  - ➢ Brg: bearing
  - ➢ By: buoy
- ❖ C.
  - ➢ C°: Celsius
  - ➢ Ch: channel VHF
  - ➢ Cm: centimetres
  - ➢ Cont: continuous
- ❖ D.
  - ➢ Dec: declination
  - ➢ DGPS: differential GPS
  - ➢ Dist: distance
  - ➢ Dr: Doctor

➤ DSC: Digital Selective Calling	
➤ DW: deep water	
➤ DWT: dead weight tonnage	
❖ E.	
➤ Ent.entrance	
➤ EP: estimated position	
➤ ETA: Estimated time of Arrival	
➤ Explos: explosive	
❖ F.	
➤ F°: Fahrenheit	
➤ FCC: Fully Cellular Container Vessel	
➤ Ft: feet	
➤ FW: Forward	
➤ FWS: fresh water supply	
❖ G.	
➤ GA: General Aviation	
➤ GMDSS: Global Maritime Distress and Safety System	
➤ GMT: Greenwich Mean Time	
➤ GPS: Global Positioning System	
➤ GRT: Gross Registered Tons	
❖ H.	
➤ H: hour	
➤ HF: high frequency	
➤ HF: Heavy fuel Oil	
➤ HrMr: harbour master	
➤ Hz: hertz	
❖ I.	
➤ Ident: identification signal	
➤ IMO: International Maritime Organisation	
➤ INMARSAT: Intern. Marit.Satelite Organisation	
➤ INT: international	
➤ IQ: interrupted quick flashing light	

➤ ISO: isophase light	
➤ ISPS: International Ship and Port Facility Port Security Code	
❖ K.	
➤ Km: Kilometer	
➤ Kn: knots	
➤ kW: Kilowatt	
❖ L.	
➤ Lat: latitude	
➤ LF: low frequency	
➤ LNG: liquefied natural gas	
➤ LOA: Lenght over all	
➤ LPG: *Liquefied/Liquefied Petroleum/Propane Gas*	
➤ LT: Local time	
➤ LT: By light bouy	
❖ M.	
➤ M: meter	
➤ MARPOL: *International Convention for the Prevention of Pollution from Ships*	
➤ MCA: Maritime and Coastguard Agency	
➤ MF: medium frequency	
➤ MHz: Megahertz	
➤ MMSI NO: Maritime Mobile Service Identity Number	
➤ MRCC CG: maritime rescue coordination Centre	
➤ MSI: maritime safety information	
➤ MT: Mobile Terminated (Messaging)	
❖ N.	
➤ N: North	
➤ NB: North Bound	
➤ NGF: Nationalen Garantie-Fonds	
➤ NM: notice to mariners	
➤ No: number	
➤ NRT: net registered tonnage	
❖ O.	

➢ OBO: Oil Bulk Oreb	
❖ P.	
➢ PA: position approximate	
➢ Pass.: passage	
➢ PR: port radio	
➢ Pos:position	
➢ Prohib: prohibited	
➢ PV: pilot vessel	
❖ Q.	
➢ Q: quick flashing light	
❖ R.	
➢ Ra: coast radar station	
➢ Racon: racon transponder beacon	
➢ Ramark: radar becon	
➢ Rep: reported	
➢ RORO: Roll-on -Roll-off	
❖ S.	
➢ SAR: search and rescue	
➢ SB: South Bound	
➢ SC: Suez Canal	
➢ SCA: Suez Canal Authorities	
➢ SCNT: Suez Canal net Tonnage	
➢ SDR: Standard Dimension Ratio	
➢ SGRT: State Gross Receipts Tax	
➢ Sig: signal	
➢ SOLAS: Safety of Life At Sea Convention	
➢ Subm: submerged	
❖ T.	
➢ T: tonne	
➢ TEL: Telephone	
➢ TEU: Twenty-foot container Equivalent Unit	
➢ Tfc: traffic	

> ## GENERALITIES

- ### Art. 1.Transit through the Suez Canal

Transit through the SC is open to vessels of all nations subject to their complying with the conditions stated in the present Rules of Navigation. All references and circulars which shall be issued by the SCA will constitute an integral part of these rules.

Vessels also have to comply with the provisions of the International Regulations for SOLAS and its amendments. MARPOL 73/78, as well as the provisions of the International Regulations for Preventing Collisions at Sea and all laws, orders, and regulations issued by the Egyptian Government. The SCA reserves the right to refuse access to Canal waters, or order the towage or conveying of vessels considered dangerous or troublesome to navigation in the Canal. (None or erroneous declaration of dangerous cargo see Art. 47).

By the sole fact of using the Canal waters, masters and owners of vessels bind themselves to accept all the conditions of the present Rules of Navigation, with which they acknowledge being acquainted, to conform with these conditions in every respect, to comply with any requisition made with a view to their being duly carried out, and to adhere to CA private Code of Signals as shown in Part III of these Rules.

- ### Art. 2. Agents:

Every vessel (other than navy ships) intending to transit the Suez Canal or staying at Port Said or Port at the Suez, or at the Suez Canal basins or docks must have a shipping agent.

SCA confirms that it has no agents or representatives abroad. The Egyptian Authorities are to be notified of intended transit of navy ships in SC viz., Ministry of Foreign Affairs, Ministry of Defense as well as Ports and Lights Administration.

- ### Art. 3 .Canal Waters:

Canal Waters mean the Canal proper, and the waters within the Canal Authority concession adjacent to the Canal proper, Port Said Harbor and Port of Suez.

The Canal proper: As to its length, is reckoned to run from Km 3.710 West Branch for vessels entering from Port Said Harbor and from Km 1.333 East Branch for vessels entering through the East Approach Channel to Hm. 3 at Suez, including the two channels of the G.B.L and all Canal by-passes.

As to its width, the Canal is bounded by two banks when they are immersed in water. If the banks are submerged, the width of the Canal is limited to the perpendiculars at the point of intersection of the submarine bank with the horizontal plane corresponding to the maximum draught authorized including squat access channels there to Port Said Eastern and Western entrance channels, Suez Entrance channel which includes the Port of Suez Eastern channel leading to the Canal entrance.

- ### Art. 4. Responsibilities:

See also: Art. 16, P. A / Art. 55, P. 5 / Art. 59, P. 3 / Art. 60, P. 4-5 / Art. 62, P. 4

When on Canal Waters or at its ports or roads, any vessel or floating structure of any description are responsible for any damage and consequential loss she may cause either directly or indirectly to herself or to CA properties or personnel or to third party.

The vessels' or floating structures' owners and /or operators are responsible without option to release them from responsibility by limited liability. The words (owners and/or operators) for the purpose of the present article shall be considered to mean person/persons or corporate body responsible for the vessel at the time of navigational accident or incident.

Moreover, the vessel guarantees to indemnify the CA in respect of any claim against the latter by reason of any damage, whatever, she may cause either directly or indirectly to third party.
The vessel waives the right to claim the SCA for any damages caused by third party that she may sustain while on Canal Waters.

- ### Art. 5. Temporary delaying of vessels:

The Canal Authority may delay a vessel for the purpose of investigating any claim or dispute that may arise, or any formal or informal complaint, or allegation of violation of the laws of the Canal or for security reasons.
A vessel may be delayed until, in the opinion of CA, its tenderness, trim, list, cargo, hull, machinery have been put into such condition as will make the vessel reasonably safe for her passage through the Canal.
No claim for damages is accepted or considered because of any such temporary delaying of vessels.

- ### Art. 6. Pilotage:

Pilot age is compulsory for all vessels, whatever is their tonnage, when entering, leaving, moving, changing berth or shifting on Canal Waters or Port Said and Suez harbors. Any exemption must be explicitly authorized by the Suez Canal Authority (See Art. 11, Item D).
Except it is an Egyptian vessel under 300 tons S:C.G.T. Authorized to work in Canal Ports and Accesses, also Egyptian fishing vessels less than 300 tons SC.G.T. (At Port of Suez: 300 tons S.C.G.T.) However, if transiting Canal, the above is not applied.

- ### Art. 7. Changing Berth in Roads Anchorage:

Vessels at Port Said Anchorage Areas (Northern and Southern) Suez Roads, the Bitter Lakes and Timsah Lake are not authorized to change berth, anchorage or make fast alongside other vessel or carry out any cargo operations without explicit authorization

- **SECTION I – APPROACHES**

  o **Art. 8. Port Said:**

GENERAL:

Fifteen miles before arrival to FAIRWAY Buoy *("All buoys in the Canal and Access Channels may be replaced by other smaller size".),* all vessels arriving from sea should contact the Harbor Office by V.H.F. (channel 16), if not able to R/T (2182 KHZ) or by W/T, or by R. Telex and Inmarsat Via SC Marine Communication Center SUQ for instructions (See part III Art. 86 and 87).

FAIRWAY BUOY Position:
Lat.: 31° 21'.32 N
Long. : 32° 20'.81 E
Characteristics: V. Q.

A - Anchorage Areas:

All vessels arriving from sea have to anchor in the berth allocated to them, by the Suez Canal Port Authority.

The incoming vessels have two anchorage areas:

(1) Northern Area: comprises two zones:

a) Zone One: For vessels with draught over 42 feet.
This zone is limited as follows:

North Limit: Lat. 31° 28'.50 N
South Limit: Lat. 31° 27'.00 N
East Limit: Long. 31° 20'.00 E
West Limit: Long. 32° 18'.00 E

Vessels at anchor in this area, when entering the Eastern Channel, will proceed between the East and West buoys at Hm. 195 (course 194°) *"All buoys in the Suez Canal and its approaches are fitted with Radar reflectors".*

Hm. 195:
East West
Lat 31° 25'.06 N Lat 31° 25'.16 N
Long 32° 24'.30 E Long 32° 23'.85 E
Isophase (4 sec.)

b) Zone Two: For VLCC'S, 4th generation containerships, 3rd generation containerships and vessels over 39 feet draught up to 42 feet.
This zone is limited as follows:

North Limit: Lat. 31° 25'.00 N
South Limit: Lat. 31° 23'.20 N
East Limit: Long. 32° 20'.00 E
West Limit: Long. 32° 16'.00 E

Vessels at anchor in this area, when entering the Eastern Channel, will proceed between the East and West Light buoys at Hm. 135.

Hm. 135:
Lat. 31° 21'.95 N
Long. 32° 23'.10 E

The berths of this zone are called (V) berths and comprise the following:
Center of circle (Radius 750 meters)

Berth V1:
Lat. 31° 23'.70 N
Long. 32° 19'.50 E

Berth V2:
Lat. 31° 24.50 N
Long. 32° 19'.50 E

Berth V3:
Lat. 32° 19'.50 E
Long. 32° 18'.50 E

Berth V4:
Lat. 31° 24'.50 N
Long. 32° 18'.50 E

Berth V5:
Lat. 31° 23'.70 N
Long. 32° 17'.50 E

Berth V6:
Lat. 31° 24'.50 N
Long. 32° 17'.50 E

Berth V7:
Lat. 31° 23'.70 N
Long. 32° 16'.50 E

Berth V8:
Lat. 31° 24'.50 N
Long. 32° 16'.50 E

(2) Southern Area:
For all other vessels, area is limited as follows:

North Limit: Lat. 31° 23'.05 N
South Limit: Lat. 31° 21'.25 N
East Limit: Long. 32° 20'.50 E
West Limit: Long. 32° 16'.70 E

Vessels at anchor in this area, when entering the Port of Port Said through the West Approach Channel proceed:
Take on their starboard „Fairway Buoy" (No. 8) (No. 7) and (No. 6) Buoys.
On the port there are 3 yellow buoys showing yellow lights, on reaching No. 5 pair of buoys at Hm. 80 showing F. Gr. & R. they will proceed through the old channel to Port (Course

217.5°).
Berths in Southern area called (C):
Center of Circle: (Radius 500 meters).

Berth C 1:
Lat: 31° 21'.50 N
Long: 32° 20'.00 E

Berth C2:
Lat: 31° 22'.10 N
Long: 32° 20'.10 E

Berth C3:
Lat: 31° 22'.70 N
Long: 32° 20'.10 E

Berth C4:
Lat: 31° 21'.50 N
Long: 32° 19'.40 E

Berth C5:
Lat: 31° 22'.10 N
Long: 32° 19'.40 E

Berth C6:
Lat: 31° 22'.70 N
Long: 32° 19'.40 E

Berth C7:
Lat: 31° 21'.50 N
Long: 32° 18'.70 E

Berth C8:
Lat: 31° 22'.10 N
Long: 32° 18'.70 E

Berth C9:
Lat: 31° 22'.70 N
Long: 32° 18'.70 E

Berth C10:
Lat: 31° 21'.50 N
Long: 32° 18'.00 E

Berth C11:
Lat: 31° 22'.10" N
Long: 32° 1 8'.00 E

Berth C 12:
Lat: 31° 22'.70 N
Long: 32° 18'.00 E

Berth C13:
Lat: 31° 21'.50 N
Long: 32° 17'.30 E

Berth C14:
Lat:. 31° 22'.10 N
Long: 32° 17'.30 E

Berth C15:
Lat: 31° 22'.70 N
Long: 32° 17'.30 E

(3) Prohibited area for anchorage:
The area between the East Limit of the two anchorage areas and the approach channels is prohibited for anchorage to all vessels and floating units.

(4) Anchorage area for transshipment operations:

a) Vessels up to 60 feet draught:

North Limit: Lat. 31° 25' .00 N
South Limit: Lat. 31° 24' .00 N
East Limit: Long. 32° 27' .00 E
West Limit: Long. 32° 26'. 00 E

b) Vessels over 60 feet draught:

North Limit: Lat. 31° 27' .00 N
South Limit: Lat. 31°' 26' .00 N
East Limit: Long. 32° 28'. 00 E
West Limit: Long. 32° 27' .00 E

(5) Dangerous Areas

a) Wreck:
A wreck buoy is situated on the western side of a sunken ship at Hm. 195 west of the approach channels:

Lat: 31° 25'.24 N
Long: 32° 22'.98 E
Height 5 meters, painted black and red horizontal bands, with Day mark 2 black balls, showing group FL,.W. (2) every 10 sec.

b) Dumping areas:
The hopper dredgers dredge underway for several months every year the entrance channels and dump in the following areas:

3140 meters east of the axis of the East Channel at Hm. 140.
Lat: 31° 20'.80 N
Long: 32° 25'.80 E

4000 meters east of the axis of the East Channel at Hm. 80. Approximately.
Lat: 31° 18'.70 N
Long: 32° 24'.70 E

B - Port Said approach channels

(1) Buoy age:
The Port Said West approach channel extends from the port of Port Said till Hm. 80 where it joins the east approach channel *"Height of the buoy at Hm. 80 Green is 10 meters"*. The Port Said East Approach Channel extends front the land boundary, east of Port Said, till Hm. 195. The two channels are marked, on each side, by light buoys of 5 meters height (except from Hm. 195 till Hm. 135 east channel, the height of the buoys is 10 meters). The light is Red on the eastern side and Green on the western side.
The buoys are as follows:

a) East approach channel:
The East Approach channel is buoyed as follows:
- In the West: Green Day-mark: Cone point up. FL. Gr. Lights.
- In the east: Red, Day-mark: Can F L. R. Lights.
The 2 buoys indicating the northern end of the channel, at Hm. 195, are Isophase (2 sec. ON, 2 sec. OFF). The distance between them is 745 meters.

b) Junction of east and west approach channels
Three Yellow buoys mark the junction of the East and West approach channels. They are placed at Hm. 83, Hm. 95 and Hm. 105.
Buoy at Hm. 83: Yellow and Black in color, is fitted with N-Cardinal 2 Cones point up day mark and shows by night Q. FL. W (5) every 20 sec.
Buoy at Hm. 95: Yellow in color, shows a F.Y. light.
Buoy at Hm. 105: Yellow in color is fitted with a yellow St. Andrews Cross day mark and shows by night Group FL.Y (4) every 15 sec.

c) West approach channel
The Buoy age of the west approach channel of Port Said harbor is as follows:

I.   Port Said „Fairway Buoy":
Off Port Said, a fairway light buoy, height 10 meters, painted Black with Yellow Horizontal stripes, surmounted by a day mark 2 cones point up, and showing V. Q.
Lat.: 31° 21'.32 N
Long.: 32° 20'.81 E

Buoy No.8 Green Day mark: Cone point up. F.Gr.Light.
Lat.: 31° 21'.13 N
Long.: 32° 21'. 04 E

Buoy No.7 Green Day mark: Cone point up. F.Gr.Light.
Lat.: 31° 20'.52 N
Long.: 32° 21'.31 E

Buoy No. 6 Green Day mark: Cone point, up. F. Gr. Light.
Lat.: 31° 19'.09 N
Long.: 32° 21'.58 E

II.   The west approach channel : is buoyed as follows:
-**In the west:** Green Day mark: Cone point up .F.Gr.Light.
-**In the east:** Red, Day mark: Can F.R.Light.
-**Buoy No.5** of Hm. 80 East Red: Day mark: Can F.R.
Lat: 31° 19'. 13 N
Long: 32° 22'. 11 E
-**Buoy No. 5** of Hm. 80 West Green: Day mark: Cone. F. Gr.
Lat: 31° 19'.30 N
Long: 32° 21'.85 E

d) El Bahar Tower
A guidance tower in position between the East and West approach channels:
Lat.: 31° 18'.16 N
Long: 32° 21'.58 E
Height 42 meters, painted white with red horizontal stripes.
Characteristics:
Beacon Call sign "Q", Range 15 miles.
Beacon light Iso. W (2) S, Range: 15 miles.
Auto. Fog -Horn.

(2) Navigation

a) Northbound Vessels
1. All northbound vessels use the east approach channel. The end of the
   Navigable channel is marked by 2 pair of Buoys at Hm. 195, Course: 014°.
   From Hm. 195, vessels are to steer North (000°) for 5 miles before altering to
   destination.
2. Vessels leaving Port Said harbor to sea, use the west approach Channel. Course
   : 037.50 till Hm. 80 (Buoys No. 5) then steer (000°) to 5 miles north of tire
   buoy of Hm. 195 west
   Lat. 31° 25'.16 N
   Long. 32° 23'.85 E
   before altering to destination.

Vessels of the northbound convoys wishing to enter Port Said Harbor may proceed through
the west channel (direct to their allocated berth in Port Said Harbor, only, if the situation of
traffic permits. Otherwise they have to proceed through the east approach channel till Hm.
195, then steer north (000') for 5 miles and head for the anchorage berth allocated by the
Harbor office. *"This is to avoid crossing incoming vessels to the northern anchorage area"*.

b) Southbound vessels
The maximum draught authorized for southbound vessels is limited to 42 feet *"Southbound
vessels may be authorized to transit with a draught from 42 feet up to 56 feet with special
arrangement"*. On condition to comply with the tables of Art. 52, Table 2, giving the
maximum draught according to the vessel's beam.
VLCC's, in ballast or partially loaded. 4th Generation Containerships and 3rd Generation
Containerships, LASH over 35.000 S.C.G.T, L.P.G & L.N.G. (Loaded or N.G.F) and vessels
having a draught of more than 42 feet and up to 56 feet maximum, have to use the east
approach channel, Course: 194°. The said vessels enter the channel between FL.GR. Buoys:
Hm.165 and Hm.135.
All other vessels, transiting the canal or berthing at Port Said, have to enter through the west
approach channel. Course: 180° from the entrance, passing between the west green buoys and
the east yellow buoys till Hm. 80, then alter course to 217.5' passing between green and red
buoys, till Port Said Harbor

A fixed red light on a pylon on the North Quay of Abbas Basin in line with an occulting red Light on a pylon West of the Fuel Oil Tanks at Raswa, indicates the axis of the entrance channel to the harbor

(C) Breakwaters:

(1) The West approach channel is protected by two breakwaters:

    a) The Western breakwater protecting the west approach channel is situated to the west of the channel and extends from land boundary till Hm.73 with a submerged part from Hm. 50. This part is marked by cigar shaped unlit buoys.

    b) The eastern breakwater extends from land boundary till Hm. 21.2, and has an occulting red light at its northern end.

(2) Two breakwaters protect the east approach channel. The eastern extends for 2 Km from the land boundary, and the Western extends. For: 53 Km from the land boundary. Each breakwater has a small fixed white light on its end.

    o **Art. 9. Suez:**

Five miles before arrival to the first separation Zone Buoy, all vessels coming from sea should contact the Suez Canal Harbor Office by VHF (channel 16), if not able to, by R/T (2181 KHZ) or by W/T, or by R, Telex and Inmarsat via SC Marine Communication Center SUQ for instruction (See Part III, art. 86 and Art. 87).

(A) Separation Zone:
A separation zone has been established, extending 0.3 mile on each of the line connecting the two separation buoys mentioned hereafter. All vessels arriving or leaving have to pass the separation zone Buoys (No. l) on their Port Side.

The separation zone buoys are:

Separation zone buoy No. 1 (southern buoy):
Lat. 29° 39'.49 N
Long. 32° 32'.12 E
Height 6 meters, R. W. color with top mark Red ball and a fog horn. Showing LFI 10s and fitted with 5 miles Beacon (0). (3.10 cm)

Separation zone buoy No. 2 (northern buoy):
Lat. 29° 48'.55 N
Long. 32° 32'.12 E
height 6 meters, R. W. Top mark Red ball, showing Iso 6s with 5 miles Beacon horn (D) (3.10 cm)

(B) Anchorage areas:
The incoming, vessels have two anchorage areas

(1) "V" Area:
For VLCC's,4th Generation Containerships, 3rd Generation Containerships, Lash Ships over 35000 SC.G.T., vessels over 38 feet draught, L.P.G and LNG vessels (loaded or N.G.F.)
This area is indicated by:
The Conry Rock Buoy:
Lat: 29° 48'. 11 N
Long: 32° 34'.22 E
Height 5 meters, Y.B.Y. West Mark showing Q (9) 15s

South Shoal Buoy:
Lat: 29° 38'.87 N
Long: 32° 35'.98 E
Black, cone point up, shows Gr., Isophase (2 sec. ON - 2 sec. OFF).
Berths of this area are called "V". Center of circle: (Radius 833 meters).

Berth V1:
Lat. 29° 46'.50 N
Long: 32° 35'.00 E

Berth V2:
Lat. 29° 45'.50 N
Long: 32° 35'.00 E

Berth V3:
Lat: 29° 45'.50 N
Long: 32° 36'.00 E

Berth V4:
Lat: 29° 45'.00 N
Long: 32° 37'.00 E

Berth V5:
Lat: 29° 4'.50 N
Long. 32° 36'.00 E

Berth V6:
Lat. 29° 44'.50 N
Long: 32° 35'.00 E

Berth V7:
Lat: 29° 44'.00 N
Long: 32° 37'.00 E

Berth V8:
Lat: 29° 43'.50 N
Long: 32° 36'.00 E

Berth V9:
Lat: 29° 43'.50 N
Long: 32° 35'.00 E

(2) Waiting area:
For Other Vessels:
This Area is limited by the following buoys:

Conry Rock: Lat:
29° 48'.11 N Long:
32° 34'.22 E
Height 5 meters, Y.B.Y - West Mark showing Q (9) 15s

Buoy "M":
Lat: 29° 50'.00 N
Long: 32° 35'.29 E
Height: 5 meters, yellow cross and showing, F. Y.

Buoy "N":
Lat: 29° 50'.63 N
Long: 32° 351.29 E
Height: 5 meters, yellow cross and showing Qk. F. Y.

Buoy "D":
Lat: 29° 51.28 N
Long: 32° 35.29 E
Height: 5 meters, yellow cross and showing F. Y.

Buoy "C":
Lat: 29° 51'.93 N
Long: 32° 35'.29 E
Height: 5 meters, yellow cross and showing FL. Y.

Buoy "B":
Lat: 29° 52'.06 N
Long: 32° 34'.54 E
Height: 5 meters, yellow cross and showing F. Y.

Buoy "A":
Lat: 29° 52'. 17 N
Long: 33° 33'.86 E
Height: 5 meters, Yellow Cross and showing F. Y.

Light Buoy:
Buoy Hm. 60.00 East HM. 60.00 West:
Lat. 29° 52'.27 N Lat. 29° 52'.26 N
Long 32° 33'. 16 E Long 32° 32',96 E
Height 5 meters, Green
Cone point up and showing FL. Gr. Height 5 meters, Red
Can and showing FL. R.

Light Buoy:
Buoy Hm. 70.50 East HM. 70.50 West:
Lat. 29° 51'.70 N Lat. 29° 51'.69 N
Long 32° 33'.26 E Long 32° 33'.05 E
Height: 5 meters, Green
Cone point up, and showing FL. Gr. Height 5 meters, Red Can
and showing FL. R.

Light Buoy:
Buoy Hm. 80.50 East Hm. 80.50 West:
Lat. 29° 51'.16 N Lat. 29° 51'.15 N
Long 32° 33'.33 E Long 32° 33'.13 E

Height: 5 meters, Green Cone point up, and showing Occ. Gr. (1) 4 sec, Height: 5 meters, Red Can and showing Occ. R. 4 sec.

Position "R": Lat:
29° 48'.52 N Long:
32° 33'.18 E

(C) Anchorage area for trans-shipment operations "S.T.S"

(1) "A" area:
Lat: 29° 43'.00 N
Long: 32° 37'.00 E

Lat: 29° 43'.00 N
Long: 32° 38'.00 E

Lat: 29° 42'.00 N
Long: 32° 37'.00 E

Lat: 29° 42'.00 N
Long: 32° 38'.00 E

(2) "B" area: Lat:
29° 37'.00 N Long:
32° 37':00 E

Lat: 29° 37'.00 N
Long: 32° 38'.00 E

Lat: 29° 36'.00 N
Long: 32° 37'.00 E

Lat: 29° 36'.00 N
Long: 32° 38'.00 E

(D) Arrival to Suez for northbound vessels:
Vessels coming front sea to transit the Suez Canal or enter the Port of Suez, have to pass east of the separation zone. VLCC'S, 4th Generation Containerships, 3rd Generation Containerships and vessels over 38 feet draught have to anchor in the anchorage area specified for these vessels ("V" berths) in the berth allocated to each vessel by the SCA. Other vessels have to pass east of the separation zone and anchor in the waiting area as previously indicated.

(E) Prohibited area for anchorage:
It is strictly forbidden for all northbound vessels to anchor in the area limited as follows:

In the north:
Two buoys marking the dredged channel position
Western Buoy: Lat.
29° 51'.15 N Long.
32° 33'.13 E
Eastern Buoy:

Lat. 29° 5 1'. 16 N
Long. 32° 33'.33 E

In the West:
By the line joining the West buoy and position "P"
"P":
Lat. 29° 48'.52 N
Long. 32° 30'.90 E

In the East:
By the line joining the East buoy and position "R":
"R":
Lat. 29° 48'.52 N
Long 32° 33'.18 E

In the South:
By the line joining position "P" and position "R".

(F) Suez Entrance Channel
Including the Eastern Channel leading to the Canal Entrance.
This channel is used for vessels entering or leaving Suez Canal and also by those entering Port of Suez and using its anchorage.

This Channel is buoyed as follows:
A pair of light buoys at Hm. 80.5 "entrance buoys"
The eastern buoy: Height 5 meters, Green, cone point up and showing oc. G 4 sec.
The western buoy: Height 5 meters, Red. Can day mark and showing oc. Red 4 sec. The distance between the eastern and western buoys is 340 meters
Preceding northward the channel is marked on both sides by light buoys, of 5 meters height.
On The eastern side of the channel: the buoys are Green, cone point up and showing FL. Gr.
They are placed in the following locations
Hm. 70.50
Hm. 60.00
Hm. 44.40
Hm. 24.00
Hm. 14.00
Hm. 7.00
Km. 162.150 (Occ. Gr.)
On the western side: the buoys are red, Can day mark, and showing Fl. red.
They are placed in the following locations:
Hm. 70.50
Hm. 60.00
Hm. 44.40
Hm. 21.00
Hm. 17.20
Hm. 1.00 (Occ. Red.)
Course: From the Entrance Buoys (Hm. 80.50), (New Port Rock Channel), till the Green light buoy of Hm. 24.00
Northbound course is 352.5'
southbound course is 172.5'

(G) Canal south entrance:
The Canal south entrance is marked by two light buoys of 7 meters height.
The Eastern Buoy at Km. 162.150: is Green, cone point up and showing oc. Green light (1) every 4 sec.
the western buoy at Hm. 1.00: Red, Can day mark and showing occ. Red light (1) every 4 sec.

(H) Port of Suez:

(1) Navigation:
Port of Suez is delimited by the imaginary line which extends from Ras Adabeya to Eyoun Mousse and comprises the coastal zone north of this up to SC entrance.

❖ **General rules**
All vessels shall conform to the International Regulations for Preventing Collisions at Sea.
Navigation in the port is limited to approve channels only.
Crossing or overtaking at the channels is strictly forbidden.
Vessels must proceed in the port with caution and at a reduced speed.
Vessels must not let go their anchors except in the anchorage areas.

❖ **Traffic Regulations**
Vessels entering or leaving the port:
- For vessels entering the port from sea and vessels leaving the port for sea, all movement shall be effected through the western channel, except for vessels anchored in 1C, 2C, 3C, 4C, 5C, which should use the eastern channel.
Vessels entering the Canal:
- From the Port and from Zone North West of Green Island. They must comply with the following:
Anchorages 8C to 16C and anchorage groups A and B.
Vessels shall pass through the western channel, then south of Green Island to join the eastern channel and then proceed to the entrance of the Canal.
- From zone north east of green island:
Anchorage IC to 7C:
Vessels shall proceed directly from their anchorages to the entrance of the Canal. If the number of vessels exceeds number of anchorages, vessels in excess shall anchor south of the western channel, parallel to anchorages 2A, 4A, 6A, 4B, 7B, making sure to leave the western channel clear for navigation at all times.
- From zone South of Green Islands:
Anchorages 1D to 6D:
Vessels shall proceed directly from the anchorages to the Canal or to sea through the eastern channel.

❖ **Vessels leaving the Canal:**
-Direct to sea:
They shall proceed through the eastern channel.

-Anchoring in the Port:
Anchorages Groups A & B. Zone N. W. of Green Island 8C to 16C:
They shall proceed through the Eastern channel, then the Western channel and shall follow it till the place fixed for their anchorage.
Zone N. E, of Green Island from 1C.to 7C.Vessels shall come out of the Canal and proceed directly to this area.

❖ **Priority of movement at the Port :**
Priority of movement in the port shall be as follows:
-Vessels leaving the Canal.
-Vessels proceeding to the Canal.
-Vessels coming from sea must wait outside the port till the Eastern Channel is clear,
-Vessels leaving the anchorages of the Port of Suez.
-Vessels coming out of the Basins (Ibrahim Basin - Adabeya - Petroleum Basin).
-Vessels using the New Petroleum Jetty.

❖ **Priority of Passage in the Eastern Channel:**
-Vessels leaving the Canal.
Vessels in anchorages of Port of Suez, and proceeding southward to sea, have to pass through the Eastern Channel. Ships approaching Port of Suez From Sea should wait outside until the Channel is clear.

❖ **When harbor is Closed due to Bad Weather:**
-Vessels coming from sea:
It is recommended not to enter the Port of Suez when it is closed due to bad weather which prevents the pilots from boarding the vessels.
However, any vessel which would like to enter on her own responsibility will have to contact the SCA wireless station (SUQ) and ask permission for doing so, giving her draught and length in feet, by the following cable:
"*I wish to enter Suez Anchorage on my own responsibility. Length ... Draught ... feet*".
If permission is granted, the Master will receive the following cable.
"*Port is closed. Entering on your own responsibility. Available anchorage. .* "

Vessels leaving the SC :
In case when the embarkation of the Roads pilot is not possible, the following cable will be sent to the ship :
"*Owing to bad weather Roads pilot will not board your ship*"
The following will be added in case the vessel would ask for an anchorage :
"*Available anchorage...*"
Vessels Anchored in the Port of Suez Leaving for Sea:
Vessels which would like to sail on their responsibility, will have to hoist the signal for pilot, send the following cable to SUQ and wait or orders.
"*I wish to go to sea on my own responsibility. Please Confirm*".
They may proceed if they receive the cable:
"*You may proceed to sea on your - own responsibility*".

(2) Buoy age:

a) Buoy 2A 281.5o - 20.9 cables from New Port Rock Light.

b) Buoy 3A 278.5o - 26.9 cables from New Port Rock Light.
These buoys show flashing red (1) every 5 sec.

c) Buoy age of Port of Suez position of Green Island Light:
Lat.: 29° 54'.59 N
Long: 32° 31'.80 E

i - Eastern channel (East of Green Island) is limited by the following buoys:
- In the East:
Buoy from Green Island Light Distance
Hm. 07.00 East 062° 2440 m.
Hm. 14.00 East 080° 1820 m.
Hm. 24.00 East 111° 1720 m.
Hm. 44.00 East 144° 3300 m.
Hm. 60.00 East 153° 4720 m.
Hm. 70.50 East 166° 5720 m.
Hm. 80.50 East 159° 6680 m.

- In the West:
Buoy From Green Island Light Distance
Hm. 1.00 West 050° 2600 m.
Hm. 17.20 West 082° 1390 m.
Hm. 21.00 West 108° 1260 m.
Hm. 44.40 West 150° 3110 m.
Hm. 60.00 West 157° 4640 m.
Hm. 70.50 West 160° 5630 m.
Hm. 80.50 West 162° 6630 m.

ii - Shallow water in the Green, Island Zones is limited as follows:
North Buoy bearing 000° at a distance of 1490 meters from Green Is land Light, showing flashing Green (1) every 2 sec.
Red Buoy of Hm. 17.20
Red Buoy of Hm. 21.00

South West Buoy bearing 239.5° at a distance of 780 meters from Green Island Light, and showing group flashing Green (3) every 7 sec.
West Buoy bearing 308 at a distance of 820 meter from Green
Island Light And showing group flashing Green (2) every 5 sec.
Oil Jetty Quick flashing white.

(3) Anchorage of Port of Suez:

-Group "A":
1A 306.5° 6.1 cables to Green island Light
2A 330°, .2 »
3A 331.5°, 4.1 »
4A 357°, 6.3 »
5A 018°, 3.8 »
6A 023°, 6.8 »
7A 050°, 5.8 »
8A 042°, 8.7 »
9A 062.5°, 8.1 »
10A 084°, 7.2 »

-Group "B":
1B 102.5° , 14.3 cables to Green island Light
2B 093° , 12.0 »
3B 079° , 12.5 »

4B 064.5° , 13.8 »
5B 090.5° , 15.1 »
6B 098.5° , 17.3 »
7B 075° , 16.8 »
SB 095.5° , 20.2 »
9B 086° , 20.3 »
1OB 080° , 15.0 »
11B 090° , 17.8 »
12B 091° , 22 0 »
13B 079° , 19.2 »

-Group "C":
1C 218.5° , 11.8 cables to Green Island Light
2C 208.5° , 11.6 »
3C 188° , 11.4 »
4C 234.5° , 8.6 »
5C 213.5° , 8.1 »
6C 170.5° , 9.6 »
7C 161° , 10.8 »
8C 159° , 9.0 »
9C 143° , 9.4 »
10C 143.5° , 12.4 »
11C 134° , 12.0 »
12C 145° , 6.58 »
13C 123° , 6.5 »
14C 105.5° , 6.7 »
15C 100° , 4.7 »
16C 075° , 4.8 »

-Group "D":
1D 345.5° , 12.7 cables to Green Island Light
2D 004° , 12.4 »
3D 021° , 13.1 »
4D 033° , 14.7 »
SD 043° , 16.0 »
6D 047°, 18.3 »

-Group "H":
1H 296.5°, 12.5
cables to Green Island Light
2H 306°, 14.8 »

- Adabeya Anchorage:
1 059°, 28.3
cables to Green Island Light
2 054.5°, 28.8 »

o **Art. 10 - Roads and Harbor Pilot Signals:**
Vessels requiring a pilot for: Entering from sea. Sailing out to sea. Changing berth. Entering the Canal. Should hoist a Black Ball over G, by day and 3 White Lights by night in a vertical line. These signals are to be hoisted where they can best be seen.

65

- **SECTION II - PILOTAGE**

Art. 11 Pilot age:
A - General:
All vessels entering or leaving Canal Waters, must take a pilot (Pilot age is compulsory). However, the SCA reserves the right to assign a tug master on board vessels under 1 500 tons Gross, and less than 800 tons gross a coxswain, instead of a pilot.
Navy ships and vessels carrying dangerous cargo must have a pilot regardless of their tonnage.
Roads pilots on board vessels arriving from sea shall hand over to the Master, the Declaration of State of Navigability and the Pilot age Form.
Masters are held solely responsible for all damage or accidents of whatever kind resulting from the navigation or handling of their vessels directly or indirectly by day or night.
The pilot must inform the Movement Control Office or the Port Office immediately by W/T, R. TELEX, Inmarsat and/or V.H.F. or U.H.F. if his advice regarding the safety of navigation is not accepted or not respected by the vessel.

B - Port Said:
(1) Southbound vessels :
a) VLCC's, 4th Generation Containerships, 3rd generation Containerships, LASH vessels over 35 000 SC.O.T., L.P.G & L.N.G and vessels over 42 feet draught are piloted from Northern Anchorage Area for Canal transit through the East Approach Channel.
b) Other vessels, either for local trade or proceeding to transit the Canal, are piloted from Fairway Buoy to berths in the harbor through the West Channel.
c) Vessels are piloted between Port Said Harbor and Port of Suez by Canal pilots who are relieved at Ismailia.

(2) Northbound vessels:
a) through east branch, vessels are piloted till Kin. 3,000. However, on Master's request, Pilot age may extend till Hm. 80.
b) Through west branch vessels are piloted till Hm. 80 if weather permits. However, on Master's request, Pilot age may end at Hm. 22 on Master's responsibility.

C-Port of Suez :
(1) Northbound vessels :
a) VLCC's, Large Bulk Carriers, 4th Generation Containerships, 3rd Generation Containerships, LASH over 35.000 SC.G.T., L.P.G. & L.N.G (Loaded or N.G.F,) and vessels over 38 feet draught are piloted from anchorage area south of Conry Rock for Canal transit
b) Other vessels are piloted from waiting area till anchorage area in the Port of Suez.
c) Vessels are piloted from Port of Suez and Port Said Harbor by Canal pilots who are relieved at Ismailia.

(2) Southbound vessels:
a) southbound convoy and vessels at Port of Suez Anchorage sailing south are piloted till Hm

80.50. However, on Master's request, piloting may end at Hrn. 44.4 (New Port Rock).

b) Vessels have to maintain course through the channel till the last pair of buoys keeping the Separation Zone on the Port Side.

D-Master and pilot:
(1) Master:
When a vessel is transiting the Canal, the Master or his qualified representative should be present at all times on the bridge. He has to keep the pilot informed of any individual peculiarities in the handling of the vessel so that the pilot might

(2) Pilot:
The duties of pilots commence and cease at the entrance buoys of Port Said and Port of Suez. He only gives advice on maneuvering the vessel, course to steer, etc. He puts at the disposal of the Master his experience and practical knowledge of the Canal.

a) The articles of Rules of Navigation.

b) The orders of transit given by Movement Control.

The maneuver and orders are carried out under the dictation of the Master who is solely responsible for the ship. It is. therefore for the Master, taking into account the indications given by the pilot, to give the necessary orders to the helmsman.

Moving in Suez Canal Waters without Pilot's Assistance:
(1) Unless explicitly Authorized by the Suez Canal Authority, the following must be considered:
a) Whenever a 'vessel moves in Canal Waters or Port Said Harbor without having a pilot on board, she shall be charged an additional due of(21 500 US_ Dollars)d)

b) An additional due of (3200 US Dollars) shall be charged to vessels moving in Port of' Suez Anchorage, or entering or leaving at Port of Suez without having a pilot onboard.

c) These dissensions do not apply in the event if the pilot being suddenly unable to carry on with his duties due to sickness or death. In this case the Master must:

   i) - Warn the vessels astern of his intended maneuver by means of the visual and sound signals as well as U.H.F, or V.H.F, or W/T, or R. TELEX and or Inmarsat via SUQ.

   ii) - Reduce speed and contact Movement Office to have advice for making fast if in the Canal, or the entrance channels; or dropping anchor at the Lakes.

   iii)- The Movement Office hi Ismailia is to be informed at all times by U.H.F, or V.H.F, and confirmed by W/T, or R. TELEX and or Inmarsat via SUQ.

(2) Exceptions:
In case of bad weather to the extent of not allowing Pilot age in Canal approach channels, Masters will be authorized by notice from the Suez Canal Port Office, to sail with their vessels on their own responsibility at the Following positions:

1) Vessels under 300 tons S.C.G.T, are subject to Rules of Navigation for Small Craft.
2) Vessels tender 300 tons S.C.O.T. arc exempted as per law 161/59.

a) For southbound convoy, from Kin. 162 to sea.
b) For northbound convoy, from Km. 3.000 east of Port Said channel northward to sea.
c) For vessels leaving Port Said Harbor through west approach channel, from Km. 22 northward.
d) For vessels anchoring in Port of Suez anchorage wishing to head to sea, also, for vessels in waiting area wishing to enter Port of Suez Anchorage Area.
e) For vessels entering Port Said Harbor either for transiting the Canal or for trade, through west approach channel till Hm. 50 approx., where Roads pilot will board vessels.
f) For vessels entering Port Said east approach channel, between Hm 165 and Hm 135 from VLCC's Anchorage area to join southbound convoy, Canal pilots will board vessels at Kin. 0 of east Port Said channel.
g) For VLCC's and other large vessels joining northbound convoy from New anchorage area south of Conry Rock, Canal pilots will board vessels at Km. 161 approx.
h) For other vessels joining northbound convoy from Port of Suez anchorage, Canal pilots will board vessels at Kin. 161 approx. N.B.: For items c, d, f, g and h the time of proceeding will be fixed by Suez Carnal Port Authority.
i) An extra pilot for assisting the pilots in charge may be assigned on Master's request or by the CA if deemed necessary.
j) A due of (300 US Dollars) for every additional Canal Pilot and (150 US Dollars) for every additional Roads pilot is charged. (See Part IV).
k) In all cases, advice will be given if necessary by shore radar to vessel´s Master.

F- Calling Pilots Unnecessarily:
When a vessel signals for pilot, and if is found when boarding that she is not ready to get underway at the limit time, the vessel is liable to be delayed and pilot disembarked, The vessel will pay extra Pilot age dues for the new pilot as mentioned hereof

G- Extra Pilots:
(1) Extra pilots shall be assigned in tile following cases:
    a) Vessels over 80000 run S, C.G, and T.
    b) Fourth generation containerships, Third generation containerships
    (over 60000 S.C.G.T) and Lashers of 35000 S.C.G.T and over.
    c) Vessels having cargoes or installations impeding visibility from inside the wheelhouse (Bad View).
    d) If a pilot is disembarked and relieved by another pilot in case of slow speed vessels, vessels having trouble which prevents to continue transit with the same convoy, or vessels that have to transit by day light only.
    e) If a vessel has no accommodation for the pilot to rest while anchoring in Bitter Lakes or making fast in mooring places for a long period.
    f) On Master's request or by SCA if deemed necessary.

> CHAPTER II: ARRIVAL AND PREPARATION FOR TRANSIT
- SECTION I - PRE-ARRIVAL OF VESSELS
  o **Art. 12 - Booking for Transit :**

Vessels may book for transiting the Canal.

The booking notice shall reach the SCA Offices not later than four days prior to the transit date. It must contain the name, nationality of the vessel, her type (Container, RO-RO, etc.), her draught, SC.G.T. And DWT Vessels booking for fixed date will have priority to join the convoy on that date, if they arrive within the limit time defined by the present Rules. Booking can be canceled or altered by notice to the SCA Offices at least 24 hours before the date booked for, otherwise, the vessel shall be charged off (150 US Dollars).

In case of VLCC's and similar vessels this charge will be (1500 US Dollars) on account of the special arrangements made by the SCA. Vessels arriving without previous booking will catch the convoy if the capacity of movement in the Canal permits. Otherwise they may join the following convoy.

  o **Art. 13 - Notice of Arrival :**

Masters of vessels fitted with wireless apparatus are requested to transmit the following information to their agents 48 hours prior to the vessel's arrival and to SCA via SUQ: The name and nationality of the vessel, her ex-name if any. Suez Canal Gross Tonnage and Deadweight Tonnage, Draught and Beam. Whether they intend transiting or merely stopping in the harbors and in this case, mention the duration of stay required. The E.T.A. Whether they carry dangerous cargo stating quantity and class according to I.M.0's regulations (see part V)

In case dangerous cargo is not declared or erroneous declaration See Art. 47 bis.

  o **Art. 14 - Contacting with Port Offices on Arrival :**

A - Vessels have to contact the Harbor Office by *V.H.F Port Said and Port of Suez on channel 16*

- Fifteen miles before arrival to Fairway Buoy of Port Said.
- Five miles before arrival to Separation Zone Buoy No. I off Port of Suez.

   B - When in touch, give the following information:

-Lat. and Long.

-Vessel's name. And vessels call sign.

-Suez Canal official number and code number.

-S.C.G.T. And DWT

-Draught.

-Loaded or not.

-Kind of cargo.

-Any defects affecting the safety of navigation.

If transiting the Canal for the first time, she has to send:

-Date of building. Suez Canal Tonnage Certificate, if available.

-Call sign or official number.

-Length over-all.

-Beam.

-Type of engine.

In all cases, the Master must inform if aiming to transit the Canal or just stay in the harbor. This information will assist the Harbor Master to identify the vessel through his radar, acquire and assign her identification "ID" tag which will follow her path till the other end.

    C - Failing to contact on the assigned channels, Masters may use, with the consent of the Harbor Master, through the International R/T (2182 KHZ) or via SUQ by W/T, or R. TELEX or Inmarsat and/or any of the following VHF frequencies :

Port Said:
156.650 MHz (Channel 13).
156.600 MHz (Channel I2).

Port of Suez:
156.550 MHz (Channel 11).
156.700 MHz (Channel 14).

    D - Any vessel which does not contact the Port Offices during her approach is subject to delay in joining the convoys.

    E - When berthing, changing berth or sailing, the Master must handle the mooring ropes by mooring boats of a firm approved by the SCA.

      ○ **Art. 15 - Documents and Requirements :**
    A - Documents to be produced are:
-Suez Canal Special Tonnage Certificate and Calculation Sheets (3 copies in the first transit).
-Certificate of Registry & ship's drawing.
-Statistical Declaration.
-Extract from the vessel's official documents and information concerning the vessel's type and her cargo (Containers, barges, etc ...).
-Declaration concerning the use of double bottom tanks and the lower parts of the high tanks.
-Declaration concerning vessels in ballast.
-Declaration of State of Navigability.
-The last Classification Certificate issued.
-Any other information necessary for transiting the Canal.
-Piping plan and general arrangement plan for LPG and LNG vessels.
- (I.O.P.P.) International Oil Pollution Prevention Certificate of Compliance and its supplement for the record of construction and equipment as amended for tanker vessels.

    B - Vessel wishing to transit the Canal must declare at the CA Offices and pay the various dues mentioned in Part IV Chap. XIII of the present Rules. She must furnish the CA Officials wit.1-i all the particulars requested by her agent's.

    C - The vessel must in addition comply with the requirements of the A.R.E. Government Authorities.

    D - In case the CA deems it necessary to be supplied with a new Seaworthiness Certificate issued by a recognized classification society belonging to I.A.C.S. Seaworthiness Certificates to be accepted by SCA, if in native language, are to be translated into Arabic or English and duly certified by the Embassy or Consulate in the ARE.

E - Navy ships transiting the SC Waters must be provided with a Suez Canal Special Tonnage Certificate showing the SC.G. And N.T. If such document is not on board, the Commanding Officer has to give, in writing, the following information:
-Name of Ship.
-Name of Commanding Officer.
-Call sign of the ship (Radio Call).
-L. 0. A., B.O.A. and depth of the ship. (As long as the ship is not provided with the SC Special Tonnage Certificate, transit dues will be levied on the temporary Gross Tonnage product of the empirical formula without any allowance till the presentation of the documents required).

F - Erroneous Declarations:
(See also Art. 47 bis.). If the SCA Officials find out *(e.g. The carriage of sweet water as cargo and declared as ship's ballast water; the omission of declaring the presence or quantity of containers. on the weather deck or any cargo on board, passengers, etc. wrong information concerning the cargo carried)* or the ship's situation ballast or loaded, resulting from the shipping clerk's or the Master's negligence, and all documents held, the tolls difference will be doubled. The tolls difference means the difference between the correct and the wrong amount of transit dues.

   o   **Art. 16 - Stay in the Harbor :**
A - The Master is responsible for the mooring of the vessel in Port Said harbor and Port of Suez.

B - Mooring lashing ropes :
For the safety and quick berthing of vessels in Port Said Harbor, the only Lashing ropes allowed to be used for fixing ship's ropes on the buoys are those provided by the Suez Canal Mooring and Light Company. For this purpose, the said company provides vessels making fast in the harbor with 2 inch Manila or Sisal ropes. This service is against 40 US Dollars per vessel to be added to the invoice of the Suez Canal Mooring and Light Company.

C - The Master is to pay attention to the instructions hereunder:
-When the vessel is moored to the buoys, the mooring ropes must be watched to ensure safe mooring. If two vessels are moored to the same buoy, when one leaves, the other must adjust her mooring.
-Masters must comply with the Harbor Master's advice regarding mooring ropes during the stay of their vessels in port; especially when, in case of expected bad weather, it is necessary to increase the mooring if required.
-When a vessel is moored with her stern to the bank, the Master must keep himself continuously informed of the depth of water aft, to avoid grounding on the submerged slope either as result of the settling of the vessel as she loads, or her proximity to the bank.
-At night, the vessel, whether moored or maneuvering, must show the lights prescribed by the International Regulations for Preventing Collisions at sea, in addition to the SC light signals.
-Unless authorized, barges alongside a vessel must not be more than two abreast each other.
-It is forbidden to try projectors, or to turn the propellers during the process of warming up, in the absence of the pilot, or without informing him when on board.
-Vessels must not put their engines out of working order for any reason whatsoever without permission from the CA.

-The Master must always keep on board sufficient crew to ensure efficient handling of the moorings, fire fighting and damage control.

-The Harbor Master or his delegates should have free access on board to ensure application of the Regulations, to verify the vessel's Seaworthiness, and to ascertain that dangerous cargo on board complies with the SC.R.

-Vessels canceling booking berth at Port Said for commercial operations, bunkering, etc..., must do so 6 hours prior to arrival, and otherwise an additional due of (300 US Dollars) will be charged.

- o **Art. 17 - Change of Berth :**

If the Master wishes to change the Berth of his vessel, he should notify the Harbor Office stating the desired time when the shift should take place. A tug or more will be imposed to assist in the maneuvers. The change of berth will take place at the time fixed by the Harbor Office. A pilot will board the vessel in due time. Shifting at the Master's request and the tugs used are charged for as per rates set out in Part IV. Art. 105 of these Rules. Charges for shifting due to erroneous or incomplete declarations by the Master must also be paid by the vessel. When necessary, the Harbor Master may order a vessel to shift, when so ordered, it should be made as quickly as possible. In such a case it is free of charge.

- • **SECTION II - PREPARATION FOR TRANSIT**

- o **Art. 18 - Measures Taken Before Entering the Canal :**

All vessels ready to enter the Canal must have their ladders and jib booms run in, their boats swung in and any derricks or cranes obstructing the view forward, lowered.

- o **Art. 19 -Mooring Ropes :**

At least 6 flexible floating mooring ropes of appropriate size for the vessel, in good condition, fitted with spliced eyes must be in readiness for any emergency, at suitable points on deck. All arrangements must be made for their quick handling.

For vessels equipped with tension mooring wires, the number of floating ropes may be reduced to 4. It is to be noted, however, that any mooring lines, likely to produce sparks by their manipulation are absolutely forbidden on board petroleum tankers, LPG, LNG or any vessel carrying inflammable substances. **It is recommended that :**

1. One of the ropes which is selected as „First Line Ashore" must be of floating material to ensure quick securing to the shore.
2. Wires should not exceed 5.5" circumference to facilitate handling.
3. All vessels should have Two fire ropes (wire) made fast one forward and one aft, hung over the vessel's side ready for use in case of emergency.

- o **Art. 20 -Mooring Boats :**

-Vessels transiting the Canal must have mooring boats as mentioned hereafter hired from the Suez Canal Mooring Company approved by SCA.

-In case no mooring(Open type lifeboat)boats from the said company are available, ship's boats if suitable for mooring in the Canal can be used and must be manned by shore crew, hired from the SC mooring company, each boat is to be manned by three men.

-One mooring boat or one motor boat for vessels under 2500 tons gross, SC.G.T.

-One motor boat for vessels from 2500 to 5000 tons gross, SC.G.T.

-Two motor boats or one motor boat and one mooring boat for vessels from 5000 SC.G.T. To 30000 SC.G.T.

-Two motor boats for vessels over 30000 tons gross, SC.G.T.

-Ships may ask for additional motor boats or mooring boats according to Master's request. These mooring boats must be in constant readiness for lowering to run the ropes to the mooring posts without any delay during the transit of the vessel.

-Ships must be fitted with well maintained lifting appliances capable of lifting mooring boats of 4 tons weight (Including crew members).

-Ships may carry extra mooring boats as passengers for the interest of navigation. However, LPG LNG, and Loaded Tankers are not allowed any extra boats.

-The handling of mooring boats must be carried out well clear from the ship's propellers.

-Masters are requested to reduce speed during lifting or lowering operations of mooring boats, an officer must be in charge, to avoid accidents that may endanger the life of mooring men.

-If the vessel has no means for lifting mooring boats and ship's boats are not suitable for mooring in the Canal, the vessel shall not be allowed to transit the Canal.

o **Art. 21 - Spreaders (Slings) :**

Containerships are advised to have their own spreaders (slings) to assist unloading and reloading containers in case of necessity. But those carrying different sizes of containers must have their own spreaders.

o **Art. 22 - Indicators:**

There must be a rudder angle indicator and an engine R.P.M. indicator in the wheelhouse so located and illuminated as to be easily visible by the pilot. *Erroneous indicators are considered defective (See p. 212, para. 14)*

o **Art. 23 -Bow Anchors:**

(See Circular No. 6/1996)

1. Any transiting vessel must be equipped with two classed anchors located forward of the collision bulkhead. Each anchor must be fitted with its own chain or wire cable, and be capable of being released, and raised by means of a windlass or capstan. If only One anchor, (see Art. 57, para 6)

2. In lieu of 1, vessels of less than I 000 SCGT must be equipped with one working anchor.

o **Art. 24 - Accommodation and Pilot Ladders :**

A - Pilot Ladder:

In Anchorage Areas, outside the Canal North or South, pilot ladders can be used to embark, and disembark pilots. The ladder shall be secured in such a position. That each step rests firmly against the vessel's side and so that the pilot can have safe access to the vessel. Whenever the distance from sea level to the point of access to the vessel is more, than 12 feet (or 3.65 meters), access from the pilot ladder to the vessel shall be by means of an accommodation ladder or other equally safe and convenient means.

The treads of the pilot ladder shall not be less than 19 inches long, 4.5 inches wide and 1 inch in thickness. Steps shall be joined in such a manner as will provide a ladder of adequate strength with treads maintained in a horizontal position and not less than 12 inches or more than 15 inches apart.

A man-rope properly secured, and a safety line shall be available and ready for use if required.

Handholds are to be provided to assist the pilot to pass safely and conveniently from the head of the ladder into the vessel or onto the vessel's deck and vice versa.

If necessary spreaders shall be provided at such a distance as will prevent the ladder from twisting.

Arrangements shall be such as:

a) the rigging of the ladder, the embarkation and disembarkation of the pilot is supervised by a responsible officer of the vessel.

b) A self igniting life buoy is to be available at hand.

B - Accommodation Ladders:

Accommodation ladders are to be used in the Canal harbors, and lakes to embark and disembark pilots.

In case no accommodation ladder is available, or difficult to rig, the vessel has to inform SCA before entering harbor or Canal. The change of pilot which is originally carried out at Ismailia, will take place in the Bitter Lakes after anchoring. In such case. The vessel will be charged extra (300 US Dollars) as Pilot age dues for each relieving pilot.

Ships with freeboard of less than 10 feet may use pilot ladder.

o **Art. 25 - Efficiency of Vessel's Equipment :**

Before entering the Canal, it must be ascertained that main engines, compasses, steering gear, engine room, telegraph, rudder angle and R.P.M. indicators, W/T, VHF and radar are in good working order.

Every vessel navigating in the SC Waters under the advice of SC Pilot, should maintain a bridge and engine bell books,

In the bridge bell book, each engine movement and the time of its transmission from the bridge to the engine room is recorded as well as in the engine room bell book.

No Vessel is required to maintain any bell book if equipped with an automatic device which produces a permanent legible record of every engine movement.

The bell books and the automatic records must be handed, upon request. To SC Officials for the purpose of investigation if necessary.

o **Art. 26 - Deck Cargo :**

1. Deck cargo See Art. 106 (15). Is to be stowed in a way, so as to provide clear view from the navigating bridge while transiting the Canal, as well as not to affect the vessel's stability.

2. The deck cargo should not protrude more than half the vessel's breadth on any side, with a maximum of 15 meters on each side if breadth exceeds 30 meters.

a) Containers on containerships are not considered as deck cargo.

b) Special built vessels and barges carrying drillers or bulky deck cargo to be studied each separately. (See Appendix, para. B).

3. If the protrusion exceeds the maximum allowed, each case is to be studied separately and an additional due of 2% of the transit dues is levied on each foot or fraction of foot in excess.

o **Art. 27 - Ballast Water :**

Vessels in ballast must fill spaces intended to be used for carrying water ballast in such proportion as the Officials of the SCA may direct.

o **Art. 28 - Searchlight :**

Before transiting the Canal, the vessel should be provided with a searchlight (projector) complying with the following conditions, and specifications.

(1) It should be placed on the bow in the axis of the vessel and show the Canal clearly.

(2) Specifications are as follows:

-Minimum range of radiation of single beam 1800 m. ahead (Brightness of 1 LUX approx., at the atmospheric transmission factor T = 0.85).

-The power of the lamp must give a luminous intensity of single light beam not less than 3x106 (3 million) candles, which is equivalent to a high efficiency incandescent lamp of 2000 watts for vessels up to 30000 SC.G.T./3000 watts for vessels over 30000 SC.G.T. Or any kind of lamps which fulfill the specifications, under item (2) and to be of the non-explosive type.

-The drum and stand should be of high corrosion resisting material and can be operated both, horizontally and vertically.

-The front glass must be of hardened type and can and can stand rapid cooling.

-The reflector must be in two halves of precise ground glass mirror of highest quality or of polished aluminum having at least 95% the reflective capacity of the glass mirror.

-The two halves of the reflector can be brought together (zero position) to make a single reflector light beam and can be parted to give two separate light beams each of 5 degrees at least on the horizontal level with adjustable dark sector from 0 to 10 degrees.

-The searchlight drum must be watertight (pressure test 0.25 kg/cm^2) and gastight (according to the classification rules for the vessel's electric appliances within the dangerous area) and provided with a vent - out of which a flexible hose can be fitted on the drum to dissipate the heated air out of the searchlight in addition to a safety vent. On vessels carrying Petroleum products, LNG or inflammable substances or vessels Not Gas Free. Exit of hot air must be effectuated in a place devoid of inflammable gas.

-The searchlight must be equipped with 2 lamps carrier that can be turned into position to let the lamp exactly in the focus of the reflector, and the current must be switched on automatically.

-The electric system (switches, plug, socket and cables) must be of 1st class marine type. The degree of protection IP 55 or similar standards.

-The searchlight must have a certificate for the "Type Test". This type test must include illuminate test to fulfill the above specifications. Issued by one of the Classification Societies (Lloyd's Register, etc). The original to be submitted to Suez Canal Officials and thereby, after test by SCA Inspector, the searchlight can be accepted.

(3) On all vessels of whatever type, electric cables installations for searchlight and all electric connections leading to it must be permanently fixed, insulated and gastight.

At the end of the cables, a fixed and gastight socket should be installed close to the searchlight.

(4) On board vessels, electrically propelled or having electrically driven gear (steering, winches, etc.) the number of generators and their individual power output must be sufficient to ensure uninterrupted functioning of the searchlight in the event of stoppage of the generators, No exception to this rule will be allowed except when there is an independent generator and circuit on board specifically set apart for the searchlight.

(5) A portable projector can be hired locally from the Canal Mooring and light Company (weight of projector about 22 kg).

(6) For vessels fitted with their own projector, two shore electricians should operate it during the transit.

(7) Vessels with special cases:

LPG and LNG vessels, without any exceptions, must be provided with their own searchlight. Vessels entering the Canal, direct from sea, must be provided also with their own searchlight.

(8) If electrical connections and/or searchlight are not in conformity, the vessel is liable to transit only in day-time and therefore, subject to delay. An additional due of (4300 US Dollars) will be imposed when the searchlight and/or electrical connections are not conforming for the 3rd transit and each following.

- ### Art. 29 - Overhead Lights (Deck Lights) :
Overhead lights visible all round the horizon with a minimum range of 200 meters (roughly 650 feet).

- ### Art. 30 - Bridge Wing Projectors :
Bridge wing projectors on either side of the bridge must be fitted to show the Canal banks clearly during the transit and mooring operations, it must have the following characteristics: Power about 4 LUX at an atmospheric transmission factor (T = 0.74) and minimum range 200 m.

- ### Art. 31 - Funnels :
Funnels must be lit to facilitate the identification of the vessel by night.

- ### Art. 32 - Bridge and Engine Room Communications :
Communication system between engine room and bridge must be in good working condition.

- ### Art. 33 - Pumping-Draining Arrangements :
The pumps and pumping arrangements including valves, pipes and strainer from several holds as well as from the engine and boiler spaces must be in good working condition.

- ### Art. 34 - Watertight Bulkheads and Doors:
All watertight bulkheads and doors are required to be in good efficient condition.

- ### Art. 35 - Draught Marks :
All vessels shall have the draught plainly marked and painted upon the stem, amidships (including Plimsoll mark and Deck Line) and stern post or rudder post according to load line convention.

- ### Art. 36 - Whistles and/or Sirens :
Whistles and sirens must be always ready for use, as prescribed in Part III, Art. 92.

o **Art. 37 - Fire Fighting Equipment on Vessels :**

-Vessels transiting the Canal should be equipped with the firefighting equipment in accordance with the requirements of the SOLAS and it's amended. All equipment should be in a good and efficient condition.

-Fire hoses with suitable nozzles attached shall be connected to the outlets of fire lines at all times while in Canal Water. Sufficient hoses shall be connected to reach all parts of the vessels.

-Approaching Canal Waters, as precautionary measures, all vessels must have a fire wire See Art. 19 para. (3) c. hanging over the side ready for use fore and aft, before entering Canal Waters.

o **Art. 38 - Side Doors :**

When side doors are used for boarding, and the minimum vertical distance between the waterline and the bottom of the side door is less than six feet, they should be closed immediately after embarking and disembarking of pilot and during transit through the Canal.

o **Art. 39 - Manning Vessels:**

The crew of vessels intending to transit the Canal should have efficient and good knowledge of their vessel and be sufficient in number to permit handling of the vessel during transit.

o **Art. 40 - Deck Watch and Engine Room :**

When under way in Canal Waters, the vessel shall keep a full watch in the bridge and in the engine room, as well as anchor watch.

o **Art. 41 - Special arrangements for VLCC'S**

(See Art. 58)

o **Art. 42 -Accommodations :**

-A suitable (Officer Class) accommodation is to be put at the pilot's disposal while anchoring in the Bitter Lakes or making fast in mooring places alongside the Canal. In case of no suitable accommodation available, the vessel will pay extra dues of (300 US Dollars) for each relieving pilot. She may be delayed if no relieving pilot is available.

-A sheltered place is to be provided for the mooring boatmen (3 to 6 men according to the size of the vessels) and two shore electricians for the projector, during transit.

o **Art. 43 - Vessels Carrying Timber :**

-The timber deck cargo shall be compactly stowed, lashed and secured in a way that it shall not hinder the navigation and allow safe access on deck.

-The loading must not exceed the Tropical Timber Load Line (L.T.). The height of the deck cargo above the weather deck shall not exceed one third of the extreme breadth of the vessel.

o **Art. 44 - Life Saving Appliances :**

Life Saving appliances for vessels navigating in the Canal Waters should meet with the requirements of the SOLAS and amended.

    ○ **Art. 45 - Anchor Watch :**

Anchor station is to be established during bad weather or poor visibility and when advised by the pilot.

    ○ **Art. 46 -Stoppage in Canal :**

-When anchored in the Bitter Lakes, Lake Timsah or stopped in the Canal, the engines should be always ready for use.

-**NOTE:** In case of failing to comply with any of the previous requirements, a vessel may be delayed from joining the convoy and/or may be subject to special arrangements for her transit.

-This includes imposing convoying tugboats. Access to the Canal may also be refused.

- **SECTION III - INTERDICTION TO ENTER CANAL**

    ○ **Art. 47 - Vessel not Allowed to Transit :**

A vessel will not be allowed to transit the Canal in any of the following cases:

  1. Any vessel whose Tropical Load Line is submerged, or Plimsoll Marks not plainly visible (Overloaded).

  2. Any vessel considered by the Suez Canal Officials, dangerous for navigation.

  3. If carrying dangerous cargo and not conforming to Part V of these Rules or carrying prohibited cargoes.

  4. If having a list more than 3 degrees.

  5. If trimmed in a way causing bad maneuverability.

  6. If having deck loads protruding from vessel's sides in a manner endangering the safety of transit. See Art. 26.

  7.If the vessel is so tender or loaded in a manner that dangerously affects her stability.

  8. If her draught is in excess of maximum permitted according to these Rules.

For VLCC's and ULCC's if there is bad weather.

The SCA may consider delaying the vessel's entry to the Canal in case of bad weather or any vessel without anchors.

    ○ **Art. 47 - Bis :**

  1. The SCA reserves the right to refuse access to Canal Waters for any vessel in case of carrying prohibited cargoes, and in case of none or erroneous declaration on the presence of dangerous cargo on board, such as ammunition, explosives, radioactive substances, etc.

  2. If the dangerous cargo mentioned in para. (1) Is discovered during the transit, the SCA reserves the right to refuse access to Canal Waters to this vessel for a period not exceeding two years. An additional due of (43 000 US Dollars) will be imposed for this violation

- **SECTION IV - PROCEEDING TO THE CANAL**

    ○ **Art. 48 - Generalities :**

Masters shall ask for pilots by clearly displaying the signal described in Part III, Art. 93 at least two hours before the time they expect their vessel to be ready to get underway.

Single up should not be before the pilot is on board.

When several vessels are ready to get underway at the same time, the order of their sailing will be fixed by the CA.

All vessels must stop whenever the passage ahead is not clear, at repairs banks, as well as when passing all vessels in sidings, hoppers, dredges and other floating plant made fast. They must slow down passing collapsed or UN

As soon as a vessel is made fast, she must hoist the signals described in Part III, Art. 92: the vessel must be ready to slack down rope or cut them in case of need. Engines must always be ready to start.

> ➤ CHAPTER III: CONVOY SYSTEM

- SECTION I- CONVOY SYSTEM

  o **Art. 49 - Formation of Convoys:**

(See Circular No. 4/1995)

A - Northbound Convoy:

(1) Starts at 0600 at Km. 160 and consists of two groups of vessels.

Group A:

i - Navy ships, 4th Generation Containerships, 3rd Generation Containerships over 40.000 SC.G.T. & similar, LASH over 35.000 SC.G.T, LPG and LNG (Loaded or N.G.F) and loaded chemicals carriers (See Art. 54).

ii - Loaded VLCC'S, conventional loaded Tankers and Bulk carriers (Draught over 38 feet or length over 950 feet B.P.)

Group B:

Cargo and other vessels anchored in Suez Anchorage's.

N.B.: For safety measures, L.P.G. and L.N.G. Vessels, in ballast or loaded and loaded chemicals in bulk are included in the Loaded Tankers group.

(2) The North bound convoy has a free run from Port of Suez till Port-Said. It passes through the East Kabrit channel, the Eastern dredged channel in the Bitter Lakes, the East channel of the Diversion, the East channel of Lake Timsah, the East channel of Ballah loop and the East channel from KM. 17 Northward.

(3) In case the northbound convoy has to stop in the Bitter Lakes due to traffic situation of southbound convoy or emergency, the following must be considered:

Container vessels heading the convoy will drop anchor in the suitable East Anchorage Areas of the Bitter Lakes.

VLCC's will anchor in the suitable East Anchorage according to their draught.

All other vessels will anchor in the East Area corresponding to their draught.

Three berths are available in Kabrit East Branch in case of emergency.

NOTE: L.P.G., L.N.G. in ballast or loaded, and chemicals loaded in bulk for safety measures, they are included in the Tankers Group.

B - Southbound First Convoy (N1)

(1) Starts from 0000 hrs to 0500 hrs and consists of 3 groups of vessels

Group A: Vessels in Port Said Harbor.

Group B : Vessels anchored in the Northern Anchorage Area consisting of 4th Generation Containerships, 3rd Generation Containerships, VLCC's in ballast over 42 feet draught, LPG, LNG, N.G.F *(LPG, LNG, N.G.F. vessels may join group A.)* . Vessels in ballast or loaded and LASH over 35.000 SC. G.T. This group will be headed by the Containerships and the first vessel will enter through Port Said East Approach channel in due time to join Group A at Km. 17.

Group C: Vessels anchored in Southern Anchorage Area will enter through Port Said West channel in due time to join Group B at Km. 17.

(2) This convoy has a free run to the Bitter Lakes, passes through the East branch of Ballah by-pass, the East channel of Lake Timsah, the Diversion West channel and anchors in the Western Anchorage's in Bitter Lakes.

(3) The sequence of continue route from the Bitter Lakes will be Warships, LPG, LNG vessels, the 4th Generation Containerships, 3rd Generation Containerships over 40.000 SC.G. And LASH over 35.000 SC. G.T. followed by VLCC's in ballast and then other vessels. The first ship of the southbound convoy will regulate speed to cross the last northbound vessel abeam of Kabrit station.

C - Southbound Second Convoy (N2):

(1) Starts from 0630 hrs to 0900 hrs. The forming and depth of this convoy is subject to situation of traffic and limit time. A third group may enter Canal from 0300 to 0430 hours according to traffic situation.

(2) 3rd & 4th Generation Container ships with more than one propeller astern shall be ahead of this convoy to anchor at Temsah Lake (maximum two vessels).

(3) Vessels will make fast in Ballah West Branch *(Maximum capacity 15 vessels according to the NR. of berths at Ballah Loop.)*, and continue route after the last Northbound vessel clears Km. 61.

(4) Dimensions of vessels that can make fast at Ballah West Branch should not exceed those indicated in the following table, excluding Tankers over 90000 Tons SC.G.T.

BEAM			DRAUGHT	
ft	m	cm	ft	in
135	41	15	42	-
136	41	45	41	8
137	41	76	41	5
138	42	6	41	1
139	42	37	40	9
140	42	67	40	6
141	42	98	40	3
142	43	28	39	11
143	43	59	39	8
144	43	89	39	5
145	44	20	39	1
146	44	50	38	10
147	44	80	38	7
148	45	11	38	4

(5) Vessels not allowed to join this convoy are the following

-Loaded Tankers (or Bulk carriers) carrying Petroleum Grade A or similar substances (Flash point below 23°C or 73°F, ascertained by an open test or any equal degree of accuracy).

-Liquefied inflammable gas vessels (LPG, LNG, or similar Loaded or Ballast N.G.F. vessels).

-Vessels not fitted with double bottom carrying chemicals in bulk.

-Vessels carrying radioactive substance Group 1.

-Vessels carrying dangerous wastes.

-Heavy lifters (semi-submersible) carrying heavy lift units with tonnage exceeding the lifting capacity of their individual cranes.

-Vessels carrying deck cargo protruding more than what is stated in Art. 26 of these Rules.

-Vessels over 90 000 tons SC.G.T. Or navy ships.

- ○ **Art. 50 - Limit Time of Arrival to Join Convoys :**
(See Circular Updates, SCA Circular. No. 13/1995)

A - Southbound Convoy:

1. 4th Generation Containerships, 3rd Generation Containerships and VLCC's in ballast and loaded vessels over 42 draught who will anchor in the New Anchorage Area (V Berths) North West of Port Said and declared by Agents ready for transit, have to reach the anchorage Area within the limit time of 1900 hours.

2. Other, vessels entering from Port Said Harbor have to reach the Anchorage Area (C berths) within the limit time of 1900 hours.

3. Ships arriving after the limit time of 1900 hours and not later than 0300 hours will join the second southbound convoy either from Port or direct from sea and be declared by Agents ready for transit, provided that the capacity of the Canal permits.

Ships arriving from 1900 to 2100 hours may join first Southbound Convoy (N1) against an additional charge of 3% of transit dues. b) Ships arriving after 2100 until 2230 hrs can also join the first Southbound Convoy (N1), against an additional charge of 5% of transit dues.

B - Northbound Convoy

1. Ships anchoring South of Conry Rock : 4th Generation Containerships, 3rd Generation Containership, VLCC's Super Tankers, Heavy Bulk carriers LASH over 35.000 SC.G.T., L.P.G & L.N.G (Loaded or N.G.F) and vessels over 38 feet draught, have to reach the Anchorage Area (V Berths) and be declared by Agents ready for transit within the limit time of 0100 hours.

2. Other vessels who will anchor North of Conry Rock have to reach the waiting area and be declared by Agents ready for transit within the limit time of 0300 hours.

   a) Ships arriving from 0300 to 0400 hrs may join the second Southbound Convoy (N2) against an additional charge of 3% of transit dues.

   b) Ships arriving after 0400 until 0500 can join the second Southbound Convoy (N2) against an additional charge of 5% of transit dues.

C - in all cases,

The documents required should be produced before the passage of the vessel by the Canal Office at Port Said or Port of Suez.

- ○ **Art. 51 - Courses to Keep on Leaving for Sea :**

A - Port Said:

Vessels of Northbound convoy have to maintain course through the East Approach channel till Hm. 195 then alter course north 000' for five miles before altering to destination.

B - Port of Suez:
Vessels proceeding to sea have to maintain through the channel till the last pair of buoys, and then keep the separation zone on the port side till the separation zone Buoy No. 1.

MAXIMUM DIMENSIONS
VESSEL'S SIZES AND DRAUGHTS (For drilling and towed units:
(See Appendix Special Cases).

- **SECTION II - MAXIMUM DIMENSIONS**

    - **Art. 52 - Dimensions of Vessels Authorized to Transit:**

(See Circular Updates, Cir. No. 1/1998)
These dimensions are given hereunder:
A - Maximum Length: No restrictions.
B - Maximum Beam: 245 feet.
Vessels with beam over 210 feet are allowed to transit in calm weather, i.e. beam wind- not exceeding 10 knots. Vessels with beam over 245 feet may transit Canal under special request.
C - Maximum Draught:
Tables, I, II, give the maximum draught authorized in relation to the beam of vessel according to the following:
(1) Table I: For vessels in ballast transiting in either direction
(2) Table II: For Loaded vessels transiting southbound & northbound

DRAUGHT TABLE
NORTH/SOTHBOUND VSLS
LADEN CONDITION

<table>
<tr><th>BEAM</th><th colspan="2">MAX DRAUGHT</th></tr>
<tr><td>Up to210 ft.
(64.0 m)</td><td colspan="2">TABLE I</td></tr>
<tr><td rowspan="3">Over 210 ft.
(over 64.0 m)</td><td>For.</td><td>Aft.</td></tr>
<tr><td>33 ft</td><td>36 ft</td></tr>
<tr><td>(9.45 m.)</td><td>(10.67 m.)</td></tr>
</table>

End of table.

Vessels with a beam Over 210 ft. transit the canal in a beam wind not exceeding 10 Knots.
Vessels with a beam Over 245 ft. may be allowed to transit the Canal under special request.

DRAUGHT TABLE
NORTH/SOTHBOUND VSLS
LADEN CONDITION

BEAM		DRAUGHT	
ft. in.	m cm	ft. in.	m cm
163 09	49 91	58 00	17 68
164 00	99	57 11	65
03	50 06	10	63
06	14	09	60
09	22	08	57
165 00	29	07	55
03	37	06	52
06	44	05	49
09	52	04	47
166 00	60	03	44
03	67	02	42
06	75	01	39
09	83	00	36
167 00	90	56 11	34
03	98	10	31
06	51 05	09	29
09	13	08	26
168 00	21	06	23
03	28	05	21
06	36	04	18
09	44	03	16
169 00	51 51	56 02	17 13
03	59	01	11
06	66	00	08
09	74	00	06
170 00	82	55 11	03
03	89	10	01
06	51 97	55 09	16 98
09	52 04	08	96
171 00	12	07	93
03	20	06	91

06	27	05	88
09	35	04	86
172 00	43	03	83
03	50	02	81
06	58	01	78
09	65	00	76
173 00	73	54 11	74
03	81	10	71
06	88	09	69
09	96	08	66
174 00	53 04	07	64
03	11	06	62
06	19	05	59
09	26	04	57
175 00	34	03	54
03	42	02	52
06	49	02	50
09	57	01	47
176 00	64	00	45
03	72	53 11	43
06	80	10	40
09	87	09	38
177 00	53 95	53 08	16 36
03	54 03	07	33
06	10	06	31
09	18	05	29
178 00	25	04	27
03	33	03	24
06	41	03	22
09	48	02	20
179 00	56	01	17
03	64	00	15
06	71	52 11	13
09	79	10	11
180 00	86	09	08

03	94	08	06
06	55 02	08	04
09	09	07	02
181 00	17	06	00
03	25	05	15 97
06	32	04	95
09	40	03	93
182 00	47	02	91
03	55	01	89
06	63	01	86
09	70	00	84
183 00	78	51 11	82
03	85	10	80
06	93	09	78
09	56 01	08	76
184 00	08	08	74
03	16	07	71
06	24	06	69
09	31	05	67
185 00	56 39	51 04	15 65
03	46	03	63
06	54	02	61
09	62	02	59
186 00	69	01	57
03	77	00	55
06	85	50 11	52
09	92	10	50
187 00	57 00	10	48
03	07	09	46
06	15	08	44
09	23	07	42
188 00	30	06	40
03	38	06	38
06	45	05	36
09	53	04	34

189 00	61	03	32
03	68	02	30
06	76	02	28
09	84	01	26
190 00	91	00	24
03	99	49 11	22
06	58 06	10	20
09	14	10	18
191 00	22	09	16
03	29	08	14
06	37	07	12
09	45	06	10
192 00	52	06	08
03	60	05	06
06	67	04	04
09	75	03	02
193 00	58 83	49 03	15 00
03	90	02	14 98
06	98	01	96
09	59 06	00	94
194 00	13	00	92
03	21	48 11	90
06	28	10	89
09	36	09	87
195 00	44	09	85
03	51	08	83
06	59	07	81
09	66	06	79
196 00	74	06	77
03	82	05	75
06	89	04	73
09	97	03	72
197 00	60 05	03	70
03	12	02	68
06	20	01	66

09	27	00	64
198 00	35	00	62
03	43	47 11	60
06	50	10	59
09	58	10	57
199 00	66	09	55
03	73	08	53
06	81	07	51
09	88	07	49
200 00	96	06	48
03	61 04	05	46
06	11	05	44
09	19	04	42
201 00	26	03	40
03	34	02	39
06	42	02	37
09	49	01	35
202 00	61 57	47 00	14 33
03	65	00	32
06	72	46 11	30
09	80	10	28
203 00	87	10	26
03	95	09	24
06	62 03	08	23
09	10	07	21
204 00	18	07	19
03	26	06	18
06	33	05	16
09	41	05	14
205 00	48	04	12
03	56	03	11
06	64	03	09
09	71	02	07
206 00	79	01	05
03	87	01	04

06	94	00	02
09	63 02	45 11	00
207 00	09	11	13 99
03	17	10	97
06	25	09	95
09	32	09	94
208 00	40	08	92
03	47	07	90
06	55	07	89
09	63	06	87
209 00	70	05	85
03	78	05	84
06	86	04	82
09	93	03	80
210 00	64 01	03	79

End of table.

- ## Art. 53 - Conditions of Transit :
(See Circular Updates, Cir. No. 1/1998)

The Maximum draught for loaded vessels is according to Table II (must not exceed the Tropical Load Line). For vessels without tropical load Line indicated in the load Line Certificate, the maximum draught allowed will be the summer load Line.

Vessels allowed to transit with a draught of over 50 feet up to 56 feet must, for the first passage, effectuate successful sea trial before entering the Canal either at Suez or Port Said Roads. Sister-ships are not to get benefit of authorization granted to a particular ship of the group.

For safety measures, LPG, LNG in ballast or loaded, and loaded dangerous chemical in bulk are included in the "Tankers" group and they are placed ahead of the loaded tankers.

- ## Art. 54 - Speed :

Station	Tanker's group other vessels
1. Port Tewfik-Geneva, head current	11 Km/hr 13Km/hr
2. Port Tewfik- Geneva, stern current	14 Km/hr 15Km/hr
3. Geneva - Kabret,	14 Km/hr 15 Km/hr
4.Kabret - Deversoir	15 Km/hr 16 Km/hr
5. Deversoir - Port Said	14 Km/hr 15 Km/hr

- **SECTION III - TOWAGE AND ESCORTING**

  ○ **Art. 55 - Canal Authority Tugs :**
1. At Port Said Harbor, tugs may be placed at the disposal of Masters if the CA deems it necessary. No charge is made for the assistance given by these tugs to transiting vessels, for mooring and getting underway. In all other cases, a charge is levied as indicated in Part IV, Art, 105. Vessels maneuvering in the harbor are required to provide their own ropes. Wire tow ropes are prohibited. Wire tow ropes should not be confused with the fire wire ropes made fast on board and fitted with the eye splice or connecting shackle hanging over the side as required. See Art. 19.
2. In other cases, tugs may be hired for mooring, towing or for getting a vessel afloat. Charges paid by vessel will be according to rates indicated in Part IV, Art. 105.
3. In accordance with the terms of Art. 57 of the present Chapter, the Officials of the CA may impose on certain defective vessels, or vessels carrying dangerous cargo a tug or more for towing or escorting during the transit of the Canal. In such cases, charges are paid according to Part IV, Art. 105 and follow the present Rules.
4. The Master of a vessel using a tug placed at his disposal has the exclusive direction and control of the maneuvers of both the vessel and the tug.
5. Whatever may be the conditions or circumstances under which the Canal Authority tugs are made use of by a vessel, the Master of the vessel is responsible for any damages or accidents whatsoever resulting directly or indirectly from the use of the said tugs, including damage which may occur to tugs themselves, and to equipment.

  ○ **Art. 56 - Use of Private Tugs :**
1. In case the SCA tugs are not available, shipping companies will be allowed to tow their "towed units" by tugs to be provided by them. (See Appendix Special Cases).
Such tugs should be approved by the Suez Canal Authority, prior to transit.
2. Apart from the special towage dues, tugs belonging to private owners are subject to the strict observance of all Parts of the Rules relative to vessels maneuvering, in transit or berthing.
3. Towing arrangement must be supervised and approved by SCA personnel.

  ○ **Art. 57 - Cases of Imposed Tugs:**
(See Circular Updates, Cir. No. 6/1996)
Chargeable tugs shall be imposed during Canal transit in the following cases: At the tariff of hire rate see Art. 105, Para. C.
The CA may require any vessel to take a tug or tugs through the Canal, when in its judgment such action is necessary to ensure safety of the vessel or to the Canal.
Any vessel without mechanical power, or the machinery of which is/or becomes disabled, or steers badly, or which is liable to become unmanageable for any reason, shall be towed through the Canal.
Vessels having engine or steering gear trouble for the second time during the same passage.
Bad view vessels owing to deck cargo, containers, cranes or constructions impeding the view from the wheelhouse and wings.

a - Vessels unable to use one or both their bow anchor. (Ref. Art: 23)

b - Vessels over 1000 SC.G.T. Built with one anchor.

c - Vessels over 1000 SC.G.T. built with more than one anchor if only one of them on the bow Drilling vessels.

e - Vessels with two engines on one propeller of which one is out of order for any reason and cannot maintain speed of 10 knots at least without current after sea trial to assure the speed and valid sea worthiness certificate.

f - Vessels with two engines on two propellers of which one is out of order on Master's request for one tug or more.

- ### Art. 58 - Escorting:
(See Circular Updates, Cir. No. 8/1996)

The escort of VLCC'S, ULCC'S, LPG, LNG, Large Bulk carriers and other vessels, will be as follows:

1. Loaded vessels less than 130,000 DWT will be escorted by one tug if for technical reason SCA finds it necessary, or when the vessels draught is more than 47 feet.
2. Loaded vessels from 130,000 DWT to 170,000 tons will be escorted by one tug.
3. Loaded vessels over 170,000 DWT will be escorted by two tugs.
4. Vessels in ballast over 250,000 DWT will be escorted by one tug. LPG, and LNG over 25,000 DWT (except G.F), will be escorted by one tug.
5. Vessels in ballast with beam over 218 feet up to 233 feet will be escorted by one tug. Vessels in ballast with beam over 233 feet will be escorted by two tugs.
6. Towed scrapped vessels in ballast 150,000 DWT and over will be escorted by

Nota Bene (1):

Reference to Art. 57 and Art. 58

1. Any vessel escorted by one tug and the situation requires another imposed tug, same tug is considered imposed needless for a second tug.
2. Any vessel escorted by two tugs and the situation requires a third imposed tug, one of the two escorting tugs will be for escort and the second is imposed needless for a third tug.

Nota Bene (2):

The prementioned vessels in Art. 57 and 58 have to prepare two Polypropylene ropes 16"(For vessels under 100,000 tons D.W.T. if their draught is over 47 feet.) circumference to join the stern of the tug during stopping operations.

The ropes should be eye spliced to fit in the quick release hook on the tug with adequate length to give distance between fore of the tug and stern of the vessel at about 50 meters.

On the vessels, these ropes will be made fast on stern bitts port and starboard. Their eyes will be hanging over the stern about 2 meters above water and lashed with rope stoppers to break loose when necessary.

Responsibility in cases mentioned before : Either imposed or escorted tug, the Master is responsible for any damage that may happen to SC tugs, directly or indirectly during the voyage, whatever the reasons of the damage may be.

> ➤ **CHAPTER IV: ACCIDENTS AND SAFETY PRECAUTIONS AGAINST FIRE AND POLLUTION**

  o **Art. 59 - Accidents :**
1. Whenever a vessel is underway and accidentally stopped, she must, if other vessels are following, attract their attention by giving five or six short blasts on the whistle or siren. This signal is to be repeated at short intervals. It means:
   "I am reducing speed and may have to stop and make fast"
   Vessels stopped accidentally at night, must in addition, immediately replace their White light astern by a Red light.
2. In case of grounding, the Master must immediately hoist the signal shown in Part 111, Art. 93 of these Rules, and send a radio message whether a tug is required or not, whether or not passage is clear for the tug and whether lightening is necessary, etc
3. When a vessel runs aground, CA Officials are alone empowered to order and direct all operations required to get the vessel afloat and in case of need, to get her unloaded and towed. Nevertheless, Masters remain responsible for all damages or accidents of any kind which may be direct or indirect consequent to the grounding.
4. All attempts on the part of other vessels to get off a vessel aground are strictly prohibited.
5. When a vessel stops in the Canal itself in consequence of an accident other than (collision, engine troubles auxiliary and steering gear troubles) CA, in order to clear the way with all possible speed, and to get her underway, will assist by the necessary tugs to afloat her, free of charge .
6. If once afloat, and the Canal Officials find it necessary to tow or escort the vessel by a tug or more, she must from that moment, pay towage charges as mentioned in Part IV. Moreover, it is understood that the vessel bears all expenses necessary for repairs of any damage or breakdown which might interfere with her getting underway, regardless of the time when such damage or breakdown takes place.
7. When a vessel grounds or stops outside the Canal itself or if the grounding or stoppage is due to a collision, all charges for getting the vessel afloat, towing, unloading, etc.... are payable by the vessel and must be settled as per statement drawn up by CA before the vessel leaves Port Said or Port of Suez.
8. Whenever a collision appears probable, vessels must not hesitate to run aground should this be necessary to avoid it.
9. When a vessel or floating structure of any description runs aground or strands or sinks or is left abandoned, either in the Canal itself or in one of its ports, Waiting and Anchorage Areas and CA deems an obstruction or a menace to navigation in Canal Waters, the Authority has the right to take of its own accord such action as may be necessary for the purpose of removing or destroying the vessel or floating structure by whatever means CA may select and at the risk and expense of the owner of, or the person responsible for the vessel or the floating structure. The SCA has in this case, the right to sell the vessel or the floating structure or the wreck salvaged or all of them together in public auctions with a view to covering all kinds of expenses

  o **Art. 60 - Leak :**
1. In Case of leak, when the ship in approaching channel, sea waiting areas and Harbor the Master must inform the Harbor Office at once.
2. When in Canal or anchored in lakes, the Master must inform immediately the Movement Office. At the same time he must make the appropriate International Signal and call attention by sounding a prolonged blast on the whistle or siren; and take all

necessary measures to stop the leakage and ensure the safety of the vessel and environmental protection.

3. The SCA officials, whose decision shall be final, may order any action deemed necessary in the best interest of all concerned; change of berth or mooring, beaching or taking the vessel out to sea.

4. The Master, the owner and/or operators of the vessel is nevertheless responsible for all damages or accidents arising directly or indirectly from the salvage operations.

5. The Master, the owner and/or operators of vessel shall be liable to indemnify any damage that may occur from pollution directly or indirectly to the environment and shall pay all expenses incurred for its removal, cleaning costs and all costs and compensation for any damage to the environment. (E.E.P.A No. 4, 1994 shall be applied)

- ### Art. 61 - Fire Fighting :

1. Vessels transiting the Canal should be equipped with the fire fighting equipment in accordance with the requirements of the SOLAS. All equipment should be in a good and efficient condition.

2. Fire hoses with suitable nozzles attached shall be connected to the outlets of fire lines at all times while in Canal Waters. Sufficient hoses shall be connected to reach all parts of the vessel.

3. Approaching Canal Waters, as precautionary measures, all vessels must have a fire wire hanging over the side ready for use fore and aft, before entering Canal Waters.

- ### Art. 62 - Fire on Board :

1. In case of fire on board, when in harbor, the Master must inform the Harbor Office at once.

2. When underway in the Canal or anchored in the Lakes or made fast in Canal, Master must inform the Movement Office. He must at the same time, make the appropriate International Signal and call attention by sounding a prolonged blast on the whistle or siren. Also, he must make ready to get underway if required to do so.

3. Neighboring vessels must in such cases also be ready to change berth.

4. Masters are responsible for the use of, on board their vessels, the fire fighting appliances and installations for the stability and safety of their vessels .

5. The SC officials will cooperate with the Master for the purpose of directing the fire fighting operations.

6. If in the opinion of CA officials, whose decision shall be final, there is a risk of fire spreading, they may order any action deemed necessary in the best interest of all parties concerned; change of mooring, beaching or taking vessel out to sea. It is understood that Masters are nevertheless responsible for all damages or accidents arising directly or indirectly from outbreaks of fire or salvage operations.

- ### Art. 63 - Fueling :

1. A vessel at fuel berth or while being supplied by fuel in waiting areas, shall at all times be ready for immediate fire fighting. She shall keep up steam and be ready to move on short notice.

2. The Master, the owners and/or operators of the vessel shall be liable to indemnify any damage that may occur from pollution during fueling operation.

o **Art. 64 - Pollution :**

A - Discharge of substances polluting waters

Vessels must not discharge or throw into the Canal waters any polluted ballast water, heavy slops, engine or fire room polluted bilge water, oil or any other substances that will cause pollution.

The Egyptian Environmental protection Act. No. 4, 1994 Prohibits the discharge of any polluting substances into waters. The Provisions of this Act will apply for any discharge of polluting substances.

B - Oil pollution notification :

Whenever a vessel observes oil slick or oil mixture discharge in the sea waiting areas, Approach Channels, Port said harbor, Canal water and anchorage areas in lakes, she must at once inform SCA with the following information if possible

1. The Time of observation.
2. The location and place and area covered by the slick.
3. The directions of movement of the slick.
4. The approximate oil thickness if possible.
5. If known, the name of vessel causing the slick.
6. The meteorological and oceanographic conditions, if possible.
7. Any other information.

➢ CHAPTER V: PROHIBITIONS, DEFECTS AND CHARGES

○ Art. 65 - Use of Anchors, Thrusters, Gyro pilot and Whistle or Siren :

1. Masters must avoid anchoring or using the thrusters in the Canal, except in case of absolute necessity.
2. The use of Gyro-pilot (Automatic steering) in the Canal is absolutely forbidden.
3. Vessel unable to use both of her anchors is prohibited to transit Canal on her own power. She may transit as a towed unit after survey (See Appendix).
4. The sounding of a whistle or siren is prohibited except for giving any authorized or required signal, as mentioned in Part III, Art. 92.

○ Art. 66 - Firing Shots :

1. Firing shots are not allowed.
2. An additional due of (300 US Dollars) will be imposed for violation of this rule.

○ Art. 67 - Picking up Objects from Water :

1. Whenever any object or merchandise whatsoever falls overboard, it must be immediately reported to the Canal Authority. If it is considered that the picking up cannot be affected by the vessel without impeding transit, CA will proceed to carry it out, at the expense of the vessel.
2. An additional due of (300 US Dollars) will be imposed for violation of this rule.

○ Art. 68 - Riveting, Welding, etc. :

1. Riveting, welding, burning, metal cutting or similar operations requiring the use of heat, are not allowed unless authorized by SCA.
2. An additional due of (750 US Dollars) will be imposed for violation of this rule.

○ Art. 69 - Pollution :

1. See Art. 64.
2. In case of leakage of any polluting material from a vessel, due to any reason, the Master, the owners and/or operators of the vessel shall be liable to indemnify any damage that may occur from the pollution directly or indirectly to the environment and shall pay all expenses incurred for its removal and all compensations. Moreover, she shall pay for all claims regarding cleaning costs and all environmental economic losses caused from the pollution.

○ Art. 70 - Direct Lights :

Under no circumstances shall the rays of any blinding lights be directed to the bridge or any other direction which would interfere with the safe navigation of other vessels.

○
Art. 71 - Embarking and Disembarking of Persons :

1. Unless authorized by CA or Port Officials, no person shall embark or disembark from a vessel while passing through the canal or in Ballah, Timsah Lake or the Bitter Lakes.
2. An additional due of (300 US Dollars) will be imposed for violation of this rule.

○ Art. 72 - Boats, other than the Canal Authority's Own :

1. Not allowed to come alongside vessels underway or maneuvering except the following at their risk :
2. Quarantine and Police boats.

3. Mooring boats .
4. The ship's agent's boats.

o   Art. 73 - Vessel Overtaking Another :

1. Vessels proceeding in the same direction are not allowed to overtake one another while underway in the Canal Waters and ports unless authorized by the Suez Canal Control Office.
2. In additional due of (750 U.S. Dollars) will be imposed for violation of this rule.

o   Art. 74 - Boat Drills :

1. No boat drills are allowed except after authorization.
2. An additional due of (300 US Dollars) will be imposed for violation of this rule.

o   Art. 75 - Venting :

1. Venting of toxic and explosive gases is prohibited in Canal Waters.
2. An additional due of (20,000 US Dollars) will be imposed for violation of this rule.
All tank's openings should be closed through the whole transit.

o   Art. 76 - Long Stay :

Unless due to conditions of traffic or incidents in the Canal, transiting vessels should not remain more than 24 hours in Port Said berths, anchorage in Port Said and Port of Suez roads, Timsah Lake or Bitter Lakes (See berthing dues Part IV, **Art. 102**).

o   Art. 77 - Vessels Having Damaged Container with Dangerous Cargo:

If upon arrival of a vessel in Waiting Areas or Port or while transiting the Canal, it is found that a container of dangerous cargo has been damaged or leaking, the Master of the vessel has to notify the Suez Canal Port Authority at once. In case of dangerous situations, the vessel may be ordered to leave the Port or Waiting Area to sea.

o   Art. 78 - Declaration of State of Navigability :

The Master shall hand in duly filled and signed, the declaration of state of Navigability, this form to be handed to him by the pilot on his arrival on board.

- **DECLARATION FORM**

I, the undersigned, Master of the..................

(1) Certify that my ship satisfies the conditions laid in Part I Article 18 to 45 of the Navigation Regulations and that in particular, the engines and the steering gear are in Good working order.

(2) I declare that my ship has, at the present time, the following defects in engines or Steering gear.............................

(3) I declare, also, that the wireless installations on my ship permit to transmit on the Frequencies, in KHz:

Telegraphy.......................... KHz.

Telephony.......................... KHz.

(4) I state also that my ship is/is not fitted with a Rudder angle indicator and Engine R.P.M. indicator on the bridge in such a position that the pilot may read both without Having to move away from his station, and that the

(**Rudder angle indicator**/Engine R.P.M indicator) is/are in good working condition.

I undertake to bring to the notice of the Suez Canal Authority, before my ship

Enters the Canal, any defects, not specified above, which may appear.

Made at Port ...., the signature:

> APPENDIX: SPECIAL CASES

○ **A - Drilling Rigs "They consist of":**

1. Drilling vessels: To be convoyed by SC Imposed tug. (See Art. 57, item 7)
2. Drilling Rigs :
   - Self steering or on self steering,
   - Legs that can be lifted: No extensions under the rig's keel.
   To be assisted by Suez Canal tugs:
   One aft and another - or more - as escort. In addition, a powerful tug forward to maintain a minimum speed of 12 Km/h over the ground. The rigs must be in stable condition.
   - Legs that cannot be lifted and a part remains under the rig's keel :

Each case is to be studied separately to decide whether or not the unit is allowed to transit the Canal.

○ **B - Heavy Lift Ships Carrying drillers, or floating units, or large units are submitted to the following conditions:**

(See Circular Updates, Cir. No. 50/1995)

1. Be able if needed, to reduce, easily and safely, the draught by one meter (3 feet 3 inches) by way of discharging clean ballast water.
2. Be escorted by one or more tugs according to the decision of the Suez Canal representatives, after survey on arrival (6600 SDR per tug).
3. The following additional dues are levied to cover special precautionary measures for the safety of navigation and vessels :
   - 125% of the transit dues and in addition.
   - 2% of the transit dues, for each foot, or fraction of a foot in excess of the maximum breadth prescribed by Art. 26.

○ **C - Self Steering Vessels Carrying Floating Units :**

1. Vessels carrying on board floating units within an adequate period. before vessels transit must introduce the following documents of their floating units :
   ○ Suez Canal Tonnage certificate and calculation sheets.
   ○ Recommended plans.
   ○ A detailed statement on the floating units loaded on board.
   ○ Cargo weight statement specifying its location on board and the way of its loading as per cargo manifest.
2. In Case of absence of the prementioned documents in para. (1) The gross tonnage will be calculated according to linear dimensions, Length, Beam and Depth.
3. Self steering vessels carrying on board floating units of 300 tons or more SC.G.T. Are subject to the following additional dues
   a) A300% of transit dues of the floating units SC.G.T.
   b) 2% of transit dues for each foot or fraction of a foot in excess of the maximum breadth authorized by Art. 26.
4. Such vessels will be able to join the second southbound convoy if their dimensions allow.

○ **Navy Ships :**

Navy and auxiliary ships belonging to different countries, an addition of 25% of transit dues is to be added owing to special arrangements.

- o **E - Integrated Units :**

Integrated Units may transit SC and berth in its harbors on the following conditions:
1. A valid Seaworthiness Certificate issued by one of I.A.C.S. recognized by SCA.
2. Additional dues of 25% of the transit dues will be charged.
3. Vessels to be escorted by a Suez Canal tug, on the first transit (experimental) against 6600 SDR.
4. If unable to maintain convoy's speed, additional dues for slow speed vessels are applied.
5. If the Integrated tug is disconnected and the unit towed by normal tugs, this unit will be considered as towed vessel and dues for towed vessels will be applied.
6. In Harbors: Berthing, loading and discharging operations are possible, after getting Harbor Authority authorization.

- o **F - Towed units :**
1. All enquiries concerning the possibility and/or approval of transit of towed units, drilling rigs, dredgers, etc..., are to be submitted by the owners of the units or their officially recognized representatives in Egypt or one of the Suez Shipping Agency Companies accompanied by a General Arrangement plan and all particulars of the unit: name, L.O.A., beam, draught, height, self steering, etc. The application must reach SCA (Transit Department, Ismailia, and Egypt) not less than two weeks before the sailing of the unit from its base.
2. Towed units are not allowed to transit the Suez Canal, unless they are towed by a tug suitable to the size of the unit and powerful enough to maintain a speed in the Canal not less than 12 Km/h over the ground, in addition to the assisting SC. tugs, whenever find necessary by SC Officials (see Chapter XIII, Art. 101)
3. Any towed unit must be supplied with floating mooring ropes in good condition and suitable in number (more than six) and size according to the dimensions of the unit.
4. A responsible person and a crew of at least 10 persons must be on board the unit during the transit.
5. A valid Seaworthiness Certificate for the towage through SC must be available.
6. The unit must comply with SC Regulations
7. A survey of the unit shall be made on the arrival, in order to take the definite steps and make the final arrangements for the transit, if it complies with SCA Rules.
8. The transit is subject to the circumstances of the Navigation in the Canal, and the weather conditions.

- o **G - Special Requests :**

Owing to the request of owners for the transit of vessels with beam over 245 feet, the SCA undertook careful studies to comply with the said request.

In this connection above mentioned, vessels may transit the Canal under the following conditions:
1. A pre-approval to be obtained in good time prior to transit.
2. Transit to be effectuated in good weather (wind not exceeding 10 knots).
3. One escorting tug against 6600 SDR for vessels with beam up to 233 feet.
4. Two escorting tug against 6600 SDR per tug for vessels with beam over 233 feet.

> CHAPTER VI: CANAL AND LAKES

- Canal And Approaches

  o **Art. 79 - Canal and Approaches :**
  o **A - Length of the Navigable Channel**

  East Approach Channel (Port Said) :

(a) Distance from outer pair of light buoys (East Branch) at Hm. 195 to Hm. 94.90 where it joins the West Approach channel is 10.010 Km

(b) Distance from Hm. 94.90 to the pair of revolving light beacons at Km. 2.738 E is 12.228 Km

  West Approach Channel (Port Said):

a) Distance from Fairway buoys to Port Said Lighthouse is 11.040 Km. (Bearing 017°)

b) Distance from Port Said Lighthouse (Km. 0.000) or (Km. 3 East branch) to Ismailia is 78.500 Km

c) Distance from Ismailia to Port Tewfik (Km.162.250) is 83.750 Km

d) Distance from Port Tewfik (Km. 162.250) (Hm.000) to the outer pair of buoys Hm. 80.50 is 8.050 Km

TOTAL length of the Navigable Channel 192.548 Km

  o **B - Characteristics of the Navigable Channel (Canal and Approaches)**

  (1) North Approaches:

a) Port Said East Approach Channel from Hm. 195 to Km. 1.000:

Depth of water 21.00 m.

Channel width measured at 21 m. depth

Hm. 195.00 745 m.

Hm. 80.00 E 400 m.

Km. 1.000 E 130 m

Side Slopes:

Natural land side slopes, ranging from 5/1 near shore to about 15/1 in the offshore part.

b) Port Said West Approach Channel from Hm. 95.00 to Port Said:

Depth of water 16.50 m.

Channel width measured at 16.50 m. depth:

Hm. 80.00 520 m.

Hm. 25.00 230 m.

  (2) Canal Cross Sections:

a) The Canal cross sections are trapezoidal in shape, having side slopes of 4/1 in the northern part, up to Km. 61.00 and 3/1 in the southern part. Toussoum Zone is the only place where the western slopes are 2.5/1.

b) Tables of main dimensions of cross sections all through the Canal (See Depths and Widths)

c) Both sides of the Canal are provided with mooring bollards.

  (3) South Approach from Hm. 0.00 (Km. 162.250) to HM. 80.50

a) Depth of water 23.50 m.

b) Channel width measured at 19 m. depth from Hm. 0.00 to Hm. 80.50 is 292.00 meters.

c) Side slopes 3/1.

- ### C - DEPTH AND WIDTH OF DIFFERENT PARTS OF THE CANAL:

(1) Main Canal and Bitter Lake East Channel:

Kilometric Position Origin Point of Km.		Designation of Different Parts of the Canal Axis of Port Said	Theoretical Depth	Width of Canal at 19 m. Depth
From Km.	To Km.	Lighthouse	Meters	Meters
2.400E	3.400 E	Junction	20.50	186-146
3.401E	15.190 E	Straight line	20.50	146
15.402E	15.540 E	Junction	20.50	Var.
17.000	19.000	Southern entrance to Port Said by-passes	20.50	Var.
19.000	30.430	Straight line	20.50	161
30.430	32.350	Northern approach to encoche (siding)	20.50	161-238
32.350	32.950	East encoche Km. 32 (siding of Km 32)	20.50	238
32.950	35.110	Southern approach to encoche (siding)	20.50	238-146
35.110	49.512	Straight line	20.50	146
49.512	51.477	Northern approach to Ballah Loop	20.50	Var.
51.449E	51.785 E	Curve of Km 51 East	20.50	146
51.450E	59.943 E	Straight line	20.50	146
60.308	60.333	Curve of Km 61	18.5-20.50	Var.
60.333	63.419	Curve of Km 61	20.50	Var.
63.419	64.514	Approach to curve	20.50	187.96- 162
64.514	71.164	Straight line	20.50	162
71.164	71.964	Approach to curve	20.50	162-182
71.964	75.311	S Curves	20.50	182
75.311	76.033	Straight line	20.50	182
76.033	76.519	Straight line	20.50	182
76.519	78.900 E	Curve of Timsah	20.50	182
78.900E	80.949 E	Encoche of Km 80 (East)	20.50	Var.
80.901E	81.692 E	Curve of Timsah	20.50	182
81.000	82.000	Junction	20.50	Var.
82.000	85.027	Straight line	20.50	182
85.027	87.414	Curve of Km 85	20.50	182
87.414	88.814	Approach to curve	20.50	182-147
88.814	92.950	Straight line	20.50	147

92.950	93.050	Junction to Syphons Zone	20.50	147-192
93.050	93.446	Syphons Zone	20.50	192
93.446	95.000	Junction to Diversion by-pass	20.50	Var.
95.000	95.250	Junction to East Branch	20.50	237.55-204.99
95.250	96.000	Junction to East Branch	20.50	204.99-142
96.000E	100.666 E	Straight line	20.50	142
100.666E	102.600 E	Straight line	20.00	142
102.600	105.030	Curve	19.50	Var.
105.030	112.860 E	Main Channel (straight line)	19.50	358
112.860E	114.200	Junction	19.50	Var.
114.200	114.957	Junction with Kabrit-Loop	20.00	Var.
114.957	115.320 E	Junction	20.50	Approx. 250-152
115.320E	121.937 E	Straight line	20.50	152
121.321E	122.100 E	Beginning of Km 122 Curve	20.50	162
122.100	125.507	Curve of Km 122	20.50	Var.
125.507	129.499	Straight line	20.50	162
129.499	131.975	Curve of Km 130	20.50	162
131.975	133.175	Approach to curve	20.50	162-132
133.175	144.714	Straight line	20.50	132
144.714	147.146	Encoche of Km 146 (siding of Km 146)	20.50	204-132
147.146	149.500	Straight line	20.50	132
149.500	153.524	Straight line	25.00	157
153.524	154.724	Approach to curve	25.00	157-187
154.724	155.724	Curve of Km 154	25.00	187
155.724	156.274	Straight line	25.00	187
156.274	159.998	Curve of Km 157	25.00	187
159.998	161.050	Straight line	25.00	187
161.050	162.250	Southern approach of the Canal	25.00	187-348

(2) Canal West Branches and Bitter Lake West Channel:

Kilometric Position Origin Point of Km.		Designation of Different Parts of the Canal Axis of Port Said	Theoretical Depth	Width of Canal at 19 m. Depth
From Km.	To Km.	Lighthouse	Meters	Meters
0.000	1.450	Ismailia Basin	15.50	Port
1.450	3.650	Basins for Coal & Fuel oil vessels	15.50	Port
3.729	4.890	Junction (1)	15.50	Var.

4.890	6.000	Junction (2)	15.50	Var.
6.000	16.500	Straight line	15.50	201
16.500	16.663	Straight line	15.50-19.00	201
16.663	17.000	Junction (siding of Km 17.00)	19.00	Var.
51.477	51.800	Straight line (siding of Km 51.500)	18.50	118
51.800	52.054	Straight line	15.50	146
52.054	53.298	Curve of Km 53	15.50	Var.
53.298	54.098	Approach to curve	15.50	160.64-146
54.098	56.397	Straight line	15.50	146
56.397	56.871	Approach to curve Km 57	15.50	Var.
56.871	58.797	Curve of Km. 57	15.50	Var.
56.797	59.269	Approach to curve	15.50	157.82-146
59.269	59.900	Straight line	15.50	146
59.900	60.308	Straight line	18.50	118
76.033	77.371	Curve (Centre on West Bank)	15.50	102-173
77.371	77.672	Junction	15.50	173-226
77.672	77.912	Junction	15.50	226-259
77.912	79.800	Curve of Lake Timsah (Centre on East Bank)	15.50	259
79.800	81.000	Straight line (siding of Km 80.000)	19.00	118
95.000	95.500	Junction to West Branch (siding of Km 95.000)	18.00	170-159
95.500	100.200	Straight line	15.00	177
100.200	101.050	Junction	14.50	177-411.43
101.050	103.759	Straight line	14.50	411.43
103.759	(103.957W 104.160E)	Junction	14.50	411.43-232
104.160	114.200	West Channel	14.50	232
114.200	115.603	Junction	15.00	400-152
115.603	122.100	Straight line	15.00	152

- **D - Bends in the Canal:**

The bends in the navigable channel have the following characteristics

1. Radius of navigation line = 5000 meters.
2. Width of channel at 11.00 meters depth = 225 - 242 meters.
3. Width of channel at 19.00 meters depth, North of Km. 61.000 (side slopes 4/1) = 176 meters.
4. Width of channel at 19.00 meters depth, South of Km. 61.000 (side slopes 3/1) = 177 - 192 meters.

5. At the ends of two bends, there is usually a funnel made to allow increasing the width of the channel from the width of the straight part to the width of the curves, (At 11.00 meters depth).

6. Location of beginning and end of each bend are included in the following table:

Canal Bends	Kilometric indication of beginning point	Kilometric indication of end point
Km. 51	Km. 49.510	Km. 51.480 W
		Km. 51.790 E
Km. 53	Km. 52.050	Km. 53.520
Km. 57	Km. 56.870	Km. 58.800
Km. 61	Km. 60.310 W	Km. 63.300
		Km. 59.940 E
S Curves	Km. 71.960	Km. 75.300
Timsah Curve	Km. 76.520	Km. 81.700 E
Km. 85	Km. 85.030	Km. 87.400
Km. 103	Km. 102.600	Km. 105.030
Km. 122	Km. 121.940 E	Km. 125.510
		Km. 122.500 W
Km. 130	Km. 129.500	Km. 131.980
Km. 146	Km. 145.500	Km. 146.330
Km. 154	Km. 154.700	Km. 155.720
Km. 157	Km. 156.280	Km. 160.000

Note: At the approaches of the by-passes, bends are made with radius more than 5000 meters.

o **E- By passes and Loops:**

(1) Port Said By-Pass

A by-pass is dredged East of Port Fouad starting at Km. 17.00 and extending straight to join the existing Port Said roadstead at Hm., 94.90 and continuing till Hm. 195. This channel (By-pass) is used for the exit of Northbound ships, the entry of VLCC's in ballast, 4th generation containerships and 3rd generation containerships, LASH over 35.000 SC.G.T., L.P.G., L.N.G. tankers and Vessels with draught over 42 feet coming from North.

Characteristics and Dimensions

The kilometric marks are followed by letter "E" to distinguish them from those of the West branch. The inland part (from Km. 1.500 E to Km. 15.465 E) width (at 19.00 meters depth) is 146 meters with side slopes 4/1. Theoretical depth 20.50 meters. It fitted with bollards on the Western side, spaced every 100 meters.

The seaward part (from Km. 1.000 E to Hm. 94.90 E) with width (at 21 meters depth) ranging from 130 meters at Km. 1.000 E to 400 meters at Hm. 80.00 E with natural side slopes ranges from (5/1 - 15/1)

Two revolving light beacons on each bank, to indicate the entrance of Canal from East Approach channel at Km. 2.738E.

(2) Ballah Loop

Between Km. 51 and 61 the Canal is doubled in the East by a branch. The zone comprising the 2 branches of the Canal limited by the North and South ends where the 2 branches meet is called "Ballah Loop".

In the East Branch the kilometric marks are followed by letter "E". The length of the East Branch is 8.490 Km.

	West Branch	East Branch
Kilometric marking of North end	51.477	51.449 E
Kilometric marking of South end	60.333	59.943 E
Slope of Bank 4/1.		

In the West branch, 15 mooring berths are situated on the Eastern bank and numbered South to North.

(3) Timsah By-Pass
Between Km. 76.580 and Km 81.700 E.
Characteristics and Dimensions:
The kilometric marks are followed by letter "E"
Length: 5.110 Km. counted at right angle from
Km. 76.578 to Km. 81.700.
Width: 182 meters at a depth of 19 meters.
Slope: The side slope is 3/1.
The radius of its axis 4905 meters
the by-pass is used by North and Southbound vessels.

(4) Diversion By-Pass
A branch is dredged east of the existing channel at Diversion zone. This branch begins at Km. 95.000 and joins the main East channel in the G.B.L. at Km. 104.160. This branch is used by northbound vessels.
Dimensions:
Width: 142 meters at 19 meters depth.
Depths:
20.500 meters from Km. 95.000 to Km. 100.670.
20.000 meters from Km. 100.670 to Km. 102.600.
19.500 meters from Km. 102.600 to Km. 104.160.
Side Slope: 3/1.

(5) Kabrit By-Pass
The By-pass is situated in the East of the Main Canal. It begins at Km. 114.957 and ends at Km. 122.100. It is (250 - 152 meters) wide at a depth of 19 meters, the bank slope is 3/1.
The by-pass is separated from west branch a submerged island at a depth between 2 and 6 meters.
The width of the island varies between 200 meters in the North and 66 meters in the South.
Some mooring bollards have been installed on the submerged island to be used in case of emergency.
The two extremities of the submerged island are marked at Km. 115.025 and 122.150 by a light buoy painted horizontally Black and Yellow and showing a flashing White light.
The by-pass (East channel) is used by northbound vessels. Southbound vessels use the West channel.

- ## Art. 80 - Lakes :

A - Lake Timsah

Lake Timsah extends from Km. 76.500 to Km. 80.520. In the presence of the Timsah by-pass, Lake Timsah is used mainly as an anchorage area.

B - Great Bitter Lake

There are 2 dredged channels in G.B.L. The East is the main channel about 358 meters wide at 19.00 meters depth and dredged to 19.50 meters for northbound vessels. The West channel 232 meters wide at 14.00 meters depth dredged to 14.50 meters depth for southbound vessels. These channels divide the Great Bitter Lake into two anchorage areas:

One to the East for the northbound convoy.

One to the West for the southbound convoy.

Each convoy is to keep strictly to its assigned channel.

- ## Art. 81 - Floating Bridges :

The fixed parts of floating bridges are outside the line of navigational buoys. The bridges may be rigged day or night. Positions of floating bridges at Km. 88.200, 67.550, 47.200.

> CHAPTER VII: BUOYAGE SYSTEM IN THE CANAL

o **Art. 82 - Buoy age :**

The navigable channel is marked by pairs of light buoys.

On the east side: Green buoys showing Green light.

On the west side: Red buoys showing Red light.

In the straight parts, the distance between each pair is 1, 5 kilometers, in the north section and 1 kilometer in the south section.

In the curves, the distance will be less than 1 kilometer.

All buoys in the Canal and its approaches are fitted with radar reflectors.

o **Art. 83 - Position and Characteristics of Buoys in the Suez Canal :**

Port Said:

A - Approaches and Sea Channels:

a) "Approaches":

Position	Color	Day mark	Characteristics
Fair way Buoy:			
Lat : 31° 21'.32 N	Black-Yellow	Black	V. Q.
Long: 32° 20'.81 E	Horizon. stripes		
Wreck Buoy:			
Lat : 31° 25'.24 N	Black-Red	Black	Gp. Fl.W. (2) 1 0 sec.
Long: 32° 22'.98 E	Horizon. bands		

b) **Port Said Sea Channels:**

i – East:

Position	Color	Day mark	Characteristics
Hm. 195.0 "East": Lat:31° 25'.06 N Long: 32° 24'.30 E	Red	Can	Isophase R. 4 sec.
Hm. 195.0 "West": Lat : 31° 25'.16 N Long: 32° 23'.85 E	Green	Cone	Isophase G. 4 sec.
Hm. 165.0 "East": Lat : 31° 23'.49 N Long: 32° 23'.80 E	Red	Can	Fl. R.
Hm. 165.0 "West": Lat : 31° 23'.58 N Long: 32° 23'.40 E	Green	Cone	Fl. G.
Hm. 150.0 "East": Lat : 31° 22'.71 N Long: 32° 23'.57 E	Yellow	Yellow	Oc. (4) R. St. Andrews

Position	Color	Day mark	Characteristics
Hm. 135.0 "East": Lat : 31 ° 21'.93 N Long: 32 ° 23'.31 E	Red	Can	Q. R.
Hm. 135.0 "West": Lat : 31 ° 22'.00 N Long: 32 ° 22'.98 E	Green	Cone	Q. G.
Hm. 120.0 "East" : Lat : 31 ° 21'.14 N Long: 32 ° 23'.07 E	Red	Can	Iso. R (4)S
Hm. 120.0 "West": Lat : 31 ° 21'.21 N Long: 32 ° 22'.75 E	Green	Cone	Iso. G (4)s
Hm. 105.0 "East": Lat : 31 ° 20'.36 N Long: 32 ° 22'.83 E	Red	Can	Fl. R.
Hm. 105.0 "West" : Lat : 31 ° 20'.42 N Long: 32 ° 22'.52 E	Yellow	Yellow	Fl. Yel.(4) 15 sec. St. Andrews
Hm. 95 "East": Lat : 31 ° 19'.84 N Long: 32 ° 22'.67 E	Red	Can	Fl. R.
Hm. 95.0 "West": Lat : 31 ° 19'.89 N Long: 32 ° 22'.39 E	Yellow	Cone	F. Yel.
Hm. 83.0 "Middle Buoy": Lat : 31 ° 19'.24 N Long: 32 ° 22'.22 E	Black-Yellow	Yellow	2 Cones Point up Q. Y. N. Cardinal
Hm. 80.0 "East": Lat : 31 ° 19'.04 N Long: 32 ° 22'.41 E	Red	Can	Iso. R (4)s
Hm. 80.0 "West": Lat : 31 ° 19'.10 N Long: 32 ° 22'.17 E	Green	Cone	Iso. G(4)s
Hm. 70.0 "East": Lat : 31 ° 18'.53 N Long: 32 ° 22'.25 E	Red	Can	Iso. R (4)s
Hm. 70.0 "West": Lat : 31 ° 18'.58 N Long: 32 ° 22'.03 E	Green	Cone	Iso. G (4)s

Position	Color	Day mark	Characteristics
Hm. 60.0 "East": Lat : 31 ° 18'.00 N Long: 32 ° 22'.10 E	Red	Can	Fl. R.
Hm. 60.0 "West": Lat : 31 ° 18'.05 N Long: 32 ° 22'.88 E	Green	Cone	Fl. G.
Hm. 45.0 "East" : Lat : 31 ° 17'.25 N Long: 32 ° 21'.84 E	Red	Can	Fl. R.
Hm. 45.0 "West": Lat : 31 ° 17'.24 N Long: 32 ° 21'.66 E	Green	Cone	Fl. G.
Hm. 30.0 "East" Lat : 31 ° 16'.44 N Long: 32 ° 21'.60 E	Red	Can	Fl. R.
Hm. 30.0 "West": Lat : 31 ° 16'.47 N Long: 32 ° 21'.45 E	Green	Cone	Fl. G.
Hm. 15.0 "East": Lat : 31 ° 15'.65 N Long: 32 ° 21'.35 E	Red	Can	Fl. R.
Hm. 15.0 "West": Lat : 31 ° 15'.68 N Long: 32 ° 21'.21 E	Green	Cone	Fl. G.
Hm. 00.0 "East": Lat : 31 ° 14'.87 N Long : 32 ° 21'.10 E	Red	Can	Fl. R.
Hm. 00.0 "West": Lat : 31 ° 14'.90 N Long: 32 ° 21'.00 E	Green	Cone	Fl. G.
Hm. 1.333 "East" : Lat : 31 ° 14'.15 N Long: 32 ° 20'.93 E	Red	Can	Fl. R.
Hm. 1.333 "West": Lat : 31 ° 14'.18 N Long: 32 ° 20'.80 E	Green	Cone	Fl. G.

ii - West:

Position	Color	Day mark	Characteristics
Buoy No. 8: Lat : 31° 21'.13 N Long: 32° 20'.04 E	Green	Cone	F.G.
Buoy No.7: Lat : 31° 20'.52 N Long: 32° 21'.31 E	Green	Cone	F. G.
Buoy No. 6: Lat : 31° 19'.91 N Long: 32° 21'.58 E	Green	Cone	F. G.
Hm. 83.0 : Mentioned in Port Said Channels as "Middle Buoy".			
Hm. 80.0 "East" No. 5: Lat : 31° 19'.13 N Long: 32° 22'.11 E	Red	Can	F. R.
Hm. 80.0 "West" No. 5: Lat : 31° 19'.30 N Long: 32° 21'.85 E	Green	Cone	F. G.
Hm. 65,0 "East": Lat : 31° 18'.50 N Long: 32° 21'.52 E	Red	Can	F. R.
Hm. 65.0 "West": Lat : 31° 18'.65 N Long: 32° 11'.31 E	Green	Cone	F. G.
Hm. 50.0 "East" Lat : 31° 17'.87 N Long: 32° 20'.94 E	Red	Can	F. R.
Hm. 50.0 "West": Lat : 31° 17'.98 N Long: 32° 20'.74 E	Green	Cone	F. G.
Hm. 35.0 "East" Lat : 31° 17'.24 N Long: 32° 20'.33 E	Red	Can	F. R.
Hm. 35.0 "West": Lat : 31°17'.33 N Long: 32°20'.20 E	Green	Cone	F. G.

Position	Color	Day mark	Characteristics
Hm. 21.5 "East" : Lat : 31°16'.67 N Long: 32°19'.79 E	Red	Can	F. R.
Hm. 21.5 "West": Lat : 31° 16'.74 N Long: 32° 19'.69 E	Green	Cone	F. G.

Port of Suez Sea Channels:
   A) Approaches:

Position	Color	Day mark	Characteristics
S. Shoal : Lat : 29° 38'.87 N Long: 32° 35'.98 E	Black	Cone	Isophase Gr. 2 sec. On, 2 sec. OFF
Conry Rock : Lat : 29° 48'.11 N Long: 32° 34'.22 E	Yellow-Black-Yellow	West Mark	Q(9) 15s
Buoy "K": Lat : 29° 41'.11 N Long: 32° 38'.67 E	Black	Cone	Fl. G.
Buoy "L" : Lat : 29° 45'.93 N Long: 32° 38'.67 E	Yellow	Yellow S.Andrews	Q.Y.
Buoy "M" : Lat : 29° 50'.00 N Long: 32° 35'.29 E	Yellow	Yellow S.Andrews	F.Y.
Buoy "N" : Lat : 29° 50'.63 N Long: 32° 35'.29 E	Yellow	Yellow S.Andrews	Q.Y.
Buoy "D" : Lat : 29° 51'.28 N Long: 32° 35'.29 E	Yellow	(See Art. 9, B(2))	
Buoy "C" : Lat : 29° 51'.93 N Long: 32° 35'.29 E	Yellow	»	
Buoy "B" : Lat : 29° 52'.06 N Long: 32° 34'.54 E	Yellow	»	

Position	Color	Day mark	Characteristics
Buoy "A" : Lat : 29° 52'.17 N Long: 32° 33'.84 E	Yellow	»	

Separation Zone Buoys:

Position	Color	Day mark	Characteristics
Buoy No. 1 : Lat : 29° 39'.49 N Long: 32° 32'.12 E	R.W.	R. ball	L. Fl. 10s Racon (O) Horn
Buoy No. 2 : Lat : 29° 48'.55 N Long: 32° 32'.12 E	R.W.	R. ball	Iso 6s Racon (D) Horn

Port of Suez Lighthouse:

Position	Color	Day mark	Characteristics
(New Port Rock): Lat : 29° 53'.11 N Long: 32° 33'.08 E	Green	Framework	Gp. Fl. R. (2) 25 sec.

b) Port of Suez Sea Channels:

Position	Color	Day mark	Characteristics
Hm. 80.5 "East": Lat : 29° 51'.16 N Long: 32° 33'.33 E	Green	Cone	Occ. G. (1) 4 sec.
Hm. 80.5 "West": Lat : 29° 51'.15 N Long: 32° 33'.13E	Red	Cone	Occ. R. (1) 4 sec.
Hm. 70.5 "East" Lat : 29° 51'.70 N Long: 32° 33'.26 E	Green	Cone	Fl. G.
Hm. 70.5 "West": Lat : 29° 51'.69 N Long: 32° 33'.05 E	Red	Can	Fl. R.
Hm. 60.0 "East": Lat : 29° 52'.17 N Long: 32° 33'.16 E	Green	Cone	Fl. G.
Hm. 60.0 "West": Lat : 29° 52'.26 N Long: 32° 32'.96 E	Red	Can	Fl. R.

Position	Color	Day mark	Characteristics
Hm. 44.4 "East": Lat : 29° 53'.10 N Long: 32° 33'.03 E		Green Cone	Fl. G.
Hm. 44.4 "West": Lat : 29° 53'.10 N Long: 32° 32'.82 E	Red	Can	Fl. R.
Hm. 24.00 "East": Lat : 29° 54'.19 N Long: 32° 32'.86 E	Green	Cone	Fl. G.
Hm. 24.0 "West": Lat : 29° 54'.15 N Long: 32° 32'.60 E	Red	Can	Fl. R.
Hm. 19.0 "West": Lat : 29° 54'.50 N Long: 32° 32'.60 E	Red	Can	F. R.
Hm. 14.00 "East": Lat : 29° 54'.73 N Long: 32° 32'.94 E	Green	Cone	Q. G.
Hm. 7.00 "East": Lat : 29° 55'.13 N Long: 32° 33'.10 E	Green	Cone	Fl. G. (1) 2 sec.
Hm. 1.00 "West": Lat : 29° 55'.48 N Long: 32° 33'.02 E	Red	Can	Occ. R. (1) 4 sec.
Km. 162.150 "East": (South entrance of Canal) Lat : 29° 55'.43 N Long: 32° 33'.29 E	Green	Cone	Occ. G. (1) 4 sec.

West Branch "Port Said":

Position	Characteristics		Remarks
	East	West	
Km. 4.100	F.G.	F.R.	Canal Buoys
Km. 6.100	F.G.	F.R.	«
Km. 7.000	F.G.	F.R.	«
Km. 9.000	F.G.	F.R.	«
Km. 10.000	F.G.	F.R.	«
Km. 11.500	F.G.	F.R.	«
Km. 13.000	F.G.	F.R.	«

Position	Characteristics		Remarks
	East	West	
Km. 16.000	F.G.	F.R.	Canal Buoys
Km. 17.050	F.G.	F.R.	«
Km. 17.050	Fl.W.		End of Island, Beacon Black & Yellow Horizontal Bands Canal Buoy - Red Black, Red

East Branch "Port Said":

Position	Characteristics		Remarks
	East	West	
Km. 2.900 E	F.G.	F.R.	Canal Buoys
Km. 4.500 E	F.G.	F.R.	«
Km. 6.000 E	F.G.	F.R.	«
Km. 7.500 E	F.G.	F.R.	«
Km. 9.000 E	F.G.	F.R.	«
Km. 10.500 E	F.G.	F.R.	«
Km. 12.000 E	F.G.	F.R.	«
Km. 13.500 E	F.G.	F.R.	«
Km. 15.100 E	F.G.	F.R.	«
Km. 15.450 E	F.G.	F.R.	«

Main Canal:

Position	Characteristics		Remarks
	East	West	
Km. 18.000	F.G.	F.R.	Canal Buoys
Km. 18.500	F.G.	F.R.	»
Km. 19.000	F.G.	F.R.	»
Km. 20.500	F.G.	F.R.	»
Km.22.000	F.G.	F.R.	»
Km. 23.500	F.G.	F.R.	»
Km. 25.000	F.G.	F.R.	»
Km. 26.500	F.G.	F.R.	»
Km. 28.000	F.G.	F.R.	»
Km. 29.500	F.G.	F.R.	»
Km. 30.500	F.G.	F.R.	»
Km. 31.500	F.G.	F.R.	»
Km. 32.350	Occ.R.	Canal	Buoy West
Km. 32.950	Occ.R.	Canal	Buoy West

Position	Characteristics		Remarks
	East	West	
Km. 34.000	F.G.	F.R.	Canal Buoys
Km. 35.000	F.G.	F.R.	»
Km. 36.500	F.G.	F.R.	»
Km. 38.000	F.G.	F.R.	»
Km. 39.500	F.G.	F.R.	»
Km. 41.000	F.G.	F.R.	»
Km. 42.500	F.G.	F.R.	»
Km. 44.000	F.G.	F.R.	»
Km. 45.500	F.G.	F.R.	»
Km. 47.000	F.G.	F.R.	»
Km. 48.500	F.G.	F.R.	»
Km. 50.000	Refl.	Refl.	Conical East & West
Km. 51.000	F.G.	F.R.	Canal Buoys
Km. 51.427	Fl.W.		North end of Ballah, Beacon Yellow & Black Horizontal Bands Canal Buoy - Red, Black, Red.

West Branch "Ballah":

Position	Characteristics		Remarks
	East	West	
Km. 51.500	F.G.	F.R.	Light on Rails
Km. 52.200	F.G.	F.R	»
Km. 54.200	F.G.	F.R.	»
Km. 55.500	F.G.	F.R.	»
Km. 57.000	F.G.	F.R.	»
Km. 57.500	-	-	Conical (East)
Km. 58.000	F.G.	F.R.	Light on Rails
Km. 59.000	F.G.	F.R.	»
Km. 60.000	F.G.	F.R.	»

East Branch "Ballah":

Position	Characteristics		Remarks
	East	West	
Km. 51.449 E	F.G.	F.R.	Canal Buoys
Km. 52.000 E	F.G.	F.R.	»
Km. 53.500 E	F.G.	F.R.	»

Position	Characteristics		Remarks
	East	West	
Km. 55.000 E	F.G.	F.R.	Canal Buoys
Km. 56.500 E	F.G.	F.R.	»
Km. 58.000 E	F.G.	F.R.	»
Km. 59.500 E	F.G.	F.R.	»
Km. 59.942 E	F.G.	F.R.	»

Main Canal:

Position	Characteristics		Remarks
	East	West	
Km. 60.358	Fl. W.		South end of Ballah, Beacon Black & Yellow Horizontal Bands Canal Buoy - Red, Black, Red Canal Buoys
Km. 60.637	F.G.	F.R.	
Km. 61.000	Refl.	Refl.	Conical (East) & (West)
Km. 61.330	F.G.	Refl.	Canal Buoys (East) Conical (West)
Km. 62.000	F.G.	F.R.	Canal Buoys
Km. 62.330	Refl.	Refl.	Conical (East) & (West)
Km. 62.660	F.G.	F.R.	Canal Buoys
Km. 63.000	Refl.	Refl.	Conical (East) & (West)
Km. 63.330	F.G.	F.R.	Canal Buoys
Km. 64.000	F.G.	F.R.	»
Km. 65.500	F.G.	F.R.	»
Km. 67.000	F.G.	F.R.	»
Km. 68.500	F.G.	F.R.	»
Km. 70.000	F.G.	F.R.	»
Km. 71.400	F.G.	F.R.	»
Km. 72.330	F.G.	F.R.	»
Km. 73.000	F.G.	Refl.	Canal Buoy (East) Conical (West)
Km. 73.660	F.G.	F.R.	Canal Buoys
Km. 74.330	F.G.	Refl.	Canal Buoy (East) Conical (west)
Km. 75.000	F.G.	F.R.	Canal Buoys
Km. 75.660	F.G.	F.R.	»
Km. 76.330	F.G.	F.R.	»
Km. 76.950	Fl.W.		North end of Timsah by-pass Beacon Black & Yellow Horizontal bands Canal Buoy-Red, Black, Red

Timsah Lake:

Position	Characteristics East	West	Remarks
Km. 77.671	F.G.	F.R.	(No. 10)
Km. 77.212	F.G.	F.R.	
Km. 78.060		F.R.	(No. 10 bis)
Km. 78.315	F.G.		
Km. 78.270		Fl.Y.	
Km. 78.279		Fl.Y.	(No. 11)
Km. 78.395		Fl.Y.	(No. 11 bis)
Km. 78.542		F.Y.	
Km. 78.725		F.Y.	(No. 12)
Km. 78.895		F.Y.	(No. 12 bis)
Km. 78.925	F.G.		
Km. 79.065	F.G.	F.R.	(No. 13)
Km. 79.943	F.G.	F.R.	
Km. 80.621	F.G.	F.R.	
Km. 81.200	F.G.	F.R.	
Km. 81.250	Fl.W.		South end of Timsah by-pass Beacon Black & Yellow Horizontal bands Canal Buoy- Red, Black, Red

East Branch "Timsah":

Position	Characteristics East	West	Remarks
Km. 77.000 E	F.G.	F.R.	Canal Buoys
Km. 77.660 E	F.G.	F.R.	»
Km. 78.420 E	F.G.	F.R.	»
Km. 78.900 E	F.G.	F.R.	»
Km. 79.800 E	F.G.	F.R.	»
Km. 80.360 E	F.G.	F.R.	»

Main Canal:

Position	Characteristics		Remarks
	East	West	
Km. 82.100	F.G.	F.R.	Canal Buoys
Km. 83.000	F.G.	F.R.	»
Km. 84.000	F.G.	F.R.	»
Km. 85.026	F.G.	F.R.	»
Km. 85.625	F.G.	Refl.	Canal Buoy (East) Conical (West)
Km. 86.300	F.G.	F.R.	Canal Buoys
Km. 87.000	F.G.	Refl.	Canal Buoy (East) Conical (West)
Km. 87.700	F.G.	F.R.	Canal Buoys
Km. 88.600	F.G.	F.R.	»
Km. 89.500	F.G.	F.R.	»
Km. 91.000	F.G.	F.R.	»
Km. 92.500	F.G.	F.R.	»
Km. 93.100	F.G.	F.R.	»
Km. 94.000	F.G.	F.R.	»
Km. 94.955	Fl. W.		North end of Deversoir by-pass Beacon Black & Yellow Horizontal bands Canal Buoy-Red, Black, Red

West Branch "Deversoir":

Position	Characteristics		Remarks
	East	West	
Km. 95.000	F.G.	F.R.	Canal Buoys
Km. 96.000	F.G.	F.R.	»
Km. 97.000	F.G.	F.R.	»
Km. 97.700	F.G.	F.R.	»
Km. 98.700	F.G.	F.R.	»
Km. 99.700	F.G.	F.R.	»
Km. 100.250	Fl. W.		South end of Deversoir by-pass Beacon Black & Yellow Horizontal bands Canal Buoy- Red, Black, Red
Km. 101.272	F.G.	F.R.	Canal Buoys (West channel) G.B.L
Km. 102.600	F.G.	F.R.	Canal Buoys (West channel) G.B.L

East Branch "Deversoir":

Position	Characteristics		Remarks
	East	West	
Km. 95.000 E	F.G.	F.R.	Canal Buoys
Km. 95.250 E	F.G.	F.R.	»
Km. 96.000 E	F.G.	F.R.	»
Km. 97.700 E	F.G.	F.R.	»
Km. 98.700 E	F.G.	F.R.	»
Km. 99.700 E	F.G.	F.R.	»
Km. 101.272 E	Fl.G.	F.R.	»
Km. 102.600 E	F.G.	F.R	»
Km. 103.344 E	F.G.	F.R.	»
Km. 104.160 E	F.G.		Canal Buoy (end of East Branch)

Great Bitter Lake:

Position	Characteristics		Remarks
	East	West	
Km. 103.344	F.G.	F.R.	End of E. & W. branches
Km. 103.755	-	F.R.	Beginning of W. passage
Km. 104.160	-	F.R.	Limit of West passage
Km. 104.160	Fl.W.		Orange St. Andrews cross North Light
Km. 104.160	F.G.	-	Limit of East passage
Km. 105.550	-	F.R.	Limit of West passage
Km. 105.550	F.Orange		Orange St. Andrews cross
C1			
Km. 105.550	F.G.	-	Limit of East passage
Km. 107.700	-	F.R.	Limit of West passage
Km. 107.700	F.Orange		Orange St. Andrews cross
C2			
Km. 107.700	F.G.	-	Limit of East passage
Km. 109.500	-	F.R.	Limit of West passage
Km. 109.500	F.Orange		Orange St. Andrews cross
C3			
Km. 109.500	F.G.	-	Limit of East passage
Km. 111.000	-	F.R.	Limit of West passage
Km. 111.000	F. Orange		Orange St. Andrews cross

Position	Characteristics		Remarks
	East	West	
C4			
Km. 111.000	F.G.	-	Limit of East passage
Km. 112.870	-	F.R.	Limit of West passage
Km. 112.870	F. Orange		Orange St. Andrews cross
C5			
Km. 112.870	F.G.	-	Limit of East passage
Km. 114.200	Fl. W.		Orange St. Andrews cross
South Light			
Km. 114.200	F.G.	-	Limit of East passage
Km. 114.200	-	Fl.R.	Limit of West passage
Km. 114.750	-	Fl.R.	Limit of West passage
Km. 114.800	Fl.G.	-	Limit of East passage
Km. 115.025	Fl. W.		North end of Kabrit by-pass Middle buoy, Y. B. Y.
Km. 115.134	F.G.	F.R.	Beginning of Kabrit West branch
Km. 115.134	F.G.	F.R.	Beginning of Kabrit East branch

West Branch "Kabrit":

Position	Characteristics		Remarks
	East	West	
Km. 115.603	F.G.	F.R.	Canal Buoys
Km. 116.800	F.G.	F.R.	»
Km. 118.000	F.G.	F.R.	»
Km. 119.200	F.G.	F.R.	Canal Buoys
Km. 120.400	F.G.	F.R.	»
Km. 120.827	F.G.	F.R.	»
Km. 121.600	F.G.	F.R.	Canal Buoys
Km. 122.100	F.G.	F.R.	»
Km. 122.150	Fl. W.		South end of Kabrit by-pass B. Y. B. Horizontal bands

East Branch "Kabrit":

Position	Characteristics		Remarks
	East	West	
Km. 115.607E	F.G.	F.R.	Canal Buoys
Km. 116.800E	F.G.	F.R.	»
Km. 118.800E	F.G.	F.R.	»
Km. 119.200E	F.G.	F.R.	Canal Buoys
Km. 120.400E	F.G.	F.R.	»
Km. 120.827E	F.G.	F.R.	»
Km. 121.600E	F.G.	F.R.	Canal Buoys
Km. 122.100E	F.G.	F.R.	»
Km. 122.150E	Fl. W.		South end of Kabrit by-pass B. Y. B. Horizontal bands

Main Canal:

Position	Characteristics		Remarks
	East	West	
Km. 122.500	Refl.	-	Conical (East)
Km. 122.690	F.G.	F.R.	Canal Buoys
Km. 123.104	Refl.	-	Conical (East)
Km. 123.501	F.G.	F.R.	Canal Buoys
Km. 123.903	Refl.	-	Conical (East)
Km. 124.280	F.G.	F.R.	Canal Buoys
Km. 124.693	Refl.	-	Conical (East)
Km. 125.097	F.G.	F.R.	Canal Buoys
Km. 125.470	Refl.	-	Conical (East)
Km. 125.800	F.G.	F.R.	Canal Buoys
Km. 126.310	F.G.	F.R.	»
Km. 127.029	F.G.	F.R.	»
Km. 128.066	F.G.	F.R.	»
Km. 129.025	F.G.	F.R.	»
Km. 129.503	Refl.	-	Conical (East)
Km. 130.060	F.G.	F.R.	Canal Buoys
Km. 130.396	Refl.	-	Conical (East)
Km. 130.600	F.G.	F.R.	Canal Buoys
Km. 131.001	Refl.	-	Conical (East)
Km. 131.402	F.G.	F.R.	Canal Buoys
Km. 131.660	Refl.	-	Conical (East)
Km. 132.000	F.G.	F.R.	Canal Buoys

Position	Characteristics		Remarks
	East	West	
Km. 133.175	F.G.	F.R.	»
Km. 133.800	F.G.	F.R.	»
Km. 135.000	F.G.	F.R.	»
Km. 136.000	F.G.	F.R.	»
Km. 137.000	F.G.	F.R.	»
Km. 138.000	F.G.	F.R.	»
Km. 139.000	F.G.	F.R.	»
Km. 140.000	F.G.	F.R.	»
Km. 141.000	F.G.	F.R.	Canal Buoys
Km. 142.000	F.G.	F.R.	»
Km. 143.000	F.G.	F.R.	»
Km. 144.000	F.G.	F.R.	»
Km. 144.714	-	F.R.	Canal
Km. 145.496	F.G.	F.R.	Canal Buoys
Km. 147.146	F.G.	F.R.	»
Km. 147.975	F.G.	F.R.	»
Km. 148.985	F.G.	F.R.	»
Km. 149.660	F.G.	F.R.	»
Km. 151.000	F.G.	F.R.	»
Km. 152.000	F.G.	F.R.	»
Km. 153.035	F.G.	F.R.	»
Km. 153.554	F.G.	F.R.	»
Km. 154.310	-	F.R.	Canal
Km. 154.685	F.G.	-	Canal
Km. 155.000	-	F.R.	Canal
Km. 155.330	F.G.	-	Canal
Km. 156.258	F.G.	F.R.	Canal Buoys
Km. 156.625	F.G.	-	Canal
Km. 157.000	-	F.R.	F.R
Km. 157.375	F.G.	-	Canal
Km. 158.000	F.G.	F.R.	Canal Buoys
Km. 158.625	F.G.	-	Canal
Km. 159.000	-	F.R.	Canal
Km. 159.330	F.G.	-	Canal
Km. 160.000	F.G.	F.R.	Canal Buoys
Km. 161.050	F.G.	F.R.	»

> CHAPTER VIII - NATURAL CONDITIONS

o **Art. 84 - Tides and Currents in SC :**

The SC is divided into three main sectors according to the nature of tide in each.
The characteristics of each can be summarized as follows:

A - The Northern Sector:
This part is located between Port Said and the G.B.L.
1. The height of tide at Port Said CO-oscillates with the tide of the Mediterranean Sea with 0.50 meter extreme tidal range (Difference between highest and lowest levels) at Spring tides.
   This tidal range decreases gradually going South, to be about 0.20 meter at the entrance of Lake Timsah.
2. In this sector, the peak tidal current may reach 1.0 knot (in case of no wind).
3. Currents may be doubled by strong prevailing winds.
4. Peak currents occur about 50 minutes after predicted HW and LW at Port Said.
5. The duration and velocity of currents in this sector are greatly affected by the relative mean sea levels between the Mediterranean Sea, the Bitter Lakes and the Red Sea as follows :
   - **In summer:** between July and October, the mean sea level at Port Said is slightly higher than that of the Bitter Lakes. This difference (which reaches its maximum of about 0.20 meter in September), beside the great evaporation at the Bitter Lakes, causes the predominance of the Southward current in duration and velocity.
   - **In winter:** between December and May, the Mean sea level at the Bitter Lakes is slightly higher than that of Port Said. This difference which reaches its Maximum of about 0.30 meter in January causes the predominance of the Northward current in duration and velocity.
   -

B - The Lakes Timsah and Bitter Lakes
1. The Lakes along the Canal have an important role in dampening the effects of sudden meteorological changes.
2. The Bitter Lakes with a surface of about 250 Km^2 reduce the vertical movement of the tide to a minimum between Km. 100 and Km. 130.
3. The high spring tide range (MHWS) in G.B.L. may reach 0.25 meter
4. The phase of the vertical tide in G.B.L. is about 3 hours later than that of Port Tewfik.
5. The vertical tide in Lake Timsah is almost in phase with the tide in G.B.L.

C - The Southern Region
This part is located between Port of Suez and the Bitter Lakes
1. The height of tide in Suez CO-oscillates with the tides of the Red Sea with extreme tidal range of about 1.90 meters at spring tides. This range decreases gradually going north till the Bitter Lakes entrance to be 0. 15 meter at Genefa.
2. The tidal volume of the Bitter Lakes is very large compared to the tidal volume of the Southern section. Consequently, the currents are relatively strong and almost uniform between Port Tewfik and Genefa.
3. In this region, the Northward current is called Flood and the Southward current is called Ebb.
4. Peak currents occur about 50 minutes after predicted HW and LW at Port Tewfik.
5. At the entrance of the Canal, Km. 159, the Flood tide starts at an average of 3 hours after the Low Water at Suez. The Ebb tide 3 hours after High Water in Suez.

6. Generally in summer, the duration of the Ebb exceeds the average of 6 hours. In winter, the Flood is the predominant. The Ebb is prolonged by "Strong Northerly Winds". The Flood is prolonged by "Strong Southerly Winds".
7. In this region, the average peak current is about 1.5 knots. In Spring tides, current may reach 2.5 knots.
8. The change of current occurs 5 to 10 minutes later on the bottom of the Canal, than on its surface.

D - Current Buoys

In the Canal, there are current buoys indicating the direction of the current:

Head Current: Red & White horizontal bands or I reflector at night.

Stern Current: Black & White vertical stripes or 2 reflectors at night.

These buoys are laid in the following positions:

El Raswa	Km. 3.710	East
Port Fouad	Km. 2.750	»
Ras El Ech (E)	Km. 12.800	»
Ras El Ech (W)	Km. 14.304	»
Tineh	Km. 24.775	»
Cap	Km. 35.420	»
Kantara	Km. 45.130	»
Ballah (E & W)	Km. 54.770	»
Ferdan	Km. 64.894	»
Ismailia	Km. 76.127	»
Toussoum	Km. 86.780	»
Deversoir (E & W)	Km. 97.845	»
Kabrit (E & W)	Km. 120.827	»
Genefa	Km. 133.950	»
Chaloufa	Km. 146.125	»
Port Tewfik	Km 160.300	»

o **Art. 85 - Weather Forecast :**

Six Meteorological stations are installed on the Canal area. Information about weather will be passed to vessels through pilots, Ismailia Radio station.

> CHAPTER IX - RADIO COMMUNICATIONS

o **Art. 86 - Wireless and Inmarsat Service :**
(1) General:
Vessels must have their W/T and radiotelephony apparatus in good working order before entering the Canal.
They must also be fitted with a VHF set easily operated from the bridge. It must have the working frequency range of the marine band (156 to 174 MHz) especially channels 6, 8, 9, 10, 11, 12, 13, 14, 15, 16, 71, 73, 74. If not, they will rent one from SCA for transit.

(2) SCA Marine communication center (SUQ):
SC wireless station (marine communication center) SUQ has different communication facilities to contact with vessels in the open sea or approaching areas and while transiting the Canal.

All these communication facilities are in compliance with the latest GMDSS regulation:
I - Radio Telex:
a) Frequency allocated to contact with vessels by radio telex from open sea to inform SCA of their expected time of arrival (E.T.A.) to Port Said or Port Tewfik harbors.
ID. NO, 4820 / Hours of service: 24 H.

Transmits	Receives	Mode	Watch hours
4250	6310 4205	FIB	H 24

Vessels are requested to send the following data before arrival by 48 H and 24 H and when arriving the approaches.

Vessel name Call sign SCID ETA Draft SCGT
....
Cargo Dangerous Cargo and Flash point
....
Origin Destination Agent name
....

b) Frequencies allocated to contact with vessels by radio telex while transiting Suez Canal or from waiting areas.
ID. NO. 4820 / Hours of service: 24 H.

Transmits	Receives	Channel	Mode	Watch hours
1612	2147	211	FIB	H 24

Radio and broadcast facilities are available on the same frequencies.

II - W/T Morse:
W/T Morse will continue to contact with Vessels transiting the Canal from waiting areas.
W/T (MF) Hours of service : 24 H.

Call sign	Transmits	Receives	Channel	Mode	Watch hours
SUQ	520.5	469.5 and 454	109	A1A-A2A	H 24

III - Inmarsat communication :
Vessels have on board Inmarsat station to contact SCA's (SES) at SC marine communication center SUQ to send their E.T.A. before arrival by 48 H and 24 H and when arriving the approaches.
The SCA's (SES) identification numbers ID are as follows:
a) Telex: 581-1622570
b) Voice: 871- 1622570
c) Fax: 871 -1622574
Answer back: Suez

IV - International Land Telex and Fax:
SC Marine communication center SUQ has international
Telex No. 63528 SUQ SC UN.
And also international Fax No. 002-064-393517.

V - Weather Reports:
SUQ has broadcasting daily weather reports and navigational warnings (If exist) to vessels transiting the Canal or in the approaches.

   o **Art. 87 - VHF-UHF Radiotelephony :**
   A - VHF Radiotelephony for vessels from Sea:
(1) At Port Said:
   • Port management (Listening)
     Call sign : (Port Said 16) (HP- 1) 156.800 MHz
   • Pilot vessel and Radar guidance :
     1. Outside the harbor:
        Call sign : (Port Said 12) (HP-2) 156.600 MHz
     2. Inside the harbor:
        Call sign : (Port Said 13) (HP-3) 156.650 MHz
   • Ad measurement Office :
     Call sign : (Port Said 73) (M) 156.675 MHz

(2) At Port of Suez :
   • Port management (Listening) :
     Call sign : (Suez 16) (HP- 1) 156.800 MHz
   • Pilot vessel and Radar guidance:
     1. Outside the harbor:
        Call sign : (Suez 11) (HP- 2) 156.550 MHz
     2. Inside the harbor:
        Call sign : (Suez 14) (HP-3) 156.700 MHz
   • Ad measurement Office :
     Call sign : (Suez 74) (M) 156.675 MHz

B - UHF Radiotelephony in the Canal:
(1) UHF voice communication system was built to cover the entire Canal and its approaches to facilitate communication between pilots and the main movement office at Ismailia and the port management offices.
The Canal pilot uses a special portable UHF personal transceiver which has the following frequencies:

CH.No.	Transmission Frequency MHz	Reception Frequency MHz	Function
1	415.350	412.850	Vessels from North (SB)
2	415.600	413.100	Vessels from South (NB)
3	415.850	413.350	Emergency (EM)
4	416.600	141.100	In Port of Suez Harbor HP (T)
5	416.350	413.850	In Port Said Harbor HP (S)
6	416.125	413.600	Emergency (EMC) Critical Vessels (out of convoy)

(2) Escort tugs-towing tugs will use special portable UHF transceiver set which has the following frequencies:

Ch. 1 414.750 MHz
Ch. 2 414.775 MHz
Ch. 3 414.800 MHz

> **CHAPTER X-THE SUEZ CANAL VESSEL TRAFFIC MANAGEMENT SYSTEM (SCVTMS)**

o **Art.88 - Overview :**

Suez Canal has upgraded its VTMS installed in 1978 to readjust some of the planning movement concepts to the new generation of vessels and technology. The new system will provide complete surveillance and tracking by radar coverage of vessels throughout the Canal and its approaches at Port Said and Port Tewfik harbours, tracking by Loran-C will be used as a backup for the radar surveillance. The new developed VTMS system will provide the following services :

(1)Automatic surveillance and tracking of vessel arriving at SC approaches (15 miles faraway) until anchorage in the waiting areas.

(2)Automatic determination of arrival times at ports.

(3)Automatic continuous tracking and monitoring of vessel's position, speed and separation distances for all vessels transiting the SC.

(4)Provide the Port management centers at P.S and P.T as well as Ismailia main traffic management center with sufficient instantaneous information about vessels transiting the Canal by means of displaying complete televised radar pictures of the whole Canal and very powerful informatics system.

(5)Provide automatic displaying system for pilots at all signal station (signal state board) which display his arrival time, meteorological data, and emergency information.

(6)Provide integral data base for vessel information, transit regulations, traffic flow transit pattern, pilot assignment, vessel billing and navigation reports.

(7)Provide an efficient and quick means of communication with vessels arriving at ports and with pilots on board of vessels transiting the Canal.

This system will add more safety values for vessels and cargo during passage through the SC. The newly adopted computerized ideal/real transit pattern will ensure optimum and safety transit passage for the benefit of her world users, owners of vessels and the international trade.

o **Art.89 - System Operation :**

(1)Transit Request:

In order to assign a vessel in the system informatics a transit request must be received from the vessel owners/or agent at one of the port management offices.

Vessel transit request usually takes one of the following forms :

- Booking in advance; usually three or four days prior to arrival at port.
- SCA informed by telex or agent that ship will arrive within 48 H.
- SCA advised that ship will arrive at any time.

A vessel that has previously transited the Canal will have a unique Suez Canal file NR (SCA ID).

It is required that this ID must be provided when the request for transit is made.

If the vessel is not currently in system informatics and data base, the port management operator will create vessel particular and automatically assign a unique SCA ID.

(2)Vessel Arrivals :

- A vessel approaching the Canal at either end is requested to call the port management office on one of the frequencies listed in chapter IX Art. 88.
- The vessel is requested to declare her position, her international call sign and SCA ID.
- The vessel will be tracked automatically by the radar subsystem and displayed on the graphic display, then the port management operator will be able to infolink it with the informatics on the arrival list.

(3)Vessel Reaching The Anchorage Area :
At both Port Said and Port Tewfik, anchorage areas are indicated on radar graphic displays. Whenever a linked vessel reaches an anchorage area, the informatics will record the time the vessel reaches an anchorage area.

(4)Vessel Berth List :
The port management office will continue tracking the vessel till entering the assigned berth location and stops and vessel berth list is created in the informatics.
Each berth location will be indicated on the port management graphic displays as well as Ismailia graphic displays.
The vessel berth list will refresh periodically to reflect any going changes to the port operators.

(5)Creation of the Transit Pattern :
The main management center at Ismailia will generate the optimal convoy pattern based on the vessel currently in the waiting areas or estimated to be in the waiting areas by the limit times.
The transit pattern will determine each convoy's start time and maximum time width.

(6)Convoy Creation :
At Port Said and Port Tewfik, the harbour master will order the vessels in the convoy patterns that were generated by the main management Center at Ismailia.
The official convoy list will only be comprised of vessels that have marked as eligible for transit (paid the transit fees, performance certificate ... etc.).

(7)Assign Pilot to Vessels :
The Port management office will assign the road and Canal transit pilots. Pilot list and pilot convoy list will be printed.

(8)Pilot Boarding Order :
After the official convoy list is created, the convoy list report will be printed. After pilot (S) have been assigned, Boarding order reports will be printed.
These reports will be given to each transit and Roads pilot as part of their pilot Boarding orders.

(9)Vessel Enter the canal :
As vessels leave their berths at the port, the port management office will follow and track them till entering the Canal.
As the vessels enter into the Canal their identifiers will be automatically updated to add their ID and relative position within the convoy against their displayed picture on the display at Port office and main management office at Ismailia.

(10)Real Transit Pattern :
As the convoy progress along the Canal, the real-time transit pattern is displayed and plotted. The real-time transit pattern screen will provide the capability of viewing real time information as X, Y positions, speed, km positions and off axis for each vessel as well as the meteorological data of all signal station includes the wind speed and direction, visibility, current speed and direction, and height of the tide.

(11)Vessel passes Check Points :
Check points are the inlets and outlets of by-passes, siding, each signal station, the Canal start and the Canal end.
The ordering of vessels within the convoy is re-checked at each check point. If the vessels has changed position within the convoy, this is automatically recorded in the transit history.
The informatic data base is updated to reflect the convoy and new convoy position displayed against the target.

(12)Information Displayed on the Signal Station Board :
As each vessel passes a signal station, the informatics will then update the signal station Boards to provide convoy progress the following information (Table 1 to 5) for a vessel as it passes the station.
Information of vessels (as vessel name, convoy position, SCA ID, call sign, speed, location and meteorological data)will be displayed to the signal station operators on signal station PCs.
(13)Vessels Leaves the Canal :
When vessels get out of range of radar the informatics will close the vessel transit and is saved as a closed transit for Historical reporting purpose.
(14)In case of emergency or radar failure, the Canal pilot will board the vessel with Loran-C court to be installed on board the vessel by SCA personal.
By initializing command from the Canal main management office at Ismailia tracking by Loran-C chain is executed.
In some cases tracking by both radar and Loran-C chain will be executed to monitor the progress of vessel during their transit through the Canal in order to assure safety transit and increase Canal efficiency.

1 - PRESENTATION OF SIGNAL STATEBOARD

AND NAVIGATION INFORMATION DISPLAYED

Signal station	Boards for vessels from North (SB)	Boards for vessels from South (NB)
	(VSP) (MET,CY.NO,E)	(VSP) (MET,E)
PF	Z	Z
	Y	Y
	(VSP) (MET,CY.NO,E)	(VSP) (MET,E)
(PS)	Z	Z
	Y	Y
	(VSP) (MET,CY.NO,E)	(VSP) (MET,B,E)
KM 3.7	Z	Z
	Y	Y
	(VSP) (MET,E)	(VSP) (MET,E)
RAS EL ICH	Z	Z
	Y	Y
	(VSP) (MET,E)	(VSP) (MET,B,E)
TINEH	Z	Z
	Y	Y
	(VSP) (MET,E)	(VSP) (MET,E)
EL KAP	Z	Z
	Y	Y
	(VSP) (MET,P,M,E)	(VSP) (MET,E)
KANTARA	Z	Z
	Y	Y
	(VSP) (MET,P,M,E)	(VSP) (MET,E)
BALLAH	Z	Z
	Y	Y
	(VSP) (MET,T,TM,E)	(VSP) (MET,E)
EL FERDAN	Z	Z
	Y	Y

	(VSP) (MET,T,P,E)	(VSP) (MET,E)
ISMAILIA	Z	Z
	Y	Y
	(VSP) (MET,E)	(VSP) (MET,T,TM,E)
TOUSSOUM	Z	Z
	Y	Y
	(VSP) (MET,E)	(VSP) (MET,T,TM,E)
DEVERSOIR	Z	Z
	Y	Y
	(VSP) (MET,E)	(VSP) (MET,P,E)
KABRIT	Z	Z
	Y	Y
	(VSP) (MET,E)	(VSP) (MET,E)
GENEFA	Z	Z
	Y	Y
	(VSP) (MET,E)	(VSP) (MET,E)
CHALOUFA	Z	Z
	Y	Y
	(VSP) (MET,E)	(VSP) (MET,E,CY.NO)
SUEZ	Z	Z
	Y	Y

The characteristic Letter used are :

VSP: Variable system parameter (6 characters) which may be inserted manually on request by movement office or signaling station for navigational information and meteorological. These 6 characters must be alphanumeric characters.

Y :Your time at the signaling station.

Z :Time of passage of vessel ahead of you.

P :Estimated time to get underway for vessels stopped at crossing zones (PREVI).

M :Number of vessels mooring in the branch you are going through.

TM :Vessels already anchored at Timsah.

T :Vessels must be anchored.

CY. No.: Convoy ordering number for ship in convoy.

E :Emergency information.

MET :Meteorological information.

B :Berthing area.

STATEBOARD REPRESENTATION

---

2 - State of Southbound convoy :

S		B		☐	☐	☐	☐ Current time
☐	VSP	☐		☐	☐	☐	☐ VSP
☐		Z		☐	☐	☐	☐ Time of preceeding vessel
☐		Y		☐	☐	☐	☐ Own vessel time

3 - State of Northbound Convoys :

N	B	□ □ □ □ Current time
□ VSP □		□ □ □ □ VSP
□	Z	□ □ □ □ Time of preceeding vessel
□	Y	□ □ □ □ Own vessel time

N.B. : The stateboard will be rotated to face the NB or SB convoy.

Explanation of the stateboard display :

*1st line indicates the convoy direction and the current time.

*2nd line (VSP) indicates the Met., Emergency and the navigational information alternatively.

*3rd line indicates time of the preceeding vessel.

*4th line indicates time of the vessel in front of the signal station.

4 - Meteorological Information :

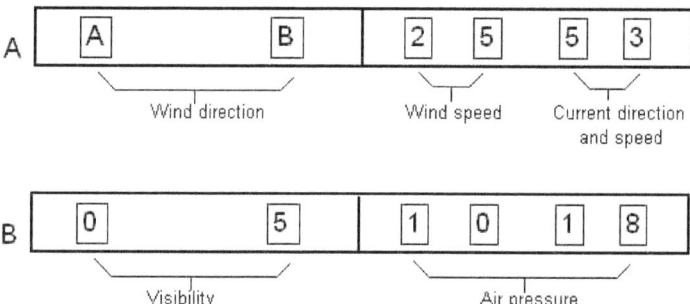

N.B.:The stateboard will be rotated to face the N.B or SB convoy.

* A and B will be displayed alternatively (One at a time) starting with A.

5 - Emergency Information :

In case of emergency the second alteration :

(B) of the (VSP) line will be replaces by the emergency or navigational information if either is needed to be displayed as the following examples :

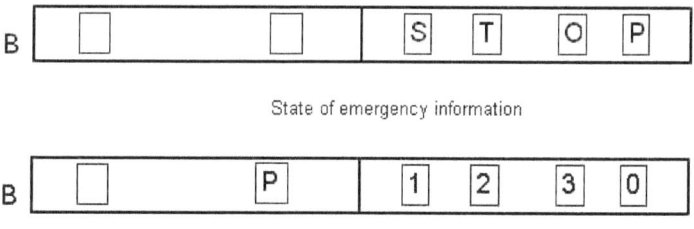

135

o Art.90 - New Information For Vessels Transiting the Canal :

(1)Each vessel has special SCA FILE NR (SCA ID) in the new informatics system in Suez Canal.SCA distributes free of charge special SCA ID card to be kept in the radio room, vessel must report SCA FILE NR on all arrival messages for transits or port calls.Any change in vessel's characteristics should be reported to SCA officially to be filled in SCA ID.

(2)Meteorological data will be displayed on signal state boards (2nd line) to inform vessels of the prevailing weather conditions as they pass the signal station.Also emergency or navigation instructions from the main management office at Ismailia can be displayed on the same line alternatively.

(3)The CORT should be mounted on either of the two wings on entrance of the Canal the area around should be clear of obstruction within 10 feet radius.A trained SCA technician will mount the CORT in place and operate before disembarking.The vessel is asked to install electrical outlet 110/220 VAC (Hubbel socket type 2356 flunged receptacle nylon casing Hubbel catalogue number 35-R-2B 37), on the two wings to supply the CORT with electrical power.Before vessel exits the Canal at either end of the Canal the CORT will be dismounted by a SCA technician.

> ➢ CHAPTER XI - SIGNALS

- ○ **Art. 91 - Generalities :**

1. All signal used in Canal Waters are mentioned hereafter.

2. All flags and pendants to be hoisted by vessels. As mentioned hereafter should be those in the International Code of Signals.

3. Night signals shall be hoisted where best be seen by other vessels.

- ○ **Art. 92 - Sound Signals:**

A - Normal maneuver:

1. The International Regulations for Preventing Collisions at Sea signals.
   One short blast: I am altering my course to **starboard**.
   Two short blasts: I am altering my course to **port**.
   Three short blasts: I am operating astern **propulsion**.
2. The signal **5 or 6 short blasts** repeated several times at short intervals to say: **I am reducing speed and may have to stop or make fast.**
   At night besides the blasts, four to five long flashes with the Aldis lamp or signal mast lamp.
3. The signal **one prolonged blast** to attract attention.
   The expression "short blast" means a blast of about 1 second duration.
   The expression "prolonged blast" means a blast of 4 to 6 second duration.

B - Obstruction in channel in all circumstances:

This under any circumstance causes of finds obstruction in the Channel must right away warn the vessels in the vicinity.

That warning is given by whistle or siren:

4 long blasts meaning: "**The channel is not free**".

That warning must he repeated every 3 minutes until vessels concerned have answered in the same manner- As soon as they hear the signal mentioned above, the vessels take steps to stop and instruct for Radio Watch, to receive full detail of the alert given by the vessel that sent the said signal.

The vessel, should maintain Radio Watch until otherwise advised.

C - Ship failure (to dredgers):

In Case of engine or steering failure making the vessel not under command, while approaching a dredger, the vessel has to give the signal : **one long blast followed by two short blast (– • •).**

D - Vessel mooring voluntarily for fog or sand storm:

During the mooring maneuver, the vessel sounds every 2 minutes a series of 6 short blasts. Once made fast (Signal No. 16 "G.V." hoisted) the vessel must ring rapidly the bell for 5 seconds at intervals not exceeding one minute. For vessels of 100 meters and over, they will have to ring the bell forward and in addition a gong aft, at intervals not exceeding one minute (a gong or any other instrument whose tone and sound will be different to that of the bell forward).

These signals are stopped when the vessel is told that all vessels concerned have been notified of her mooring.

E - Vessel aground or across:

See Art. 92 B - Obstruction in channel.

F - Between vessels and tugs:

(1) Vessel aground in the Canal:

Between a vessel aground in the Canal and a tug.

These signals are for maneuver of refloating, as long as the vessel has one of the grounding signals:

Pull slowly – •

Increase – • •

stop – –

Slack the line – – •

I am going to let go – – • •

These signals are to be repeated by the tug.

(2) Vessel towed in the Canal:

Between a vessel towed in the Canal and a tug.

Radiotelephony is used as communication between ship and tug, besides the following signals:

By Day (flag)	At Night (sound)
Slow speed : "A" hoisted above bridge	– •
Half speed : "A" hoisted halfway	– • •
Normal tow : "A" hoisted right up	– • • •
Steady : "A" lowered	– –

(Or sound signals if considered surer)

-The sound signals are to be repeated by the tug.

-The flag signal remains flying as long as the tug is to give the signaled speed.

- By day, every change of flag signals is followed by a long blast.

G - Signals between VLCCs and escort tugs:

(1) Attention to start maneuver:

Several prolonged blasts given by the ship.

(2) Stern tug

Bring my stem to starboard	•
Bring my stem to port	• •
Keep my stern in the axis	• • •
Pull my stern aft slowly	• • • •
Increase pulling my stem	• • • • –
up to half speed astern	• • • • •
Increase pulling my stern	• • • • • –
up to full speed astern	• • • • • •
Stop pulling (very long blast)	

(3) Forward tug :

Give me a push on starboard bow	–
Give me a push on port bow	– –
Stop pushing	– – –

- **Visual Signals**

  o <u>**Art. 93 - Visual Signals :A - Signals displayed on station signal masts to vessels**</u>

Signal No. 1: Stand by to proceed (general)

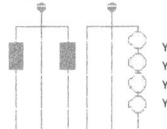

(a) Hoisted on Kabrit, Deversoir and Ras El Ech:
"Stand by to Proceed on signal No. 2".
(b) Hoisted on Ballah and repeated on El Ferdan:
"Southbound vessels made fast in Ballah West Branch, Stand by to Proceed".
(c) Hoisted on Ballah and repeated on El Kantara:
"Northbound vessels made fast in Ballah West Branch, Stand by to proceed".
(d) Hoisted on Km. 3 East branch of Port Said:
"Southbound vessels using Port Said East Branch, Stand by to Proceed".

Signal No. 2: Proceed (general)

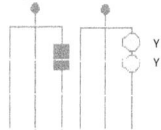

(a) Hoisted on Port Tewfik, Kabrit, Deversoir and Ras El Ech:
"Proceed"
(b) Hoisted on Ballah and repeated on El Ferdan:
"Southbound vessels made fast in Ballah West Branch, Proceed".
(c) Hoisted on Ballah and repeated on El Kantara:
"Northbound vessels made fast in Ballah West Branch, Proceed".
(d) Hoisted on Km. 3 East branch:
"Southbound vessels using Port Said East branch, Proceed".
(e) Absence of Signal No. 2 "Stay at anchor or made fast and keep continuous W/T watch".

Signal No. 3: Stand by to make fast

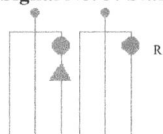

Hoisted at Km. 18 mast :
"Southbound vessels made fast in West branch Km. 4 to 14 and Northbound vessels already passed Tineh station, Stand by to make fast".

Signal No. 4: Make fast

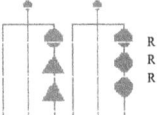

Hoisted at Km. 18 mast:
"Southbound vessels in Port Said East or West by-pass and northbound vessels already passed Tineh station, MAKE FAST".

Signal No. 5: Attention

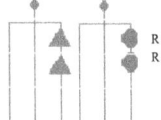

"Southbound & Northbound vessels stand by to make fast or maneuver. Keep W/T watch immediately".

Signal No. 6: Immediate stopping

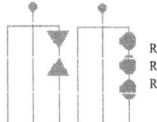

"Southbound & Northbound vessels make fast immediately".
Vessels may proceed when signal is lowered or switched off.

Signal No. 7: Make fast (vessels from North)

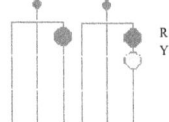

"Vessels from North: Make Fast".
(To be lowered or switched off when all concerned vessels are made fast).

Signal No. 8: Make fast (vessels from South)

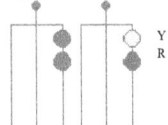

"Vessels from South: Make Fast".
(To be lowered or switched off when all concerned vessels are made fast).

Signal No. 9: Proceed (vessels from North)

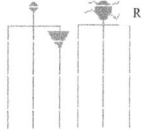

"Vessels from North made fast on Signal No. 7, Proceed".
(Southbound vessels made fast in Port Said West branch and in Ballah West branch to Proceed or, signal No. 2).

Signal No. 10: Proceed (vessels from South)

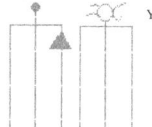

"Vessels from South made fast on Signal No. 8, Proceed".
(Northbound vessels made fast in Ballah West branch to Proceed on signal No. 2).

Signal No. 11: Current signal

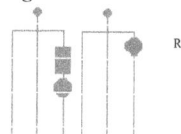

Current indication signal.
Hoisted on Challoufa and Genefa Signal masts:
"Current Running NORTH"
Absence of signal: "Current is Running SOUTH or Slack Water".

Signal No. 12: Port closed

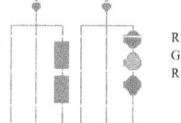

"Suez Roads closed for bad weather".

Signal No 13: W/T watch (vessels from North)
Signals No. 13 & 14 can be used at the same time addressing both convoys from North and South

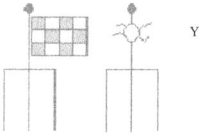

"Vessels from North establish Wireless Telegraphy Watch".

Signals No. 13 & 14 can be used at the same time addressing both convoys from North and South

Signal No 14: W/T watch (vessels from South)
Signals No. 13 & 14 can be used at the same time addressing both convoys from North and South

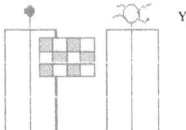

"Vessels from South establish Wireless Telegraphy Watch".

Signals No. 13 & 14 can be used at the same time addressing both convoys from North and South

Signal No. 15: Passage authorization (Ferry Boats)

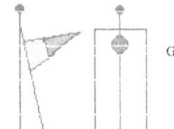

"Ferry Boat not allowed to move"
(**By night:** Light on wharf).

Signal No. 16: Isolated signal station

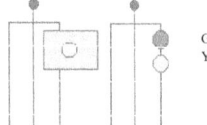

"This signal station is isolated.
All communications are made by Wireless Telegraphy".

- ○ <u>Art.93b B - SPECIAL SIGNALS USED BY VESSELS IN PORTS AND IN THE CANAL</u>

Signal No. 1: Vessels carrying bulk petroleum flash point between 73° and 150° F.
Oil tanker carrying bulk petroleum: (Flash point between 73' and 150'F.)

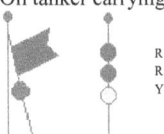

Signal No. 2: Vessels carrying explosives - vessels N.G.F.

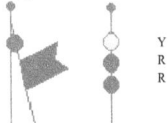

Vessels carrying 1st group dangerous goods N.G.F. tankers.
LPG-LNG- Dangerous chemicals in bulk.

Signal No. 3: Vessels carrying bulk petroleum flash point under 73ºF.

R
R
R

Petroleum in bulk: (Flash point below 73' F.)

Signal No. 4: Vessels carrying radioactive substances

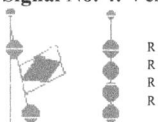

R
R
R
R

Vessels carrying radioactive substances

Signal No. 5: I require a pilot

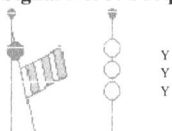

Y
Y
Y

I require a pilot
N.B.:
a) From Port to Sea or changing berth, signal to be hoisted half an hour before sailing time.
b) For the Canal at least 2 hours before the 1st Vessel is expected to enter the Canal.

Signal No. 6: I require Free Pratique

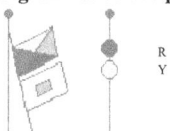

R
Y

I require Free Pratique
(only in port)

Signal No. 7: Coming from infected port

My vessel is coming from an infected port
(only in port)

Signal No. 8: Under Quarantine.

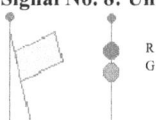

R
G

My vessel is under Quarantine.

Signal No. 9: Tug required (in ports)

I require a tug (followed by a numeral pendant to indicate the number of tugs required).
By night: A long blast on the whistle and letters "YA" flashed by Morse Lamp several times, (only in port).

Signal No. 10: Mooring boats

I have no mooring boats.
By night: numeral 3 flashed by Morse lamp several times.
(only in port).

Signal No. 11: Searchlight

I have no shore searchlight.
By night: numeral 4 flashed by Morse lamp several times.
(Signals 10 & 11 can be used in one hoist if vessel has no mooring boats and searchlight).

Signal No. 12: Last in convoy

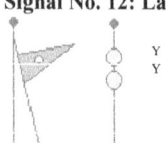

Last Vessel in the convoy.
When signal No. 13, 14, & 15 are hoisted, vessels are not authorized to overtake or cross until vessel is securely made fast and signal No. 16 (G.V.) hoisted.

Signal No. 13: Making fast

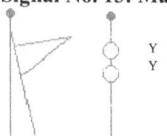

The Vessel is making fast:
N.B.: In the Canal when made fast, the 2 white lights are extinguished and a red light put on aft all the time the vessel is moored until actually underway.

Signal No. 13-bis: Doubling in G.B.L.

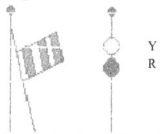

Vessels doubling in G.B.L.: (Numeral pendant indicating new turn of vessel)
When signal No. 13, 14, & 15 are hoisted, vessels are not authorized to overtake or cross until vessel is securely made fast and signal No. 16 (G.V.) hoisted.

Signal No. 14: Vessel maneuvering to sea

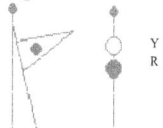

The vessel is maneuvering to get underway to Sea.
When signal No. 13, 14, & 15 are hoisted, vessels are not authorized to overtake or cross until vessel is securely made fast and signal No. 16 (G.V.) Hoisted

Signal No. 15: Vessel maneuvering to Canal

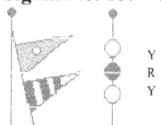

The vessel is maneuvering to get underway to Canal.
When signal No. 13, 14, & 15 are hoisted, vessels are not authorized to overtake or cross until vessel is securely made fast and signal No. 16 (G.V.) Hoisted

Signal No. 16: Voluntary stopping (G. V.)

Voluntary Stopping (G.V.) "Garage Volontaire".
Vessel is not ready and will not maintain her turn in the convoy.
If hoisted by a vessel in the Canal: "I am securely made fast and can be crossed or doubled by other vessels in the convoy".

Signal No. 17: Aground

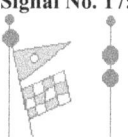

"Passage clear for tugs".
"Passage not clear for tugs"

Signal No. 18: I have a pilot:

a) I have a Pilot on board.
b) Leaving Port Said & Port of Suez:
I have a pilot to disembark.

Signal No. 19: My vessel is isolated

I have no means of communication.

o **Art.93c** C - SIGNALS USED BY DREDGERS IN CANAL WATERS

(1) DREDGERS WORKING UNDERWAY

Signal No. 1: Dredgers underway
By Day   By Night

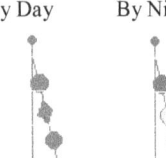

International Signal
I am dredging underway and cannot get out of the way
N.B. - In Lieu of the white masthead light.

Signal No. 2: Passage clear on side shown
By Day   By Night

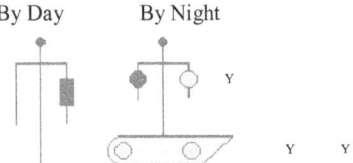

By Day: A drum at the yard arm on the side on which the passage is clear.
By Night: A white light at the yard arm on which the passage is clear. A red light at the yard arm on which the passage is not clear. Two white lights along the bulwark where passage is clear.

Signal No. 3: Passage is clear on both sides

By Day   By Night

By Day: A drum at both yard arms

By Night: A white light at both yard arms and tow white lights along the bulwark both sides.

Signal No. 4: Passing not allowed on either side

By Day   By Night

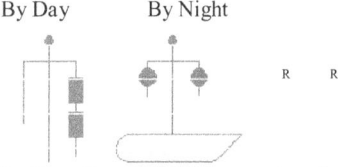

By Day: Two drums one over the other at the yard arm.

By Night: A red light at both yard arms.

Signal No. 5: I am going about

By Day   By Night

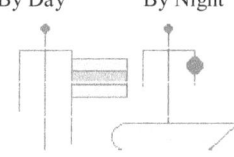

By Day: Flag D hoisted at the yard arm on the side to which she is turning.

By Night: A red light shown at the yard arm on the side to which she is turning. Signal IP by Morse lamp.

Signal No. 6: I am not under command

By Day   By Night

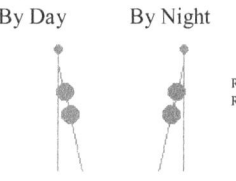

International Signal

This signal may be hoisted together with the International signal K (sound & visual) meaning: "STOP IMMEDIATELY".

(2) STATIONERY DREDGERS, FLOATING CRANES, ETC.

Signal No. 1: Passage clear on side shown
(I am at work or moored).

By Day   By Night

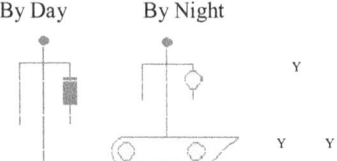

By Day: A drum at the yard arm on the side on which the passage is clear
By Night: A white light at the yard arm on the side on which the passage is clear. Two white lights along the bulwark on the side on which the passage is clear.

Signal No. 2: Passage clear on both sides
(I am at work).

By Day   By Night

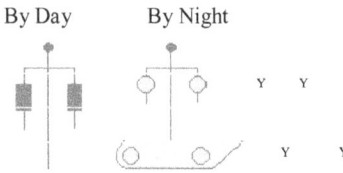

By Day: A drum at both drum yards
By Night: A white light at both yard arms. Two white lights along the bulwark on both sides.

Signal No. 3: Passage clear on side shown, with speed reduction
Passage is clear on the side shown but only to proceed at the lowest possible speed.
This signal is also used by "Warehouse" string of barges. The International Signal TE may also be hoisted. In this case the decrease of speed is imperative. By night the imperative decrease of speed is shown on the Pilot's boarding order.

By Day   By Night

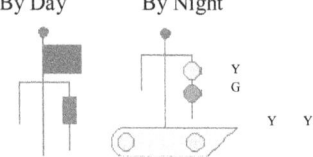

By Day: A red flag at the masthead. A drum at the yard arm on the side on which the passage is clear
By Night: A white light over a green light on the side on which the passage is clear. Two white lights along the bulwark on the side on which the passage is clear.

Signal No. 4: Passing not allowed on either side

passing not allowed on either side

By Day   By Night

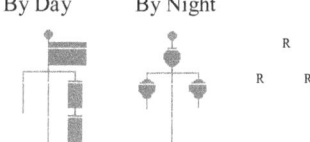

By Day: Two drums one over the other at the yard arm.
By Night: A red light at both yard arms

Signal No. 5: Passing not allowed: maneuvering to clear passage

passing not allowed. I am maneuvering to make fast to clear the Passage.

By Day   By Night

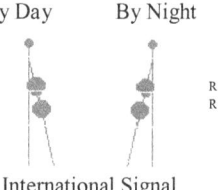

By Day: A red flag at the masthead & 2 drums one over the other at the yard arm.
By Night: A red light at the masthead. A red light at both yard arms.

Signal No. 6: I am not under command - passing not allowed

passing not allowed. I have a breakdown & cannot get out of the way.

By Day   By Night

International Signal

- **Art. 93** -SIGNAL LIGHTS REQUIRED FOR VESSELS TRANSITING THE CANAL

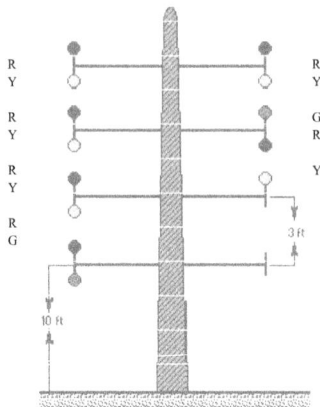

NOTE: When made fast in the Canal, a R. Light in lieu of the stern light.

> ➤ CHAPTER XII - COMPUTATION OF TONNAGE

> o **Art. 94 - Extract from the Regulations for the Measurement of Tonnage recommended by the International Tonnage Commission assembled at Constantinople, in 1873.**

(Minutes of proceedings XXI, Appendix II)

A - Rule 1: General Principles:

1. The gross tonnage or total capacity of ships comprises the exact measurement of all spaces (without any exception). Below the upper deck, as well as of all permanently covered and closed - in spaces on the deck.
   N.B.: By permanently covered and closed - in spaces on the upper deck are to understood all those which are separated off by decks or coverings, or fixed partitions and therefore represent an increase of capacity which might be used for the stowage of merchandise, or for the berthing and accommodation of the passengers or of the officers and crew.
   Thus, any one or more openings, either in the deck or coverings, or in the partitions, or a break in the deck, or the absence of a portion of the partition, will not prevent such spaces being comprised in the gross tonnage, if they can be easily closed - in after admeasurements, and thus better fitted for the transport of goods and passengers.
   But the spaces under awning decks without other connection with the body of the ship than the props necessary for supporting them, which are not spaces "separated off" and are permanently exposed to the weather and the sea, will not be comprised in the gross tonnage, although they may serve to shelter the ship's crew the deck passengers and even merchandise known as "deck loads".

2. "Deck loads" are not comprised in the measurement.

3. Closed spaces for the use or possible use of passengers will not be deducted from the gross tonnage.

4. The determination of deduction for coal spaces may be effected either by the rules of the European Danube Commission of 1871 or by the exact measurement of fixed bunkers.

B - RULE 2 - For Laden Ships:

(Art. 9) - When ships have their cargo on board, or when for any other reason their tonnage cannot be ascertained by means of Rule 1, proceed in the following manner:

Measure the length on the upper deck from the outside of the outer plank at the stem to the aft side of the stern-post, deducting there from the distance between the aft side of the stem-post and the rabbet of the stern-post at the point where the counter-plank crosses it.

Measure also the greatest breadth of the ship to the outside of the outer planking or Wales.

Then, having first marked on the outside of the ship, on both sides thereof, the height of the upper deck at the ship's sides, girt the ship at the greatest breadth in a direction perpendicular to the keel from the height so marked on the outside of the ship, on the one side, to the height so marked on the other side by passing a chain under the keel; to half the girth thus taken add half the main breadth; square the sum, multiply the result by the length of the ship taken as aforesaid; then multiply this product by the factor 0. 17(seventeen hundredths) in the case of ships built of wood, and by the factor 0. 18 (eighteen hundredths) in the case of ships built of iron. The product will give approximately the cubical contents of the ship, and the general tonnage can be ascertained by dividing by 100 or by 2.83, according to the measurements taken in English feet or in meters.

(Art.10) - If there be a break, a poop, or other permanent covered and closed-in spaces (as defined in the general principles) on the upper deck, the tonnage of such spaces shall be ascertained by multiplying together the mean length, breadth and depth of such spaces and dividing the product by 100 or 2.83, according to the measurements taken in English feet or meters, and the quotient so obtained shall be deemed to be the tonnage of such space, and shall be added to the other tonnage in order to determine the gross tonnage or total capacity of the ship.

C - Deductions:

To be made from the Gross Tonnage in order to ascertain the Net Tonnage:

(Art.11) - To find from the gross tonnage of vessel as above set forth the official, or net registered tonnage, either for sailing vessels or for steam ships, the following mode of operations must be resorted to :

(1) Sailing Vessels :

(Art.12) - For sailing vessels deduct : the spaces exclusively and entirely occupied by the crew and the ship's officers, those taken up by the cookhouse and latrines exclusively used by the ship's officers and crew whether they be situated above or below the upper deck; the covered and closed in spaces, if there 'be any situated on the upper deck, and used for working the helm, the capstan, the anchor gear, and for keeping the charts, signals and other instruments of navigation.

Each of the spaces deducted as above may be limited according to the requirements and customs of each country, but the deductions must never exceed in the aggregate 5 percent of the gross tonnage.

(Art.13) - The measurement of these spaces is to be effected according to the rules set forth the measurement of covered and closed-in spaces on the upper deck, for result, obtained by deducting the total of such allowances from the gross tonnage, represents the net or tonnage of sailing vessels.

(2) Steam Ships :

(Art. 14) - For vessels propelled by steam or any other mechanical power, deduct:

A - The same spaces as for sailing vessels (Art. 12) with the limitation to 5 percent of the gross tonnage.

B - The spaces occupied by the engines, boilers, coal bunkers, shaft trunks of screw steamers, and the spaces between decks and in the covered and closed-in erections on the upper deck surrounding the funnels, and required for the introduction of air and light into the engine-rooms and for the proper working of the engines themselves.

Such deductions cannot exceed 50 per cent of the gross tonnage.

(Art. 15) - The measurement of the spaces allowed for both in sailing vessels and in steam ships (section A of Art. 14) is to be effected according to the rules set forth in Articles 12 and 13 for sailing vessels.

Spaces for which allowances are made in steam ships only (section B of Art. 14) are measured according to the following rules.

(3) Ships having coal-bunkers with movable partitions :

(Art.16) - In ships that do not have fixed bunkers but transverse bunkers with movable partitions, with or without lateral bunkers, measure the space occupied by the engine-rooms, and add to it, for screw steamers 75 percent, and for paddle steamers, 50 percent of such space.

By the space occupied by the engine-rooms is to be understood that occupied by the engine-room itself and by the boiler-room together with the spaces strictly required for their working, with the addition of the space taken up by the shaft-trunk in screw steamers and the spaces between decks which enclose the funnels and are necessary for the admission air and light into the engine-rooms.

These spaces are measured in the following manner :

Measure the mean depth of the space occupied by the engines and boilers from its crown to the ceiling at the limber strake, measure also three, or, if necessary, more than three breadth of the space at the middle of its depth, taking one of such measurements at each end and another at the middle of the length: take the mean of such breadths; measure also the mean length of the space between the foremost and aftermost bulkheads or limits of its length, excluding such parts, if any, as are not actual occupied by or required for the proper working of the engines and boilers.

Multiply together these three dimensions of length, breadth and depth, and the product will be the cubical contents of the space below the crown.

Then find the cubical contents of the space or spaces, if any, between the crown aforesaid and the uppermost or poop deck, as the case may be, which are framed in for the machinery or for the admission of light and air, by multiplying together the length, depth and breadth thereof. Add such contents as well as those of the space occupied by the shaft trunks to the cubical contents of the space below the crown; divide the sum by 100 or by 2.83, according to the measures taken in feet or meters and the result shall be deemed to be the tonnage corresponding to the engine and boiler room which serves as basis for the deductions referred to.

If in any ship in which the space aforesaid is to be measured, the engines and boilers are fitted in separate compartments, the contents of shall be measured separately in like manner, according to the above rules, and the sum of their several results shall be deemed to be the tonnage of the engine-rooms which serves, as aforesaid, as basis for the total deductions.

(4) Ships with fixed coal-bunkers

(Art. 17) - In ships with fixed coal-bunkers measure the mean length of the engine and boiler-room, including the coal-bunkers. Ascertain the area of three transverse sections of the ship (as set forth in the rules given in Art. 3 and 4 for the calculation of the gross tonnage) to the deck which covers the engines.

One of these three sections must pass through the middle of the aforesaid length, and the two others through the two extremities.

Add to the sum of the two extreme sections four times the middle one, and multiply the sum thus obtained by the third of the distance between the sections. This product divided by 100, if the measurements are taken in English feet, or by 2.83 if they are taken in meters, gives the tonnage of the space in question.

If the engines, boilers and bunkers are in separate compartments they are separately measured, as above set forth, and the results are added together.

In screw steamers the contents of the shaft-trunk are measured by ascertaining the mean length, breadth and height, and the product of the multiplication of these three dimensions divided by 100 or 2.83 according to the measurements taken in feet or in meters, gives the tonnage of such space.

The tonnage of the following spaces between decks, and in the covered and closed-in erections on the upper deck, is ascertained by the same method:
- The spaces framed-in round the funnels.
- The spaces required for the admission of light and air into the engine-rooms.
- The spaces, if any, necessary for the proper working of the engines.

(Art. 18) - Instead of the measurement of fixed bunkers, the rules for bunkers with movable partitions as set forth in Art. 16 may be applied.

(Art. 19) - In the case of tugs the allowances are not limited to 50 per cent of the gross tonnage; all the space occupied by machinery, boilers and coal-bunkers may be deducted. Nevertheless, if such vessels are not excursively employed as tugs, the deductions in question cannot exceed 50 percent of the gross tonnage.

o **Art. 95 - Additional Deductions allowed by the Suez Canal Authority :**

The SCA allows the following spaces to be included in the deductions specified in Art. 12 of the Regulations for the Measurement of Tonnage, provided the deductions do not, in the aggregate, exceed 5 percent of the gross tonnage*(Maximum raised to 10% from 1st. April 1948.)* . And subject to the condition that they are clearly and permanently marked so as to show the purpose to which they are exclusively appropriate:

A - Spaces for the exclusive use of officers, engineers and crew:
- Master's accommodation.
- Officer's smoking room.
- Chief engineers and Chief Officer's day rooms and/or offices.
- Doctor's and dentist's cabins (if they are occupied by the doctors and dentists for whom they are intended).
- Consulting rooms.
- Hospital.
- Infirmary.
- Surgery of operating room.
- Chemist's laboratory.
- Cabins of wireless operators (if utilized).
- Stewards cabin (if the stewards are solely employed for the officers, engineers or crew).
- Cabins of the engineer's storekeepers and water tenders.
- Mess rooms. (No deduction is allowed for officers mess room in vessels having passenger accommodation which are not also provided with a passengers mess room).
- Bathrooms. (With the exception of such bathrooms as are available for passengers when no bathroom for their exclusive use is provided)
- Lavatories.
- Library.
- Bar.

- Gallery, cookhouse.
- Pantry
- Scullery,
- Bakery (only on vessels having no passenger accommodation).
- Laundry.
- Drying room.
- Heating boilers.
- Refrigerating machinery (excluding cold storage rooms and store rooms).
- Distilling apparatus.
- Disinfecting apparatus.
- Wardrobes, oilskin and lifebelt lockers.
- Ventilators (utilized neither for passengers or cargo).
- Night watchmen accommodation (provided these men are signed on as crew and are not employed in connection with passengers or cargo).
- Accommodation of fire fighting personnel. *(Fire extinguishing installations are also to be deducted.)*
- Domestic water pump rooms.
- Switchboard lockers. *(Installations used for the needs of the crew and also for the purpose of navigation are to be treated as navigation spaces.)*
- Transformer rooms. *(Installations used for the needs of the crew and also for the purpose of navigation are to be treated as navigation spaces.)*

B - Navigation spaces (if above the uppermost deck)
- Chart house.
- Master's spare room on the bridge (especially on warships).
- Searchlight spaces.
- Submarine telephone spaces.
- Direction finder spaces.
- Sounding spaces.
- Gyro compass spaces.
- Wireless telegraphy spaces.
- "Radar" spaces (exclusively used for navigational purposes).
- Lamp room (if only containing signal lamps)
- Lookout houses.
- Emergency generators.
- Emergency compressors (if used exclusively in case of accident for pumping out water and not for any commercial purposes).
- Switchboard lockers.
- Transformer rooms.

- o **Art. 96 - Measurement of Deck Spaces:**
For vessels fitted with superstructures, the following rules, which concern only such spaces as are excluded from the national tonnage, are applied.

A - Vessels with one tier of superstructures only:
  (1) Poop, bridge, forecastle:
The following exemptions (See Art. 97 - 2.) are allowed under certain conditions:
- Such length of the poop measured from the inside of the stern timber, at half height of the said poop, as shall be equal to 1/10th of the full length of the ship.

- The Portion of the bridge in way of the light and air spaces of the engine and boiler spaces is being understood that such light and air spaces are not considered to extend beyond the forward bulkhead of the stoke-hold and the after bulkhead of the main engine-room.
- Such length of the forecastle measured from the inside of the stem at half height of the said forecastle, as shall be equal to 1/8th of the full length of the ship.
- In each of the above three cases of superstructures, such portions as are in way of corresponding openings in the sides of the ship, not provided with any means of closing.

(2) Poop and bridge combined, or forecastle and bridge combined:

In each of these combined spaces, the following exemptions (See Art. 97 - 2.) are allowed under certain conditions:

- **a)** That length only which corresponds to the openings of the engine-room and boiler spaces as specified in (1b) above.
- **b)** Such portions as are in way of corresponding openings not provided with any means of closing in the sides of the ship.

(3) Shelter-decks:

In the case of shelter-decks. The following exemptions are allowed under certain conditions:

- a) The portions in way of corresponding openings in the side plating of the ship not provided with any means of closing.
- b) Such air spaces as are situated within the shelter-decks must be measured into the engine-room space and deducted together with 75% of their volume.

B - Vessels having more than one tier of superstructures:

1. The exemptions Prescribed in paragraph A-(I), (2) and (3) above are applicable in their entirety to the lowest tier only.
2. Tiers above the lowest tier are only allowed the exemption (See Art. 97 - 2.) of such portions as are in way of corresponding openings in the side plating of the vessel not provided with any means of closing.

- ○ **Art. 97 - Suez Canal Tonnage :**

(1) The tonnage on which fill dues and charges to be paid by vessels, as specified in these regulations, are assessed, is the net tonnage resulting from the system of measurement laid down by the International Commission held at Constantinople in 1873, and duly entered, on the special certificates issued by the competent authorities in each Country.

In assessing the dues, any alteration of net tonnage subsequent to the delivery of the above mentioned certificates is taken into account.

(2) In order that the exemptions from measurement shown on the special certificate may apply, there must be no merchandise, commercial stores, or supplies, of any kind in the portions of spaces which are entitled to exemption.

- Should a vessel, at anytime, transit with passengers, merchandise of any kind, or bunker coal, or commercial stores of any description, in any portion whatever of any exempted or deducted spaces, the whole of those spaces is added to the net tonnage and can nevermore be exempted from measurement?
- Nevertheless. The SCA agrees that in cases where the vessel is sold, the new owners can again claim exemption of the exemptible spaces previously taxed. The sale of the

vessel must of course be effective and bona fide. A new SC Special Tonnage Certificate must be obtained.

(3) Double Bottom :
- When any bottom space is utilized over 6 inches for the carriage of bunker during the transit of the Canal, its cubical capacity will be added to the tonnage.
- Contrary, however, to the Rules now in force, this addition will not be a permanent character, the cubical capacity of the said spaces will only be added to the tonnage when they are utilized.

(4) Verification :
- a) The CA Officials *(They are authorized to get on board ships at Port Said, Bitter Lake and during transiting the Canal.)* are empowered to ascertain whether cargo or passengers, are carried in any space not included in the net tonnage entered on the vessel's special certificate.
- b) And, generally, may verify whether all spaces which ought to be included in the tonnage are entered on the certificate and are correctly determined thereon, Seamen occasionally taken on board vessels passing through the SC are considered as passengers, unless they are duly entered on the ship's articles and certified as being intended for vessels belonging to the same owners.

(5) Dock loads:
Unfixed and unenclosed deck loads are not included in the measurement. Closed deck loads including containers on weather deck of' cargo ships are to be included in the measurement.

(6) Vessels without a valid special tonnage certificate: *(Document issued by the Tonnage Authorities of the vessel's Registry.)*
- Every vessel not provided with a valid special tonnage certificate showing the net tonnage prescribed by the Constantinople commission, is measured by the CA officials in conformity with the Rules laid down by the Constantinople Commission.
- The net tonnage thus arrived at, is provisionally used for the assessment of dues, until such time as the vessel tenders at a subsequent transit, a special certificate duly drawn up by the competent authorities.
- If there are any difficulties in assessment of the net tonnage, especially in Maiden voyage, the dues shall be levied provisionally on the gross tonnage until measured in other trips.

(7) Navy ships :
- As long as the ship is not provided with SC Special Tonnage Certificate, transit dues will be levied on the temporary gross tonnage product of the empirical formula without any allowance till the presentation of the documents required.
- Meanwhile, owing to special arrangements necessary for transit of navy ships, a surcharge of 25% of the transit dues is to be applied for Navy and Auxiliary ships belonging to the Navy of different countries.

(8) Vessels in ballast distinctive character:
- Merchant vessels :
  - o i - Which are not earning freight on their voyage.
  - o ii - Which are only carrying fuel for their own consumption.

o   iii - Carrying only its own crew, with their private provisions, are considered as being in ballast.
- Containers on containerships, trailers on vehicle carriers, and barges on lash vessels are considered as a permanent vessel's equipment if fulfilling SC Conditions.
- The presence of oil residues *(These residues must not exceed 1% of the vessels Deadweight.)* on tankers, as well as dry cargo on bulk carriers or combined carriers, does not lose the vessels privilege of being in ballast.
- A small quantity of the previous cargo*(Not to exceed more than 2 % of the Summer Deadweight.)* on the liquefied gas carriers, to maintain a low temperature inside the cargo tanks to be able of receiving the new cargo, does not lose the vessel the privilege of being in ballast.
- Small quantity remainder of previous packed cargo garbage. Dump, sweeping ... etc., not exceeding 2M/ton on general cargo vessels does not lose the vessel the privilege of being in ballast. *(Not to exceed more than 2 % of the Summer Deadweight.)*
- For human reasons, the SCA will, however, tolerate the presence of shipwreck survivors rescued at sea on board vessels in ballast. The presence on board of such survivors shall not render the vessel liable to dues at the full rate.
- A vessel landing her passengers or cargo before passing through the Canal and taking them on board afterwards will in no case be considered as being in ballast.
- Further in order to be entailed to claim the benefit of the ballast rate, the volume of bunker coal or fuel must not exceed 125 % of the engine room space as shown on the Suez Canal Certificate. Bunker coal or fuel should, primarily, be contained in the vessel's permanent or movable bunkers.
- On board vessels in ballast, the CA allows part of the bunkers to be carried in the exempted portion of the bridge without loss of the exemption.
- In any case, owners will have to take the necessary steps to ensure that the total volume of all bunkers on board can be easily ascertained. *(See Art. (16) and Art (17) of the Regulations for the measurement of tonnage.)*

o   **Art. 98 - Regulations concerning the "Containerships":**
(See Circular Updates, Cir. No. 12/1995)

A - The "Containers" are closed space increasing the carriage capacity of the ship when situated over the main deck (weather deck).
They are considered as a ship's permanent equipment. It is a matter of fact that those in the cargo holds are included in the under deck tonnage. Surcharges on Canal dues relevant to number of tiers on weather deck are taxed.

B - Conditions to consider the containers as part of the ship's permanent equipment:
1. They must belong to :
   a) the ship's owner.
   Or **b)** the time charterer.
   Or **c)** The container's consortium.
   Or **d)** Containers leasing company.
2. They must bear a serial number as well as the owner's name.
3. They must be registered on the ship's official documents.
4. The Master of the containerships must assure to SCA Representatives all facilities concerning the measurement and number of containers, their internal capacities and the kind of cargo contained.
5. Containerships are considered, in ballast :

a) If all containers on the main deck as well as those inside cargo holds are empty.

b) If the main deck is clear and there are empty containers in the cargo holds; in this case, a ratio of 6% of the SC dues is to be added.

C - Presence of uncontainerized cargo 300 metric ton or more, other than floating unit, on board (in holds and/or on upper deck) container vessels,
The actual volume of containers on deck is to be added to the taxable tonnage.

D - Con-bulker vessels:
This type of vessels will be treated, regarding dues and tonnage as follows:
1. If the vessel carries dry bulk cargo only, the rate of loaded dry bulk carriers is applied.
2. If the vessel carries containerized cargo only, the rate of loaded container vessel is applied, plus the surcharge on dues relevant to number of tiers oil weather deck.
3. If the vessel carries bulk cargo & containers, the rate of laden container vessel is applied. Meanwhile, the actual volume of containers on upper deck is taxed.
4. When the vessel is completely empty, transit dues of ballast dry bulk carriers is applied.
5. If the vessel is carrying empty containers only, the rate of ballast container vessel is applied, plus the surcharge on dues relevant to number of tiers on weather deck.

○ **Art. 99 - Regulations to be applied to cargo ships carrying containers on weather deck :**
The volume of the containers on deck is to be added to the taxable tonnage:
1. If such containers are full, the ship is considered loaded.
2. If such containers are empty and the ship is in ballast, the ship is considered in ballast.
3. If some of the containers are empty and others are full, the ship is considered loaded even if the ship is in ballast.
4. If the containers on the main deck as well as those in the holds are empty, the vessel is considered loaded.
5. If there are no containers on the main deck, but they are in the holds, the ship is considered loaded even if the containers are empty.

○ **Art. 100 - Computation of tonnage and state of vessels Roll-On/Roll-Off carrying containers :**
A - Computation of tonnage :
1. If the containers on the main deck not exceed 2 tiers :
- A ratio of 5% of the vessel's net tonnage is be added to the ship's net tonnage on the condition that the tonnage of these containers should not exceed 20% of the vessel's SC.N.T.
2. If the tonnage of the 2 tiers exceeds the 20% of the vessel's SC.N.T:
- The difference is added to the taxable tonnage.
3. If the number of tiers of containers is more than 2 tiers :
The tonnage of tiers of containers exceeding the 2 tiers is to be added to the taxable tonnage even if the tonnage of the first 2 tiers is less than 20% of the vessel's SC.N.T.

B - State of Vessel:

   1. 1.The vessel is considered in ballast, in the following conditions :

a) If all the containers and/or the ship's rolling equipment over the main deck, as well as those inside the cargo holds are empty.

b) If the main deck is clear, and there are empty containers inside the cargo holds and the rolling equipment are empty; in this case, a ratio of 5% of the net tonnage is to be added to the taxable tonnage.

   2. The vessel is considered loaded, in the following condition: The presence of any loaded containers and/or rolled cargo.

   3. These regulations do not apply to Roll-On / Roll-Off vessels carrying containers if they carry besides any bulked or stacked cargo.
   In this case, they are considered as Conventional Cargo Ships.

   4. By rolling equipment above mentioned - and which are considered as permanent ship's equipment - it is understood the ship's cranes, tractors and trailers.

> CHAPTER XIII - TRANSIT AND TOWAGE DUES

○ **Art. 101 - Canal dues :**

A - Transit dues:

(Not applicable to vessels under 300 S.C.G.T.)

1. Transit dues are assessed on SC.N.T.
2. Transit dues rates will be levied according to the last circular to be issued by SCA.
3. Transit dues are payable in advance. (See PART IV: NOTICE)

B - Division of transit :

A reduction of a quarter, half or three quarters of the transit dues is allowed to vessels using only three quarters, half or one quarter of the Canal.

Once a vessel just entered the Canal; a quarter of transit dues are to be levied.

(Northern Entrance: a) At Km. 3.710 (West Channel) b) At Km. 1.333 (East Channel) Southern Entrance: At Hm 3.000).

C - Additional dues on slow vessels:

Additional transit dues are levied on slow vessels on the basis indicated below:

Ship's speed is less than the speed of the vessels of her group in the convoy, by not more than	Additional Dues
1 Km/H	10 % of transit dues
2 Km/H	20 % of transit dues
3 Km/H	30 % of transit dues
4 Km/H	40 % of transit dues
5 Km/H	80 % of transit dues
6 Km/H or more	160 % of transit dues

D - Towage Dues:

(See Circular 2/99 Towage dues)

(1) Vessels towed or escorted in the Canal:

- Manned vessels pay transit dues as mentioned above for vessels transiting under own power.
- i - Manned vessels without steering pay 50% of the transit dues. (Transit dues are levied on SC.N.T.)
  ii - Manned vessels with engines out of order pay 75% of the transit dues. (Transit dues are levied on SC.N.T.)
  iii - Manned vessels have both cases mentioned before in para. a),b) pay 100% of the transit dues. (Transit dues are levied on SC.N.T.)
- Unmanned or scrapped vessels (dead body) pay transit dues levied on the basis of Gross Tonnage SC special Tonnage Certificate. The rates S.D.R. per ton is the same as used for vessels transiting under own power.

These vessels are subject also to the payment of extra dues for towed units mentioned. (See item 2-C)
- If towed or escorted by approved tugs not belonging to SCA, vessels have to pay towage dues of 25 US Cent per SC.N.T. In case of manned vessels and per SC.G.T in case of unmanned or scrapped vessels, in addition to the transit dues.
- Approved tugs not belonging to SCA pay transit dues as a laden vessel.
- In case of towing or escorting with a tug not belonging to SCA, a pilot is imposed against a payment of a lump sum of 450 US Dollars.
- The towed unit is charged by the Pilotage dues for the additional pilots appointed to assist the pilot on board that unit. The rate being 300 US Dollars for every extra pilot in the Canal and 150 US Dollars for every extra harbor pilot.

(2) Towed large floating units

Transiting Canal dues are to be collected as follows:
a) **Transit dues :**
    i. **Towed Large floating units:**
       Transit dues are collected on the basis of SC.N.T. The tug of the unit will be treated as conventional ship regarding dues.

    ii. **Unmanned or scrapped vessels arriving in the Canal:**
        Transit dues are levied on the basis of the SC.G.T.

b) **Towage dues:**
    Dues are collected on the towed manned unit at a rate of 25 US Cent per ton of Net Tonnage. For scrapped or unmanned vessels, they are levied on the basis of SC.G.T.

c) **Extra Charges :**
    i. **Length:**
       If the length of the towed unit, together with its deck load exceeds 200 (two hundred) feet, an extra charge equal to 0.25% of the transit dues will be collected for every foot in excess.
       This extra charge will not exceed 125% of the unit's or vessel's transit dues.

    ii. **Beam:**
        If the maximum beam of the towed unit or the deck load it carried exceeds 100 (one hundred) feet, an extra charge equal to 1% of the transit dues will be collected for every foot in excess.
        This extra charge will not exceed 125% of the unit's or vessel's transit dues.

    iii. **Draught:**
         If the draught of the towed unit exceeds ten feet, an extra charge equal to 4% of the transit dues will be collected for every foot in excess.
         This extra charge will not exceed 125% of the unit's or vessel's transit dues.

    iv. **Height:**
        If the height of the towed unit or if the cargo carried exceeds 1 5 (fifteen) feet calculated as from the water level, a charge equal to 0.5% of the transit dues is collected for every foot in excess.
        This extra charge will not exceed 125% of the unit's or vessel's transit dues.

v.   **Non self steering unit:**
If the towed unit is not fitted with an efficient apparatus self steering and its beam exceeds 50 (fifty) feet, a charge equal to 2% of the transit dues is collected for every foot in excess in beam.
This extra charge will not exceed 125% of the unit's or vessel's transit dues.

vi.   **Ocean going barges (non self steering units) :**
The above charge is reduced to 0.5% of the transit dues for every foot in excess of 50 feet in the beam of Ocean going barges if the following conditions are fulfilled :
   • The Ocean going barge should transit the Suez Canal regularly (10 round trips, at least, per year).
   • The barge is to be used for the transport of goods, containers or trailers.
   • The barge should prove in a successive number of transits, (to be determined by SCA) that the method of external steering used is efficient and allows the unit to transit SC with the regular speed of convoy without any trouble or accidents.

vii.   **Speed of transit**
The towed unit must have a sufficient ability to transit the Canal with the help of the towing units belonging to the owner or hired, at a speed not less than 12 (twelve) kilometers per hour.
All towed units other than ships not sailing in the Canal under their own power will be considered with no steering.

If the speed of transit is below this limit, the towed unit will be subject to the following charges :

Speed of Transit less than	Charges to be collected
12 Km/h	5% of the transit dues
11 Km/h	10% of the transit dues
10 Km/h	20% of the transit dues
9 Km/h	40% of the transit dues
8 Km/h	80% of the transit dues
7 Km/h	160% of the transit dues

viii.   **Pilotage dues**

The towed unit is charged with the Pilotage dues for the additional pilots appointed to assist the pilot on board that unit, at a rate of (300 US Dollars) for every extra pilot in the Canal and of (150 US Dollars) for every extra harbor pilot.

(3) Guarantee deposit
Before entering the Canal, towed units, unmanned or scrapped vessels must deposit a "guarantee deposit" (either cash or letter of guarantee, through the ship's agency). That bank

guarantee must be confirmed by any Egyptian bank. Plus to the transit dues the value of this Bank guarantee is to be calculated as follows:

- 80% of the transit dues to cover the extra expenses for slow speed. (Not applied for vessels disabled during the transit.)
- A lump sum on account of any damage occurring to SCA property and/or equipment and installations during transit as follows :

Less the	1000 SC.G.T	4000 US Dollars Small craft covered by insurance policy are exempted.
Up to	2000 SC.G.T	10000 US Dollars
Up to	4000 SC.G.T	20000 US Dollars
Up to	6000 SC.G.T	30000 US Dollars
Up to	10000 SC.G.T	50000 US Dollars Over 10000 tons gross to be studied case by case.

- In abnormal cases, a bigger amount may be imposed.
- The approximate cost of hire of assisting tugs (taking into account the number of tugs required and expected duration of the transit), on the basis of (15000 US Dollars) per tug and per day.
- Letter of Bank Guarantee... (See Art. 109).

Note: The said deposit shall be refunded after deduction of the exact extra expenses, if any.

- o **Art. 102 - Berthing Dues: (For vessels less than 300 tons SC.G.T, see Rules of Navigation for Small Craft.)**

A - Vessels in harbors and not transiting the Canal:
1. Vessels not intending to transit the Canal and anchoring or mooring in Port Said Harbor (Vessels undergoing repairs in the Authority dockyard or floating (locks and SC Affiliated Companies, are exempted from berthing dues.), Timsah Lake. G.B.L. anchorage, have to pay berthing dues follows:
   a) 1st day till 10th.
      5 US Cent / Net Ton / Day (SC.N.T.)
   b) 11th day till 20th.
      10 US Cent / Net Ton / Day (SC.N.T.)
   c) 21 1st days till 30th.
      20 US Cent / Net Ton / Day (SC.N.T.)
   d) Over 30 days.
      30 US Cent / Net Ton / Day (SC.N.T.)
      If the vessel stays more than thirty days and without crew, the has the right to shift the vessel outside the berthing area on account of the vessel's owner.

2. Units or vessels authorized by official authorities to offer services in harbor (as launches, barges, bunkering barges, tugs, floating cranes, floating silos, hopper barges or any floating unit serving the harbor); have to pay a rate of (5 US Cent/Net Ton/Day SC.N.T.).

B -Transiting vessels :

1. Berthing dues are not payable by transiting vessels for the first 24 hours in harbor of arrival. The untaxable period can be increased if the vessel is delayed from transit due to traffic conditions in the Canal.
2. If during the Canal transit. The vessel stops in any of the anchorage's of Bitter Lake, Timsah Lake or the port of Port Said for reasons from the vessel herself. Berthing dues will be paid as mentioned in para. (A) Above.

C - Changing berths :

1. Pilotage dues. See Art. 103, para. (3).
2. Tug charges (See Art. 105, para. A.) Changing berth on SCA's request is free of charge, except vessels staying more than 30 days and without crew.(See Art. 17)
3. Vessels in Port Said Anchorage Area (Northern and Southern Anchorage) the Bitter Lake or Lake Timsah, if changing berth or anchorage without explicit authorization from SCA, shall be charged an additional due of (5200 US Dollars) and (3200 US Dollars) for vessels in Suez VLCCS, 4th Generation Containerships and 3rd Generation Containerships Anchorage.

o **Art. 103 - Pilotage Dues :(For Vessels less than 300 tons SC.G.T. see Rules of Navigation for Small Craft.)**

A - Vessels not transiting the Canal:
(1) Port Said:

Pilotage is compulsory for vessels from Anchorage Area to Port or from Port to sea.

The dues are as follows :

Vessel S.C.T.	Day Pilotage	Night Pilotage
Up to 2500 tons	US Dollars 60	US Dollars 90
Up to 5000 tons	US Dollars 90	US Dollars 130
Up to 10000 tons	US Dollars 115	US Dollars 175
Up to 20000 tons	US Dollars 150	US Dollars 220
Up to 30000 tons	US Dollars 175	US Dollars 260
Up to 50000 tons	US Dollars 200	US Dollars 300
Over 50000 tons	US Dollars 230	US Dollars 350

(2) Port of Suez :

- Pilotage is compulsory from Waiting Area to Port of Suez anchorage, from Port of Suez anchorage to Basins Including Ibrahim Basin, Petroleum Basin and Adabiya Docks. , also from Basins to Anchorage areas or sea. The dues are as per port of Suez Tariff.
- In case of non-transiting vessels impeding SC Traffic, the SCA has the right to shift any vessel at the Owners and/or Operators Expenses.

(3) Changing Berth (Port Said):
For changing berth, the Pilotage rate mentioned in para (1) is doubled; in addition, the vessel will have to pay the following:

Up to 2500 tons	US Dollars 30
Up to 5000 tons	US Dollars 45
Up to 10000 tons	US Dollars 60
Up to 20000 tons	US Dollars 75
Up to 30000 tons	US Dollars 85
Up to 50000 tons	US Dollars 100
Over 50000 tons	US Dollars 115

B - Vessels transiting the Canal:
1. Pilotage dues are not payable by vessels transiting the Canal :

   a) Southbound from Port Said Anchorage Area to Km. 162.
   Pilotage dues are payable from Km. 162 to Hm. 80 South or to Port Suez anchorage.

   b) Northbound, vessels pay Pilotage dues from Anchorage Area for VLCCs or Waiting Area to Port of Suez Anchorage, also from this latter area to Km. 162 From Km. 162 Northward, no Pilotage dues are payable for transiting vessels.
2. In all cases when the pilot is disembarked and another pilot comes on board, owing to vessel stopping in Canal Waters for any reason relating to the vessel herself such as engine trouble, steering trouble, etc..., the vessel will pay tile charges for the new pilot as mentioned in para C. hereafter.

C - Extra Pilot Dues:
In case of having an extra pilot on board, the vessel shall pay extra due of (300 US Dollars) per Canal Pilot and (150 US Dollars) per Roads Pilot

In case of bad view vessels, they will pay the dues for extra pilots.

If that vessel is piloted by one pilot only, she will pay 50% these rates.

D - Moving in SC Waters without Pilot's Assistance: (For Vessels less than 300 tons SC.G.T, see Rules of Navigation for Small Craft.)
1. Whenever a vessel without authorization of the SCA moves in Canal waters or Port Said Harbor without having a pilot on board, she shall be charged an additional due of (21 500 US Dollars).

2. An additional due of (3200 US Dollars) shall be charged to vessels moving without authorization of SCA in Port of Suez Anchorage, or entering or leaving Basins at Port of Suez without having a pilot on board. Vessels under 300 tons SC.N.T are exempted as per law 161/59.

   These dispositions do not apply in the event of the pilot being suddenly unable to carry on with his duties owing to sickness or death. Word sickness includes injuries.

E - Calling Pilot Unnecessarily :
When a vessel signals for pilot, and it is found when boarding, that she is not ready to get underway it, the limited time, the vessel is liable to be delayed and pilot disembarked.

The vessel will pay extra pilot dues for the new pilot.

- **Art. 104 -Trial Charges :**

For the safety of navigation, trials may by requested by the SCA before entering the Canal or resuming the transit.

A pilot will supervise the trials.

A charge of (170 US Dollars) is to be paid by the vessel for each pilot or Canal expert for each trial.

If trials are made outside Canal Water, the charge will be (340 US Dollars).

- **Art. 105 - Charges for SCA Tugboats :**

Will be levied according to the last circular to be issued by SCA

A - Charges for harbor tugs applied at Port Said Harbor:
1. Vessels transiting the Canal are free of charge.
2. For other vessels, are payable for mooring or getting underway:
   Will be Levied according to the last circular to be issued by SCA
   These charges are payable each time the CA sends one or two tugs to assist in maneuvering the vessel; if more than two, charges will be as above.
3. In case of changing berth, the charges are doubled.

B - Rates of Escorting Tugboats (see Art. 58):
A unified Canal passage rate of 6 600 SDR is to be paid for each escorting tug in the following cases:
1. Loaded vessels under 130 000 tons DWT when for technical reasons the SCA finds it necessary.
2. Loaded vessels of 130 000 tons DWT and over.
3. Vessels in ballast over 250 000 tons DWT.
4. Vessels with draught over 47 feet.

C - Hire of Tugboats :
1. **Tariff per tug.**
   Will be Levied according to the last circular to be issued by SCA

   a) Hire is reckoned from the time of starting preparations to get underway and ceases when tug returns to its base.

   b) Fractions of an hour will be reckoned as full hour.

   C) Hire charges are increased by 10 % when tug is used after official hours and on

Fridays or Public Holidays.

D) Hire charges are increased by 100 % when tug is used outside Canal Waters.

c) Hire charges outside the Territorial Waters are to be agreed upon with SCA.

f) This tariff may be revised every 3 months without notice.

2. **The tariff is applied in the following conditions:**

   a) Towing of vessel or floating unit in Canal Waters.

   b) If the towed vessel or unit calls for the assistance of one or more of the Authority tugs to help or escort during the towing operation. Or if the Authority considers it necessary to escort the towed unit by one or more of its tugboats to ensure the safety of transit.

   c) In case SCA Officials consider the transit of a vessel dangerous to navigation due to defects in the vessel, such as engine trouble, etc. ..., or bad view. In such a case the vessel will be escorted by tug or more.

   d) In case of refloating a vessel, except for vessels aground or stopped in the Canal, in consequence of an accident other than collision, and obstructing the passage for other vessels: the refloating is free of charge.

   e) In any other cases of hiring of tugboats.

3. **Hire of Plant other than tugboats:**

   The tariff for the hire of other plant is at the disposal of clients at SC Offices.

   o **Art. 106 - Additional Dues - Various :**

All Additional Dues In US Dollars	
(1) Boat drill (Violation of the indication to carry out boat drills)	300
(2) Booking for transit alteration of date or cancellation	
a) VLCCs	1450
b) Other vessels	150
c) Booking a berth at Port Said Harbor for commercial operations, bunkering, repairs etc., cancellation 6 hours or less before arrival to Port Said	300
(3) Changing berths or anchorage without authorization :	
a) Port Said Anchorage Area, Bitter Lakes, Timsah Lake	5200
b) Suez VLCCs 4th generation Containerships and 3rd generation Containerships Anchorage	3200
(4) Declaration (erroneous declaration)	see Art. 14-F

(5) Dues of transit, change in payment currency	15
(6) Embarking-disembarking persons without authorization	300
(7) Firing shots	300
(8) Overtaking underway without authorization	750
(9) Picking objects from water without authorization	300
(10) Pilots :	
a) Accommodation for pilot unavailable	300 per relieving pilot
b) Accommodation ladder unavailable, entailing relief of pilot in Bitter Lakes instead of Timsah Lake	300 per relieving pilot
c) Extra pilots.	
Canal Pilot	300 per pilot
Roads Pilot	150 per pilot
d) Navigation or movement without pilot :	
i - in Canal Waters	21500
ii - in Port Said Harbor	21500
iii- in Suez VLCCs 4th Generation Container ships and 3rd Generation Containerships Anchorage	3200
iv - in Port of Suez Anchorage	3200
v - in Port of Suez Basins	3200
e) Pilot's advice concerning orders issued from SCA (refusal of execution)	21500
f) Pilotage dues for tug or salvage tugs not belonging to SCA, carrying out towage	450
g) Omitting or erroneous declaration of dangerous cargo and discovery during the transit (See Art. 47 bis)	43000
(11)	
a) Throwing wastes	5000
b) Venting gas	20000
(12)	
Riveting	Without authorization 750
Welding	without authorization 750
Metal cutting	without authorization 750
Operation requiring use of heat	without authorization 750

(13) Slow speed :	
a) Vessels	See Art.101-C
b) Towed units and unmanned or disabled or scrapped vessels	See Art.101-D-2
(14) Vessels indicators (rudder and/or engine RPM):	
a) Same indicators still defective or still not, installed: The 2nd consecutive transit and each following transit	3000 S.D.R
b) Both indicators still defective or still not installed: The 2nd consecutive transit and each following transit	5000 S.D.R
(15) Deck Load protrusion in excess: -2% of transit dues on each foot or fraction in excess of the maximum breadth authorized by Art. 26	
(16) Heavy Lift Ships loaded with drilling rigs or large floating units 300 SC.G.T or more (See PART I - NAVIGATION - SPECIAL CASES): 125% of transit dues, plus 2% of transit dues for each foot or fraction in excess of the maximum breadth authorized by Art. 26.	
(17) Other self steering vessels carrying floating units 300 SC.G.T. or more (See PART I - NAVIGATION - SPECIAL CASES): - 300% of the floating units SC.G.T. plus 2% of transit dues for each foot or fraction in excess of the maximum breadth authorized by Art. 26.	
(18) Navy and auxiliary ships belonging to different countries, an addition of 25% of transit dues is to be applied owing to special arrangements.	
(19) Searchlight and/or electrical connections not in conformity with SCA 4300 regulations for the 3rd transit and each following transit.	

> **CHAPTER XIV - PAYMENT OF CANAL DUES**

  o **Art. 107 Determination and payment of the Suez Canal dues:**

(1) The SC dues rates are determined on the basis of SDR Units (SDR means Special Drawing Right)

(2) Dues calculated on this basis are payable in one of the hard currency declared by the Exchange Control according to rates of currencies in relation, to SDRs as declared by the International Monetary Fund.

(3) Following are the acceptable currencies for payment of dues:

The Sterling Pound	The US. Dollar
The Canadian Dollar	The Danish Kroner
The Swedish Kroner	The Norwegian Kroner
The Belgian Franc	The French Franc
The Italian Lira	The Deutsch Mark
The Japanese Yen	The Florin (Netherlands Guilder)
The Austrian Schilling	The Swiss Franc

(4) Canal dues may be paid in Egyptian pounds in the following conditions:
- Vessels under Egyptian flag.
- The owner's nationality is Egyptian - Meanwhile he is not subject to any of the investment laws.
- If the time charter (For more than one trip.), is Egyptian, in this case chartering agreements (Contract of affreigatment) must be introduced.

(5) Accordingly, ship owners, charterers or agents dealing with SCA are requested to include in the Statistical Declaration submitted to the Authority by dues payers a statement of the kind of currency in which dues will be paid.

(6) The Central Bank of Egypt, Cairo, shall furnish SCA, Ismailia, every day with a list of rates of hard currency in relation to SDRs according to the bulletin of the International Monetary Fund taking into consideration that the latter does not issue bulletin on SDR on Saturdays and Sundays due to official and weekly holidays, as well as on official holidays of the IMF.
Accordingly, rates given in the latest IMF bulletin notified to SCA by the Central Bank of Egypt shall be applied. This consequently requires considering rates notified on Saturday morning a basis for calculating dues on Saturday, Sunday, and Monday of every week as well as on the IMF holidays. Therefore, the basic rule is to apply the latest bulletin of currency rates in relation to SDR Units, issued by the IMF and furnished to the Authority by the Central Bank of Egypt.

(7) Transit dues and services related to; have to be paid in any of the hard currency fixed for the payment of dues by the debit of the following accounts:
- Accounts for the SC transit dues.
- External nonresident accounts in foreign currency.
- Free nonresident accounts in Egyptian Pounds.

(8) Accounts for payment of transit dues -which are permissible for Banks to open.
Banks can open the following Accounts in foreign currency for the payment of transit dues and for services related to
- Transit dues accounts:
  These accounts are opened in the name of nonresident for owners or charterers of foreign ships or in the name of their consignees in Egypt. They bear no specific quality and are fed by any acceptable hard currency in which dues are payable. Re-transferring from these accounts abroad at the request of their owners of their agents in Egypt is possible.
- Accounts of advance payments for paying transit dues:
  These accounts are opened in the name of SCA and are fed by funds credited in hard currency for paying the Canal transit dues, for the account of nonresident foreign ship owner and charterers.
  These accounts are used for payment of transit dues and related services due on foreign vessels belonging to these owners.
  It is possible to re-transfer any balances of these accounts according to the request of the SCA in the same currency received from abroad to feed them.

(9) Exemption of Canal dues:
The following vessels may be exempted from Canal dues
- a) Vessels belonging to the Egyptian Government, on condition that it did not carry any cargo or passenger.
- b) Vessels belonging to United Nations, Multinational Troops. (Presidential Decree No. 450, Art. 33 Issued in 1981)
- c) Vessels under 300 tons SC.G.T. (Small Craft) in condition that:
  i - She is not carrying any passengers or cargo.
  ii - She is not replacing any ship or any small craft subject to pay Canal dues. (For example, any cargo transferred from any vessel in the Canal, waters or at its mouths, to that small craft.)
- d) Motor boats belonging to Canal shipping Agents, on condition that she is not carrying passengers.

o **Art. 108 - Determination of accounts :**
1. According to the country where the main center of the ship owners is if the vessel is king for his account or chartered for a trip or more.
2. According to the permanent residence of charterer of the ship if time chartered.

o **Art. 109 - Change in the transit dues modality :**

A sum of 15 USD is collected if the currency of the transit dues is changed after the vessel's transit.

Letter of Bank Guarantee:

We Hereby Guarantee to pay to M/S SCA

Value _____

for _____

This Bank Guarantee sum should be payable to M/S SCA upon First DEMAND without Proof or Conditions.

This Guarantee is valid till _____

and will be automatically
Renewed Till the Date of _____

> CHAPTER XV - CARRIAGE OF DANGEROUS CARGO

o **Art. 110 - DEFINITIONS :**

A - For the purpose of these regulations, the meaning of the terms and expressions mentioned in each of the following articles will be as defined in the respective subparagraph:

1. "Dangerous Cargo" Means the following:

   a) Any substance whether packaged or in bulk, intended for carriage or storage and having properties in the classes listed in the I.M.D.G. Code as amended from time to time.

   b) Any substance shipped in bulk not coming within the I.M.D.G. Code classes but is subject to the requirements of the Codes for the dangerous chemical in bulk, liquefied gases in bulk and solid bulk as amended from time to time
   .

2. "Packaged Dangerous Goods" Means any dangerous cargo contained in receptacle, portable tank, freight container or vehicle. The term includes an empty receptacle, portable tank which has previously been used for the carriage of dangerous substance, unless such receptacle or tank has been cleaned and permits transport with safety.

3. "Hazardous Wastes" Means wastes having hazardous characteristics according to Basel Convention on the control of transboundary movements of hazardous wastes.

4. "Dangerous Cargo in Bulk" Means any dangerous substance, carried without intermediate form of containment, in a tank or cargo space which is structural part of a vessel or in a tank permanently fixed in a vessel.

5. "Petroleum" : reference to Petroleum in these Regulations shall be deemed to include all products such as : Rock oil, Rangoon oil, Burma oil, oil made from petroleum, rosin, bog head, coal, schist, shale, peat and other bituminous substances and any products of petroleum, and any of the above mentioned oils, (such as benzene, kerosene, gasoline, fuel oil, toluene, paraffin wax etc.).

   For the purpose of these Regulations, Petroleum is classified:

   a) Grade A - Those of the above mentioned products or any other not mentioned and having a flash point below 23 degrees Centigrade (73 degrees Fahrenheit).

   b) Grade B - Those of the above mentioned products or any other not mentioned having a flash point between 23 degrees Centigrade (73 degrees F) and 66 degrees Centigrade (150 degrees F).

   c) Grade C - Those of the above mentioned products or any other not mentioned having a flash point above 66 degrees Centigrade (150 degrees Fahrenheit.

6. "Tanker" Means any vessel that transport bulk inflammable liquids. She shall comply with standards of "SOLAS 74/78" and must be classified in one of the Recognized Classification Societies belonging to the IACS to carry inflammable liquids (petroleum) and still under its supervision.

7. "F.P." Means Flash Point for petroleum and must be ascertained by Open Cup test or any other closed test of an equal degree of accuracy.

8. I.G. means Inert Gas used in cargo tanks and must be checked to ensure that the oxygen concentration is below the flammable limit i.e. can be considered as free from explosive gases.

9. "N.G.F." Means Non Gas Free, i.e. not sufficiently free at the time if test from toxic and explosive gas.

10. "Code for liquefied gases in bulk" Means the code for the construction and equipment of ships carrying liquefied gases in bulk, as amended, published by I.M.O.

11. "Liquefied inflammable gas carrier" Means any vessel that transports bulk liquefied inflammable gas. She shall comply with the standards of "SOLAS 74/78" and must be constructed according to IMO code for the construction and equipment of ships carrying liquefied inflammable gas in bulk, as amended from time to time or to standards at least as effective, and must be classified in one of the classification societies belonging to IACS and still under its supervision.

12. "Code for dangerous chemical in bulk" Means the code for the construction and equipment of ships carrying dangerous chemical in bulk, as amended, published by I.M.O.

13. "Dangerous chemicals in bulk Carrier" Means any vessel that transports bulk dangerous chemical. She shall comply with the standards of "SOLAS 74/78" and must be constructed according IMO code for the construction and equipment of ships carrying dangerous chemicals in bulk, as amended from time to time or to standards at least as effective, and must be classified in one of the classification societies belonging to IACS, and still under it supervision.

14. "Code for solid bulk" Means the code of safe practice for solid bulk cargoes.

15. "Prohibited Goods" Means
a) any goods which are specified by "I.M.D.G." code as carriage prohibited.
b) Bulk dangerous cargoes not listed in the code of dangerous chemical in bulk, the code of liquefied gases in bulk or solid bulk code.
c) Dangerous cargoes that are not listed on ship certificate of fitness.
d) Dangerous cargoes that are not listed in dangerous cargo manifest.
e) Any goods which do not fulfill cargo requirements in these Rules.

16. "MARPOL 73/78" Means the International Convention for the Prevention of Pollution from Ships, as amended from time to time.

17. "I.O.P.P. Certificate" Means the I.M.O. International Oil Pollution Prevention certificate, certifying that the ship has been surveyed in accordance to "MARPOL 73/78". (See Art 126.)

18. "Certificate of Fitness" Means a certificate issued by a national government, or society on behalf of government, certifying that the construction and equipment of the ship are in accordance with the code for dangerous chemicals in bulk or the code for liquefied gases in bulk or to similar recognized national provisions in bulk or to standards at least as effective.

o **Art. 111 - Preliminary Regulations :**

1. These regulations apply to the transport of dangerous goods through the Suez Canal, as amended.

2. The classifications in these regulations are in accordance with I.M.D.G. code.

3. Dangerous cargoes in these regulations are divided as follows:
   a) The dangerous packaged goods, as classified in accordance with I.M.D.G. Code
   b) The dangerous cargoes in bulk (Petroleum, liquefied inflammable gases and dangerous chemicals).
   c) The radio substances, as mentioned in Class 7 of I.M.D.G. Code

4. All dangerous cargo alarms, safety equipment and firefighting equipment must be checked within 24 hours prior to the arrival to Suez Canal. The ship's log shall be available for inspection by the boarding pilot or inspector.

5. SCA may consult a recognized surveyor where such consultation is required by the SCA.

6. Advanced notice of arrival must reach the CA's Offices at least 48 hours before the vessel's arrival to the Canal entrances.

7. The Master, owner and/or operator is responsible for any damage, direct or indirect, caused to CA or to third party, which may result by presence of dangerous goods on board of his vessel, and their stowage and handling.

> CHAPTER XVI - VESSELS CARRYING DANGEROUS PACKAGED GOODS

  o **Art. 112 - General Terms and Conditions :**

A - Grouping System:

For purpose of berthing and cargo handling each of IMDG classes (Except Class 7, radioactive, see Chapter XVIII) is further divided by SCA into three groups. These groups are as follows :

1. **Group 1:** Substances representing high danger: no handling is allowed either for ordinary goods or dangerous goods; vessels carrying these substances are only allowed to have berth at Port Said outer harbor, bunkers taking place at the outer harbor basin.

2. **Group 2:** Substances representing medium danger, handling of cargo is allowed as follows:
   a) Containers can be handled in the inner harbor
   b) General Cargo vessels (Except dangerous substances of Group 2 in Containers.) can be handled by isolating the vessel in Port Said outer harbor basin. A vessel carrying not more than 100 tons total of these substances will not be given a special berth for handling the ordinary cargoes, providing holds containing these dangerous substances is kept closed while ordinary cargoes are being handled on these vessels.

3. **Group 3:** Substances representing minor danger: vessels carrying these substances shall be considered as ordinary vessel.

B - Description of Groups in Different IMDG Classes:

1. **Group 1:** (Substances representing high danger):
   It contains the following:
   a) Class 1, explosives, (div. 1.1, div. 1.2, and div.1.3).
   b) Class 2, gases in large welded receptacles.
   c) Class 3, Inflammable liquids (div. 3.1 and div. 3.2) in large welded receptacles.
   d) Discovery of substances of its existence and/or stowage on board the ship, the Master has no knowledge. (Additional dues according to Art. 47 - Bis.)
   e) Hazardous wastes.

2. **Group 2:** (Substances representing medium danger):
   It contains all substances of the Classes which do not belong to either Group 1 or Group 3.

3. **Group 3:** (Substances representing minor danger):
   It contains the following:
   a) Class 1, explosives, (div. 1.5).
   b) Class 2, gases (non flammable compressed gas only).
   c) Class 3, Inflammable liquids (high flash point group only).
   d) Substances in Class 4, 5, 6, 8 and 9 stated in Appendix No. 4.

4. Vessels carrying more than one group at the same time will be treated as vessel of the higher dangerous group.

- o **Art. 113 - Cargo Requirements :**
1. The packing, labeling, marking, stowage, segregation, maintenance and certification of packaged dangerous goods shall be in compliance with the I.M.D.G. code, or to standards at least as effective.

2. In respect of Hazardous Wastes, transit documents must be sent to both EEAA and SCA for prior approval. The transit of the Hazardous Wastes is not granted until SCA received the E.E.A.A. approval.

- o **Art. 114 : Vessels Carrying Dangerous Goods in Limited Quantities :**
Limited quantities of dangerous goods can be carried according to I.M.D.G. code and the Certificate of Compliance specified by these Rules must be produced to SCA on arrival of the vessel to Canal entrances.

- o **Art. 115 : Prohibited Cargoes :**
(Additional dues Art. 15 - F.)
1. Packaged dangerous goods which are specified by I.M.D.G. code as Carriage Prohibited.

2. Packaged dangerous goods which are transported with dangerous cargoes in bulk.

3. Dangerous goods that are not declared in the Dangerous Cargo Manifest (See Art. 47 bis, part 1.). (See Art. 117).

4. Any Cargoes which are not fulfill with cargo requirements.

- o **Art. 116 : Vessel Requirements :**
Vessels carrying dangerous packaged goods must comply with the standards of "SOLAS 74/78" as amended and must be classified in one of the recognized classification societies belonging to the IACS and still under its supervision.

- o **Art. 117 : Certificates and Declarations :**
1. The Master of the vessel shall submit to the CA's Officials on arrival the list of the manifest or the stowage plan for the dangerous goods placed in the vessel signed by the ship-owners and/or their representatives and approved by an official authority of the port of loading and includes the following:
a) The chemical name and the quantities of the dangerous goods classified in accordance to IMDG.
b) The substances group as according to Art. 112 - B of these Rules.
c) Certificate of complying with cargo requirements.
d) The flash point for inflammable substances in degrees centigrade if applicable.

2. Further, the Master of the vessel must be furnish a signed SC declaration (See Appendix 1) which will be handed to him by the pilot when he comes on board.

- o **Art. 118 - Arrival :**
Any vessel carrying dangerous goods must hoist the special signal indicating the nature of her goods before entering SC (See Appendix 5).

- ○ **Art. 119 - Compensation warranty :**

The Master shall submit a certificate issued by an official Recognized Authority in charge of the protection and compensation of ship owners against damage, and approved by SCA, this certificate must indemnify SCA & third party against any compensation for all kinds of damage that may occur directly or indirectly, to the environment and shall pay all expenses incurred for its removal, cleaning costs and all compensations.

- ○ **Art. 120 - Berthing Places :**

Any vessel carrying dangerous goods shall be assigned a berth or mooring place at Port Said, such place will be selected by the Authority's Officials according to the information sent in advance and the declarations of the Master.

- ○ **Art. 121 - Permission to take in provisions and fuel or to handle cargo :**

1) Vessels of Group 2 and 3 enter SC, take in provisions and fuel and handle cargo within the limits set in Art. 112 - A.

2) When taking in provision or fuel, they must begin the necessary operations at once, carry them out as quickly as possible and be ready to enter the Canal immediately afterwards.

Except in case of emergency, of which CA shall be sole judge, such operations shall not last more than 12 hours.

- ○ **Art. 122 - Permission to Carry out Repairs :**

The CA's Shipyard shall be sole judge whether or not repairing operations can be done.

- ○ **Art. 123 - Control :**

1. The CA reserves the right to inspect the stowage of dangerous goods, and if the information given is found to be incorrect, access to the Canal may be forbidden or the change of berth necessary shall be at the vessel's cost.

2. For the safety of navigation, the Harbor Master is entitled to stipulate any further safety measures that are required with regard to local conditions, other vessels traffic and other circumstances

3. During the whole stay in SC, vessels carrying dangerous goods from any group shall comply with the instructions of Appendix No. 2 for their respective groups.

- ○ **Art. 124 - Responsibility of Ship's master :**

The Master is responsible for the handling and the stowage of dangerous goods on board of the vessel. He is also responsible that the dangerous goods have been packed in a good manner in accordance to Art. 112 of this Chapter. (See also Art. 111 - (6) Preliminary).

> CHAPTER XVII - VESSELS CARRYING DANGEROUS CARGOES IN BULK

o **Art. 125 - General Terms and Conditions :**

A - Tanker in Ballast or Vessels Carrying Grade C Only:

1. Tankers in ballast and vessels carrying Grade C only are deemed to be ordinary (non dangerous) vessels, if they have been rendered gas free or free from inflammable gases since they last carried Grade A or Grade B. They are not subject to any of the foregoing regulations, but the Master must sign the declaration which will be handed to him by the pilot when he comes on board and hand it to the CA Officials (See Appendix I).

2. Tankers in ballast and vessels carrying part cargo of Grade C without having been rendered gas free of free from inflammable gases since they last carried Grade A or Grade B, are subject to these Regulations.

3. Tanks which are ballasted to the level of the expansion hatch deck coating will be accepted as the equivalent of a tank which has been gas free since last transporting hazardous cargo.

4. Tankers of vessels carrying two grades of hazardous cargoes at the same time will be treated as vessels of the grade corresponding to that of the volatile product.

B - Liquefied gas Carrier in Ballast:

Liquefied inflammable gas carriers in ballast are to be ordinary vessels, if they have been rendered gas free or free from any inflammable gas.

o **Art. 126 - Pollution Prevention :**

See Articles 64, 69.

Ballast tankers required to reduce their draught for transiting the Canal shall comply with the requirement of Regulation 13 "MARPOL 73/78" and have "IOPP Certificate".

o **Art. 127 - Prohibited cargoes :**

Additional dues Art. 15.

- Bulk dangerous cargoes not listed in the codes of dangerous chemical in bulk, liquefied gas in bulk, or solid bulk.
- Dangerous cargoes not listed on vessel's Certificate of fitness.
- Dangerous cargoes that are not declared in the cargo manifest list (See Art. 117).
- Any cargoes which are not fulfill with cargo requirements.

o **Art. 128 - Safety Regulation for Tankers and dangerous cargo in bulk :**

1. Further to Regulations of Appendix No. 2, the vessel shall conform to the requirements of SOLAS 74.78 and must be constructed according to IMO codes for the construction and equipment of ships carrying (liquefied inflammable gas or dangerous chemical in bulk) as amended from time to time or to standards at least as effective, and must be classified in one of the classification societies belonging to IACS and still under its supervision.

2. The vessels must have outside her cargo tanks, non dangerous substances (clean ballast water, fuel oil, etc.) which can, if needed, be easily and safely unloaded, in sufficient quantity to reduce her draught by one foot (30 cm), for tankers and by 3 feet (90 cm), for vessels carrying liquefied inflammable gases or dangerous chemicals in bulk.

3. Vessel carrying grade A must also comply with the following requirements:
a) two mooring boats immediately available; that is to say, slung outboard, ready for lowering.
b) Fire wires made fast on forward and one aft and hung over the vessel's side ready for use, so that a tow rope can be easily fastened there to by a tug in an emergency.
c) A special searchlight for night transit (See Art 28) of the Rules of Navigation).

- **Art. 129 - Vessels Carrying Dangerous Goods in Limited Quantities :** (See Art. 115).

- **Art. 130 - Certificates and Declarations :**
1. The Master shall hand to the Authority's Officials a declaration (Declaration "A" Appendix 1) showing the following :
a) Ship safety Construction Certificate,
b) Ship safety Equipment Certificate,
c) Ship safety Radio Telegraphy Certificate, and
d) That the vessel is classed and still under supervision of one of classification societies belonging to IACS.

2. Further, the Master of a vessel must furnish a signed SC declaration (See Appendix 1), which will be handed to him by the pilot when he comes on board.

- **Art. 131 - Arrival :**
1. If a vessel carries dangerous cargoes in bulk, the Master must state the fact to pilot as soon as he arrives on board, then the Master must comply with Regulations Art. 130 concerning the declarations of Appendix No. 1 and the port of loading certificate.

2. Before entering SC, vessels belonging to this Chapter shall hoist the special signal indicating the nature of their cargo (See Appendix 5).

3. All vessels belonging to this Chapter shall be assigned special mooring berths at Port Said which will be selected by CA's Officials according to the information sent in advance and the declarations of the Master.

4. When, through failing to comply with paragraph (2) and (3) above, a vessel has been given a berth where she must not stay by reason of her carrying dangerous cargoes in bulk, the change of berth shall be at the vessel's cost. Additional dues Art. 106

- **Art. 132 - Berthing Places :**
1. Vessels coming under the regulations of this Chapter are only allowed to have a berth at Port Said Outer Harbor Basin except gas free carriers and tankers carrying Grade C only.

2. Vessels carrying Grade A of liquefied inflammable gas should avoid using anchor when berthing.

- o **Art. 133 - Permission to Take in Provisions and Fuel :**

1. All these operations are Not Allowed for N.G.F. tankers (Grade A or B) and N.G.F. Liquefied inflammable gases.

2. All these operations are Not Allowed for Tankers carrying Grade A.

3. All these operations are Not Allowed for liquefied inflammable gas carriers and dangerous chemicals in Bulk carriers.

4. All these operations are Not Allowed for Tankers in ballast and vessels carrying part cargo of Grade C without having been rendered gas free from inflammable gases since they last carried Grade A or Grade B goods.

5. Fueling is only allowed by permission from the Harbor Master for Tankers in ballast and contains Grade B vapor, also for Tanker loaded with Grade B and Tankers loaded with Grade C and contain Grade B vapour.

6. All above mentioned operations are allowed for gas free carriers, or free from explosive gases, also for tankers loaded with Grade C.

- o **Art. 134 - Permission to Handle Cargo :**

A - Cargoes of Grade A in bulk or in receptacles, and cargoes of Grade B in bulk:
Handling of cargo not allowed, except upon special application in advance. Shipping and handling of receptacles of Grade A of Grade B at specially appointed places may be carried out, provided the Regulations of Appendix No. 3 are complied with, and barges, lighters and tugs satisfy the requirements of Appendix No. 3 (IV. 6, 7, 8, 9) and are approved by the SCA.

B - Cargoes of Grade B in Receptacles:
For the purpose of cargo handling, Grade B is regarded as vessels carrying dangerous goods of the second group.

C - Cargoes of Grade C :
Vessels carrying a full or part of Grade C without having been rendered gas free since they last carried Grade A or Grade B are authorized to discharge their cargo of Grade C subject to comply with the following regulations:

1. After the previous discharge, the vessel's cargo tanks must have been properly drained to clear out deposits and sediments.
2. The tanks of the vessel must be full (to 98 %) or completely empty.
3. Empty tanks must have been filled with fuel oil and emptied; this washing out must have been following by blowing air through the tanks during the days preceding the arrival of the vessel in SC.
4. While unloading is in progress, the tank hatches must be kept closed; apart from the minimum time necessary to take soundings, sounding pipes must be covered with metallic gauze.

D - Liquefied inflammable gas and dangerous chemicals in bulk carriers:
Handling of cargo is Not Allowed.

N.B.: Limited quantities of dangerous chemicals in bulk may be handled by prior authorization from SCA.

- ### Art. 135 - Permission to Carry Out Repairs :
1. No repairs that involve burning, welding, riveting, other hot work, high speed drilling, chipping, hammering or other similar operations to any compartment or pipe line which has contained petroleum shall be begun or carried out in any vessel unless a certificate issued from a recognized chemist certifies that he finds it is free from inflammable vapor, and safe for such operations.

2. The CA's Shipyard shall be sole judge whether or not repairing operations can be done.

3. Carrying out repairs is not allowed for liquefied inflammable gas carriers or dangerous chemicals in bulk carriers.

- ### Art. 136 - Precautions on Board :
During the whole of their stay in SC, vessels carrying dangerous chemical and liquefied gases, Petroleum Grade A or Grade B or N.G.F. Carriers shall comply with the regulations of (Appendix No. 2).

The handling on board of any vessel with liquid having a flash point of or below 66 degrees Centigrade (150 degrees Fahrenheit) is strictly prohibited. The handling of receptacles of Grade A petroleum is however, allowed within the conditions specified in Art. 134-A.

Further, no craft with a naked fire shall come or remain alongside vessel carrying benzene, or liquefied inflammable gases.

- ### Art. 137 - Control :
The Master of any vessel carrying petroleum of whatever nature, liquefied gas or dangerous chemicals in bulk must help SCA's officials by all possible means to inspect the vessels installations.

The SCA reserves the right, after inspection of the vessel by its officials, to refuse transit, if sufficient precautions have not been taken, to obviate any danger of fire during her stay in S.C.

- ### Art. 138 - Responsibility of Shipmaster :
1. The Master is responsible for loading the cargo in a manner adequate or withstands the ordinary risks of transport. (See also, Art. 112 - 7).

2. The Master is responsible for and damage that may occur from the passage of the vessel (See Art. 4. and Art. 60).

> CHAPTER XVIII - VESSELS CARRYING RADIOACTIVE SUBSTANCES

o **Art. 139 - General Terms and Conditions :**
Generalities - Documents - Grouping:
1) Art. 113, 114 and Art. 118 - Shall be applied.

2) Permission is granted to carry through the SC radioactive goods on condition that the following documents are produced:
- Documents proving that vessel carrying radioactive substance has complied with conditions and prescriptions contained in those laws and rules in force in the exporting country and with the conditions and prescriptions recommended by the I.M.D.G. code or that of the IAEA.
- Compensation warranty document covering all direct or indirect damage that may be caused by the presence of radioactive substances on board.
- Document similar to the declarations of the A.E.E. (Appendix 1) concerning the shipment with all information required by the establishment, each declaration concerns one of the two basic groups :
  i.   Declaration B, Group 1 Radioactive, which includes, fissile materials, i.e. artificially produced nuclear substances such as enriched uranium, uranium-235 and plutonium-239, which under certain conditions are capable of undergoing fission, and Irradiated uranium and other fissile material.
  ii. Declaration C, Group 2 Radioactive, which includes radioactive goods stated by the I.M.D.G code as exemption, Uranium ores and concentrate, natural uranium and thorium, radio isotopes for medical, agricultural, scientific or industrial use, irradiated specimens of metals or minerals - except those which fall within declaration B above.

o **Art. 140 - Vessel Requirements :**
Vessels carrying radioactive goods shall comply with the standards of "SOLAS 74/78" and must be classed in one of the Recognized Classification societies belonging to the IACS and still under its supervision.

o **Art. 141 - Cargo Requirements :**
Loading, packing, labeling, marking stowage, segregation and inspection certificate shall be in compliance with the IMDG code.

o **Art. 142 - Vessels carrying exemption radioactive substances :**
Vessels carrying substances which are stated by IMDG code as exemption are deemed to be ordinary vessels, provided they satisfy conditions in Art. 140. 141 above.

o **Art. 143 - Prohibited Cargoes :**
See Article 15 - F.
1) Radioactive goods not carried in compliance with IMDG code.

2) Radioactive goods not declared in Cargo Manifest and SCA, declarations for dangerous cargoes.

- Art. 144 - The Authority's Approval of Transportation of the Substances :

1) In respect of substances Group 1 radioactive, Prior Approval of Authority for the transit of goods before shipment, is required and is not granted until approval of A.E.E. is notified to the Authority.

2) In respect of Group 2 radioactive, the Master of the vessel shall hand to the CA's officials on arrival, all the documents concerning the goods for checking and ascertaining the authenticity of the details contained therein. These formalities are sufficient.

- Art. 145 - Certificates and Declarations :

The Master of a vessel shall hand to the CA's officials, on arrival a list or manifest or stowage plan for dangerous goods places in the vessel signed by the ship owners and/or their representatives at the port of loading and including the following:

1) Full and clear details concerning the goods, and mentioning its kind, quantity, weight, etc. shall be furnished on declaration form to the Authority.

2) Information in respect of goods of radioactive substances which do not require special formalities and are excluded of the regulations concerning radioactive substances and those concerning protection issued by the IAEA, must also be furnished to the Authority and to the Secretary of the A.E.E. Such information must also be in the possession of the Master to be produced to the A.E.E.'s delegates on request. A copy of the correspondence directly or indirectly exchanged with the A.E.E. and the load owners and the vessel's Agents must also be furnished to the Authority.

- Art. 146 - Compensation Warranty :

1. The Master shall hand the following Warranty Documents to SCA. These documents are to be kept by the Authority.

2. In respect of substances of Group 1 Radioactive the Master shall hand one of the two following documents:
   a) Either an insurance Policy issued by an approved protection and insurance organization for a preliminary amount of twenty Million US Dollars with a guarantee certificate issued by a recognized Atomic Energy Organization. The SCA is entitled to request the increase of the insurance in any case when the circumstances of any load require such an increase pursuant to a technical study by the experts of A.E.E. or.

   b) A full engagement (guarantee) with unlimited compensation amount from the recognized exporting Atomic Energy Authority, accompanied by a guarantee certificate issued by its government, covering the compensation. The guarantee must also fulfill all legal conditions according to the laws of the guaranteeing country and bind is government.

3. In respect of substances of Group 2 Radioactive the Master shall hand a certificate issued by an official recognized Authority in charge of the protection and compensation of ship-owners against damage, and approved by SCA, this certificate must indemnify against any compensation for all kind of damage due to the passage of the vessel.

4. The following provisions must also be enforced:

a) The compensation guarantee document of whatever kind (documents - insurance - guarantee - engagements) must explicitly provide that the victims shall receive compensation for all direct and indirect damage resulting from the radioactivity of the load for the time during which the vessel stays in the SC or its lakes, including the two entrances and their vicinity and also the port of Suez and its entrance and their vicinity.

b) This document shall remain good as long as there exist a possibility that damage may occur as a result of the transit of the shipment, according to what SC will decide in this respect.

c) Payment of compensation in all cases mentioned in paragraphs above shall be based on the mere occurrence of a damage resulting from the load whether present or future and it is sufficient that damage occurs to generate the right for compensation without need for indicating the causes.

d) In case of any accident resulting from the transit of an atomic shipment or radioactive substances of any kind, courts of the A.R.E. are solely and exclusively competent to decide thereof in claims of damage compensation and in all that may be connected with the accident or its direct or indirect consequences. The sentence shall be executor in any country and the insurance mentioned in these regulations shall be a guarantee for the execution of the sentence rendered by A.R.E. courts, without any other formalities.

e) Ship owners and/or operators whose vessels carry radioactive substances transiting the Canal must undertake, in the country of registration of these vessels, all measures ensuring that the government of such country shall respect the above prescriptions.

- **Art. 147 - Notice on the Date of Arrival of the Vessel :**

1) The Agent of vessel carrying radioactive substances must advise SCA and the A.E.E. of the time of arrival of the vessel at least 48 hours in advance.

2) The vessel bears the responsibility of her delay in entering the harbor and transiting the Canal resulting from a delay in giving notice of her arrival. (Notice of arrival must include kind, quantity and number of radioactive substances.)

- **Art. 148 - Experts of the A.E.E. :**

1) Experts of the A.E.E. may go on board to inspect and examine the load, make the radioactive measures, make sure they are good and approve them before the vessel enters the port, to take a decision in the following matters:

- **a)** Authorizing the vessel to enter the port and transit the Canal.
- **b)** Handling of other goods inside and outside the vessel.
- **c)** Transporting the radioactive load to another vessel or to shore.
- **d)** Authorizing the vessel to make repairs in the port and to take supplies.

2) The A.E.E. experts may decide to accompany the load from the moment it enters the Territorial waters of the A.R.E. till it leaves. In such a case, the vessel's Agent has to arrange with the vessel for ensuring their comfort while aboard and Masters must tender every assistance requested by the representatives of the A.R.E. and those accompanying the load and comply with their advice concerning the radioactive substances.

3) The vessel bears the traveling expenses of A.E.E. experts to reach the vessel and their return expenses. The vessel's Agent shall pay these expenses if claimed by the A.E.E. and also, the value of the works in order for any operation carried out with the Authority's equipment or plant.

- ### Art. 149 - Organization of the Transit :
1) Vessels carrying radioactive substances Group 1 Radioactive; Southbound: may be put at the end of the No.1 convoy; northbound: may be put at the end of convoy.

During transit, an interval of 20 minutes at least must be put between these vessels and the preceding vessel. They may also transit convoyed by a salvage at the vessel's expenses and the Agent must in this case file an order to this effect if it is necessary for safety.

2) Vessels carrying radioactive substances Group 2 Radioactive have no special regulation with respect to their position in the convoys.

- ### Art. 150 - Responsibility of the Contravening Vessel :
A vessel arriving in the S.C. without fulfilling the required conditions shall be considered as a danger for navigation and the security of the Canal and shall bear full responsibility if not authorized to enter the harbor or handle other goods or transit the Canal. She will also bear the responsibility for any information given which may subsequently prove to be inaccurate (Additional dues Art. 106) besides the other responsibilities provided for in common law.

➤ **APPENDIX**

○ **APPENDIX NO. 1 DECLARATION VESSELS CARRYING DANGEROUS CARGOES**
(Packaged / Bulk Dangerous Cargoes)

I, the undersigned, ……………………………………………………,

Master of M/V ……………………………………………………,

Owned by ……………………………………………,

Carrying dangerous cargoes [1] ……………………………………………,

as shown on list herewith, enclosed and established according to Suez Canal Rules of Navigation for vessels carrying dangerous cargo, do hereby declare and certify, on behalf of the owners, as follows:

(1) The vessel is specially classed for the carriage of [2] ………………
in Class [3] ……………………………

(2) The vessel's safety equipment and radio telegraphy were inspected under the Authority of [4] …………………………, and are in good working conditions.

(3) The cargo [5] has been packed, stowed and segregated in accordance with IMDG code, and has not been disturbed.

(4) The vessel (has been/has not been) rendered gas free or free from explosive gases [6].

Place and Date: ……………………

Master's Signature: ……………………

[1] State the type of cargoes, packaged or bulk.
[2] State the kind of cargoes according to IMO codes.
[3] State in which of the IACS societies the vessel is classed and still under supervision.
[4] Inspector, Port authority officials, etc., as the case may be.
[5] Only for packaged dangerous goods.
[6] Only for ballast tanker which carried Grade A or Grade B petroleum or liquefied inflammable gases in bulk.

DECLARATION "A"

Date   ....
Master ....

Vessel's Name   ....
Vessel's Owner   ....
Address   ....
Vessel's Operator ....
Address   ....
Agent   ....

DOCUMENT	ISSUING AGENCY	ISSUE DATE	EXIPARTION DATE
IMO Certificate			
Classification Society Certification			
Safety Equipment Certificate			
Safety Construction Certificate			
Safety Radio Telegraph Certificate			
Other Safety Inspections			

Master's Signature: ....

ARAB REPUBLIC OF EGYPT ATOMIC ENERGY ESTABLISHMENT
DECLARATION "B"

Technical and Protection Information in Respect of Consignments of Group 1 Radioactive Substances on Vessels Transiting SC.

(All items must be completed. If any of the items in this statement is not applicable, the letters "N.A." should be inserted).

Name of vessel .... Nationality ....

Master's Name ....

Port of entry .... Date of transit ....

Port of loading .... Port of destination ....

1. Regulations according to which the packing is prepared for transportation.
2. Number of packages containing fissile materials, their marks and serial numbers.
3. Required information on packages characteristics (Similar packages with the same contents should be mentioned together with indication of their marks and serial numbers):
   a) Marks and serial number.
   b) Color category.
   c) Dimensions in cm (indicate whether it is large radioactive source).
   d) Type of packing.
   e) Nature and quantity of the fissile materials present in M.C. each package.
   f) Class category.
   g) Weight.

a -
b -
c -
d -
e -
f -
g -

a -
b -
c -
d -
e -
f -
g -

a -
b -
c -
d -
e -
f -
g -

a -
b -
c -
d -
e -
f -
g –

4. Radiation level in mr equivalent per hr at :
   a) External surface.
   b) One meter from external surface.
   c) Two meters from full load.
5. Precautions required on a routine basis.
6. Precautions to be taken in case of accident or unexpected delay.
7. Physical and chemical state of the fissile materials in the packages.
8. Max. Temperature at surface of the package during transport.
9. Any information known about the following:
   a) Coolant inside the package.
   b) Neutron absorbing material within the package.
   c) Moderate or reflecting materials inside the package.
10. Number, date and competent authority issuing the packing certificate.
11. Stowage conditions of packages (where and how).
12. Depth of screening by other cargo or bulkheads in meters,
13. Statement of presence of:
    a) Explosive materials.
    b) Inflammable materials.
    c) Spontaneously inflammable materials.
    d) Corrosive materials.
    e) Oxidizing materials.
    f) Compressed gases
    g) Liquefied gases.
    h) Any other materials.
14. The following certificate must be signed by the technical person responsible for these shipments and recognized by Master of vessel on behalf of the ship-owner:

    "We the undersigned certify that the information given in 1 to 14 is surely correct and that the packaging of these fissile materials and marking and labeling on the packages are in accordance with"

    ".."
    ".."

    - Date:................. Signature

    - Stamp of vessel Master's Signature

    N.B.: Items 1 to 12 should be filled and forwarded to the Suez Canal Authority before the vessel leaves her port of loading.

ARAB REPUBLIC OF EGYPT ATOMIC ENERGY ESTABLISHMENT
DECLARATION "C"

Technical and Protection Information in Respect of Consignments of Group 2 Radioactive Substances on Vessels Transiting SC.

(All items must be completed. If any of the items in this statement is not applicable, the letter "N.A." should be inserted).

Name of vessel .... Nationality   ....

Master's Name ....

Port of entry   .... Date of transit   ....

Port of loading .... Port of destination ....

1. Regulation according to which the packing is prepared for transportation.
2. Appropriate information related to the radioactive material:
   a) Material and group   ....
   b) Activity in M.C. per package   ....
   c) Physical and chemical state   ....
   d) Max. Temp. at the surface of the
   package during transport   ....
   e) Encapsulated state.   ....
3. Required information on packages characteristics. (Similar packages with same contents should be mentioned together with indication of their marks and serial numbers) :
   a) Marks and serial number   ....
   b) Type of packing   ....
   c) Packing category   ....
   d) Dimensions in cm (indicate whether
   it is large radioactive source)   ....
   e) Weight   ....

   a -
   b -
   c -
   d -
   e -
   f -
   g -

   ---

   a -
   b -
   c -
   d -
   e -
   f -
   g -

   ---

   a -
   b -
   c -
   d -

e -
f -
g -

---

a -
b -
c -
d -
e -
f -
g -

4. Radiation level in mr equivalent per hr. at:
   a) External surface   ....
   b) One meter from external surface ....
   c) Two meters from full load   ....

5. Precautions required on a routine basis.
6. Precautions to be taken in case of accident.
7. Number, date and competent Authority issuing the packing certificate.
8. Stowage conditions of packages (where and how).
9. Depth of screening by other cargo.
10. Statement of presence of:
    a) External materials.
    b) Inflammable materials.
    c) Spontaneously inflammable materials.
    d) Corrosive materials.
    e) Oxidizing materials
    f) Compressed gases.
    g) Liquefied gases.
    h) Any other cargo.
    N.B.: For large radioactive sources, only items from 1 to 8 should be filled and forwarded to SCA before the vessel leaves her port of loading.
11. The following certificate must be signed by the technical person responsible for these shipments and recognized by the Master of vessel on behalf of ship-owner:

    "We the undersigned certify that the information given in 1 to 14 is surely correct and that the packing of radioactive materials and marking and labeling on the packages are in accordance with"

    ".."
    ".."

    - Date:.................. Signature

    - Stamp of vessel Master's Signature

o **APPENDIX NO. 2**

I - Regulations for all vessels carrying dangerous goods (1st, 2nd and 3rd groups):
1. The vessel must fly the prescribed signal.
2. All dispositions for coping with a fire must be attended to (steam up for the pumps, fire hose in position, inspection of sluice valves, etc.).
3. The captain must keep on board sufficient crew to ensue the manning of all appliances for coping with a fire and for opening the sluice valves.
4. The signal "Fire on Board" must be kept ready to be hoisted at any moment as follows:
   By day: N.Q. of the International code, and giving in addition one long blast on the whistle.
   By night: One long blast on the whistle and at the same time, if possible, the signal N.Q. by Morse lamp.

II - Additional Regulation for:
- Vessels carry 1st Group substances.
- Vessels carrying liquefied gases or dangerous chemicals in bulk.
- Vessels carrying Grade A and Grade B petroleum.
- Vessels handling 2nd group substances. (Except ammonium nitrate and artificial fertilizers of any kind, the handling, loading or unloading of which is absolutely prohibited in SC. That of class 5 (Division 5-1) can be exceptionally allowed by SCA.)
1. The vessel must be ready to get under way at any moment, an officer remaining on watch throughout the vessel's stay in SC.
2. The use of portable heating or cooking appliances and of naked fire of any kind or incandescent objects in contact with the air is prohibited.
   Smoking on board, except at specially appointed places, is also prohibited.
   The use of portable lighting appliances is prohibited except hand fed lamos fed by dry battery, unspillable accumulator or dynamo, of not more than 6 volts, and of safety type suitable for use in fiery coal mines.
3. Only boats and other craft of the consignees or agents or those indispensable for services requirements are permitted to go alongside. (These instructions do not apply to Officials or craft of the SCA or to those of the Government.)
   Tugs or any other steam vessels going alongside the ship must have their funnels fitted with spark screens. Fuel oil tanks and water tanks supplying benzene and kerosene vessels must compulsory be motor propelled.
   Authorized tugs, lighters, tank-lighter may only go alongside the vessel at the moment of starting operations; they must remain alongside when these are completed.
4. With the exception of the consignee's agents and of persons having duties to perform on board (stores, projector, mooring boats and where undertaken, commercial operations or repairs), no stranger is allowed on board. (These instructions do not apply to Officials or craft of the SCA or to those of the Government.)
   Persons authorized to go on board (in particular the crew of mooring boats) are not permitted access to the interior of the ship, save in cases of absolute necessity.
5. The vessel must be moored by means of steel wire hawsers.(Paragraph (5) applies only to vessels carrying 1st Group cargo, Grade A petroleum, liquefied gases in bulk or dangerous chemicals in bulk.)
   Fire wires made fast one forward and one aft and hung over the vessel's side ready for use so that a tow rope can be easily fastened there to by a tug in an emergency.
6. Masters of vessels carrying Grade A petroleum or liquefied inflammable gases are advised to fir metallic spark screens on the top of the vessel's funnel during transit, to prevent the escape of insufficiently cooled flakes which might start a fire.
7. Tankers in ballast, whether gas free or not, must keep their cargo tank hatches closed during the whole of their stay in SC.

- o **APPENDIX NO. 3 Regulations for Handling and Towing Dangerous Goods**

I - Handling and towing substances of the 3rd Group is allowed, subject to the regulations of Appendix No. 2 & 1 being complied with.

II - Handling and towing substances of the 1st Group is not, as general rule, allowed in SC. When this is exceptionally allowed by the C, the Captain or the shipper must sign a declaration to the effect that the operations will be carried out at his entire responsibility, whether on board, or during the transport from the vessel to the landing place, or on land, further, the regulations of IV of this Appendix must be complied with.

III - Handling and towing substances of the 2nd Group (General Cargo vessels), of Grade A and Grade B or C petroleum is only allowed on the following conditions:
1. At Port Said the vessel shall be isolated in the Outer Harbor.
2. On being landed, dangerous substances shall be placed in stores specially fitted out for the purpose and approved by CA.
3. The regulations of IV of the Appendix shall be complied with.

IV - When handling dangerous substances of 1st or 2nd Group is allowed in accordance with paragraph II or III above, the following instructions shall be strictly complied with:
1. All holds must remain closed except those which contain the 1st or 2nd Group substances allowed to be handled.
2. These operations must be carried out without interruption during day time so as to be completed as promptly as possible. They shall never be allowed during the night.
3. Wearing boots or shoes with iron nails of shold or strengthened with iron is prohibited.
4. The tugs or any other steam vessels taking part in these operations or coming alongside the vessel must have their funnels fitted with a spark screen
5. The tugs, barges and lighters must be approved by the CA.
6. The barges and lighters must be constructed of steel plates of 6 or 7 mm. Thickness; and in both their peak and stern there be made fast to bits of clinched on board and hung over their side a connecting shackle so that a tow rope can be easily fastened thereto. The barges or lighters must be approved by the SCA.
7. Towing two boats abreast is not allowed.
8. The tow ropes must be of metal or at any rate fastened to the shackle hanging over side of the lighters or barges.
9. The use of cranes or winches for loading or unloading substances of the 1st or 2nd Group which are sensitive ti shocks like chlorate of potas must be avoided as possible.
   Packages shall be passed from hand to hand carefully and handled with the greatest care in order to avoid shocks.
   Packages weighing more than 25 kilograms shall be handled by least two men together.
   If the use of cranes or winches and the slinging of packages cannot be avoided, these operations shall be carried out in such a manner as to prevent the possibility of any package containing 1st Group substances being roughly handled or dropped.
   No substance of the 1st or 2nd Group shall remain either in barges or lighters, or on land, or on deck, except under the constant supervision of a watchman appointed by the Captain or the shipper.
10. Bins filled with sand shall be immediately at hand where receptacles of dangerous liquid (benzene, alcohol, etc.) are being handled together with foam facilities (foam concentrate), a pump and branch pipes.

11. Receptacles containing dangerous liquids shall be inspected on their being landed or put on board, and those showing traces of leakage shall be isolated at once.

12. In the interior of vessels, lighters, or boats where 1st Group substances are intended to be placed or carried, there shall be no iron or steel unless the same be covered with leather, wood, cloth or other suitable material. Tarpaulins shall be spread out both on top and under the packages of 1st Group substances.

The decks gangways, and spaces over or through which it is intended to carry 1st Group substances, shall be carefully swept and kept clean. If any category substance shall escape from the package in which it is contained, or be spilt, or if any package appears to be defective, such package or such 1st Group substance shall immediately be collected and destroyed by environmentally safe method.

13. No substances of any of the 3 Groups shall remain on land except at places specially appointed for each group.

No substances of any of the 3 Groups shall remain in lighters except by special permission obtained in writing from the Canal Authority. The CA shall appoint a mooring place to the lighters, whose place as a general rule will be near the land depot of the corresponding group.

In any case, the Egyptian Government's Regulations concerning the care and supervision of these substances, and the CA's Regulations with regard to mooring, will have to be complied with.

14. All the Regulations of Appendix No. 2 shall apply.

V - Handling of the 2nd Group dangerous packaged goods in containers can be handled in the Inner Harbor, subject to the regulations of the Appendix No. 1 and 2 being complied with.

Group 3:
(Substances representing minor danger) I.M.D.G. Class

Class 4:
(Division 4.1), Inflammable Solids.
- Aluminum powder, coated.
- Boenoel.
- Calcium resinate.
- Calcium resinate, fused.
- Celluloid in Blocks, rods, rolls, sheets, tubes, etc. (scrap excluded).
- Cigarettes, self-lighting.
- Cobalt naphthenates, powder.
- Cobalt resinate, precipitated.
- Driers, paint or varnish, in solid form, n.o.s.
- Films, nitrocellulose base, gelatin coated (scrap excluded).
- Hafnium powder.
- Hay, Straw or bhusa.
- Hexamine.
- Magnesium and magnesium alloys containing more than 50 percent magnesium in pellets, turning or ribbons.
- Magnesium resinate.
- Matches, safety.
- Matches, "strike anywhere".
- Matches, wax "Vesta".
- Metaldehyde.
- Naphthalene (Creosote salts), crude or refined.
- Phosphorous, amorphous.
- Silicon powder, amorphous.
- Sulphur.
- Titanium metwl powder.
- Toe puffs (Nitrocellulose base).
- Zirconium metal, wetted with at least 25 percent water.
-

Class 4:
(Division 4.2), Substances liable to spontaneous combustion.
- Bags having contained sodium nitrate, empty unwashed.
- Calcium dithionite.
- Charcoal of animal or mineral origin.
- Charcoal of vegetable origin.
- Copra.
- Cotton, wet.
- Fibers', animal or vegetable, burnt, wet or damp, n.o.s.
- Fibers' or fabrics, animal or vegetable, with animal or vegetable oil, n.o.s.
- Fish scrap or fish meal.
- Iron oxide, spent, or iron sponge, spent (obtained from coal gas purification).
- Lamp black, of vegetable origin.
- Paper, treated with unsaturated oils, incompletely dried (includes carbon paper).
- Plastics, spontaneously combustible, n.o.s.
- Rags, oily.
- Seed cakes (seed expellers), containing vegetable oil.

- Sulphides, n.o.s.
- Textile waste, wet, n.o.s.
- Wool waste, wet.
- Zinc dithionit.
- Zirconium, metal, dry finished sheets, or coiled wire.
- Zirconium scrap.

Class 4:
(Division 4.3), Substances which on contact with water, emit inflammable gases.
- Aluminum silicon powder, uncoated.
- Calcium Cyanamid containing more than 0.1 percent calcium carbide.
- Calcium silicon.
- Ferrosilicon, containing more than 30 percent and less
- than 90 percent silicon.
- Zinc ashes.

Class 5:
(Division 5.1), Oxidizing substances, other than organic peroxides.
- Aluminum nitrate.
- Ammonium nitrate.
- Ammonium nitrate fertilizers.
- Ammonium persulphate.
- Caesium nitrate.
- Calcium nitrate.
- Didymium nitrate.
- Ferric nitrate.
- Guanidine nitrate.
- Lead dioxide.
- Magnesium nitrate.
- Potassium dichromate.
- Potassium nitrate.
- Potassium persulphate.
- Sodium dichromate.
- Sodium nitrate.
- Sodium nitrate and potassium nitrate mixtures.
- Sodium persulphate.
- Strontium nitrate.
- Urea hydrogen peroxide (hydrogen peroxide solid).

Class 6:
(Division 6.1), Poisonous substances.
All substances in division 6.1 except:
- Poisonous gases.
- Poisonous substances stated in other I.M.D.G.
- Classes and present in Group 1 or Group 2.
- Cyanides.

Class 8:
Corrosive substances.
- Acide butyl phosphate.
- Batteries, electric storage (accumulators, electric) wet charged or filled.

- DI iso octyl acid phosphate.
- Ferric chloride.
- Hypochlorite, solutions containing more than 5 percent but less than 16 percent available chlorine.
- Iospropyl acid phosphate.
- Phosphoric acid.
- Propoinic acid.
- Soda lime.
- Zinc chloride solution.

Class 9:
Miscellaneous dangerous substances.
- Acetaldehyde, ammonia.
- Ammonium nitrate fertilizers.
- Calcium oxide.
- Carbon dioxide, solid.
- Dibromo di-fluoromethane.

o **Appendix No 5: Special signals**

These special signals must be hosted by the vessels concerned immediately on arriving off Port Said or Suez

Vessels Carrying :
- Bulk petroleum, flash point below 73° F.
- A full cargo of Grade A in receptacles.
- A mixed cargo of bulk petroleum, flash point between 73° F and 150° F and petroleum in receptacles flash point below 73° F.

BY DAY   BY NIGHT

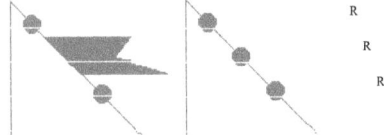

By Day: A Red Flag "B" of the International Code, between two balls.
By Night : Three Red Lights
- Vessel carrying bulk petroleum, Flash point between 73° F and 150° F.
- Nom gas petroleum tankers in ballast.

BY DAY   BY NIGHT

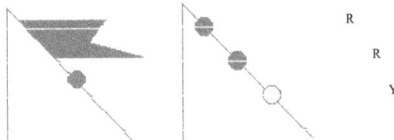

By Day: A Red Flag "B" of the International Code, over one ball.
By Night: Two Red Lights over one White Light

Vessels Carrying:
- 1st group dangerous goods.
- A part cargo of petroleum in receptacles flash point below 73° F, but no bulk petroleum.
- Liquefied inflammable gas and dangerous chemicals in bulk.

BY DAY   BY NIGHT

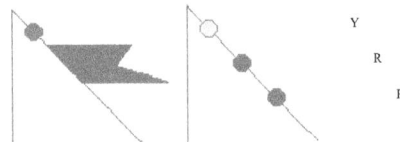

By Day: A ball over a Red Flag "B" of the International Code.
By Nights: a White light over two Red lights.

Vessels carrying radioactive substances

BY DAY   BY NIGHT

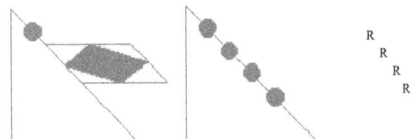

By Day: Flag "F" of the International Code, between two balls.
By Night: Four Red Lights.

1 - VESSELS CARRYING DANGEROUS PACKAGED GOODS

TYPE OF DANGEROUS GOODS IN ACCORDANCE TO IMDG CODE	S.C. GROUP	DOCUMENTS	BERTHING PLACE	PERMISSIBLE OPERATIONS	REMARKS
-More than 3000 Kilos of Class I, explosives (Div. 1.1, Div. 1.2 and Div. 1.3.). -Class 2, gases, in large welded receptacles. -Class 3, inflammable liquids (Div. 3.1. and Div. 3.2) in large welded receptacles. -Hazardous wastes. -Discovery of substances of which existence and stowage on board the ship the Master has no knowledge.	1 (High danger)	S.C. Declaration	Outer Harbour	Bunkering and water supply only (at the outer harbor).	Regarding hazardous wastes: 1. Prior authorization from E.E.A.A. 2. Approval by SCA after authorization 3. Produce compensation warranty documents.
All substances not included in S.C. Group a or S.C. Group 3.	2 (Medium danger)	S.C. Declaration	Any place in the harbor except in case of handling (handling taking place at the outer harbor for general cargo vessels and in the inner harbor for containers).	All operations allowed. (Handling taking place at the outer harbor for G.C. vessels and in the inner harbor for containers).	Handling and towing of dangerous substances to be in accordance with Appendix No. 3 of these Regulations

-Class 1, explosive, (Div. 1.5). -Class 2, gases, (non-flammable compressed gas). -Class 3, Inflammable liquids, (high flash point). -All substances listed in Appendix 4 of these Regulations. -Vessels carrying not more than 3000 Kilos of dangerous substances of each of SC three groups.	3 (Minor danger)	S.C. Declaration	Any place in the harbor.	All operations allowed.	Handling and towing of dangerous substances to be in accordance with Appendix No. 3 of these Regulations
-Class 7, radioactive substances.	1 Radio-active	A.E.E. Declaration B	According to decision of A.E.E.	According to decision of A.E.E. Expert.	1. Prior authorization from Egyptian A.E.E. 2. Approval by SCA after auth/tion of E.E.A.A. 3. Produce compensation warranty documents.
	2 Radio-active	A.E.E. Declaration C	Any place in the harbor.	All operations allowed.	1. Inform A.E.E. &SCA. 2. Produce compensation warranty document.

Notice: Vessels carrying more than one group of dangerous substances at the same time will be considered as vessel of the higher danger group

2 - VESSELS CARRYING DANGEROUS CARGOES IN BULK

TYPE OF DANGEROUS CARGOES	DEGREE OF DANGER	DOCUMENTS	BERTHING PLACE	PERMISSIBLE OPERATIONS	REMARKS
-More than 3000 Kilos of Grade A petroleum (flash point below 23 degrees C). -Liquefied inflammable gas. -Dangerous chemical in bulk. -Non gas free from Grade A petroleum. -Grade C petroleum & Grade A vapours. -Non gas free liquefied inflammable gas carrier. -Dangerous wastes.	High danger	S.C. Declaration & Declaration A	Outer Harbour	No operations allowed	At Port Said for Grade A tankers and liquefied inflammable gas carriers avoid use of anchors while berthing. For dangerous waters, pls. see remarks for packaged goods.
-More than 3000 Kilos of Grade B petroleum (flash point between 23 degrees C and 66 degrees C). -Non gas free from Grade B petroleum. -Grade C petroleum & Grade B vapours.	Medium danger	S.C. Declaration & Declaration A	Outer Harbour	Bunkering and water supply only (taking place at outer harbor).	Permission from Harbor Master must be taken before any operation.
-Grade C petroleum (flash point above 66 degrees c). -Gas free from explosive gases. -Vessels carrying not more than 3000 Kilos of Grade "B", and 9000 Kilos of dangerous good of three groups.	Minor danger	S.C. Declaration & Declaration A	Any place in the harbor.	All operations allowed.	The 3000 Kilos of Grade "A" or Grade "B" can be doubled if there are no 1st Group dangerous goods.

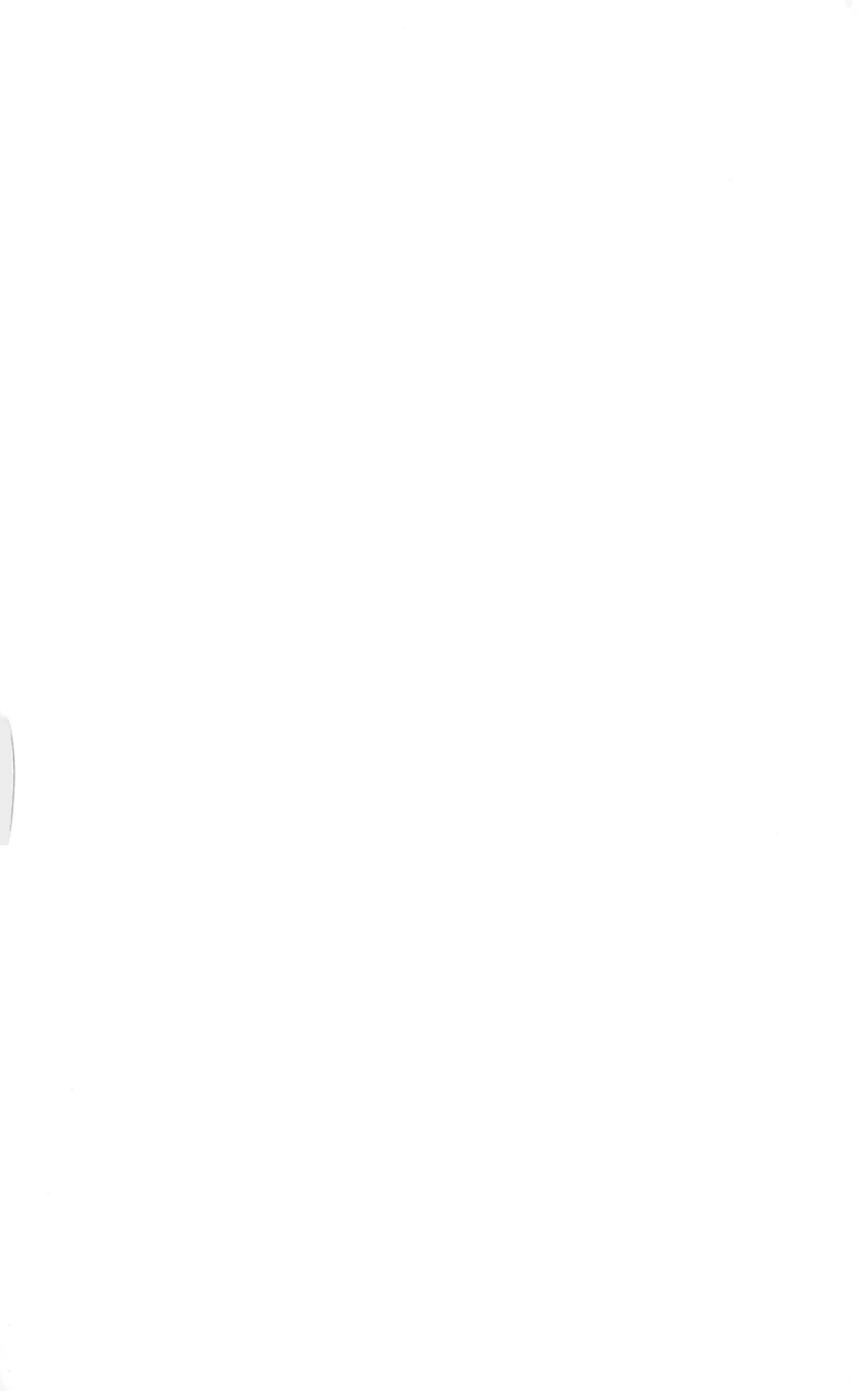

Lightning Source UK Ltd.
Milton Keynes UK
UKHW010644080421
381649UK00001B/37